CURRY

CURRY

Fragrant dishes from India,
Thailand, Vietnam and Indonesia

DK INDIA
Senior Art Editor Ira Sharma
Project Lead Editor Arani Sinha
Project Art Editor Anjan Dey
Managing Editor Alicia Ingty
Deputy Managing Editor Bushra Ahmed
Managing Art Editor Navidita Thapa
DTP Designers Rajdeep Singh, Manish Upreti
Pre-Production Manager Sunil Sharma

DK UK
Managing Editor Dawn Henderson
Managing Art Editor Christine Keilty
Senior Jacket Creative Nicola Powling
Producer, Pre-production Dragana Puvacic
Senior Producer Jen Scothern
Art Director Peter Luff
Category Publisher Peggy Vance

2006 Edition: Commissioning Editor Jeni Wright,
Art Director Peter Luff, **Project Manager and Editor**
Norma Macmillan, **Creative Publisher** Mary-Clare
Jerram, **Senior Art Editor** Susan Dowing, **Operations
Publishing Manager** Gillian Roberts, **Senior Editor**
Dawn Henderson, **Publisher** Corrine Roberts, **Project
Art Editor** Caroline de Souza, **DTP Designers** Adam
Walker, Traci Salter **Designers** Sue Storey, Simon
Daley, **Production Controller** Stuart Masheter,
Editorial Assistant Zoe Moore, **Photographer**
Hugh Johnson

First published in Great Britain in 2006 by Dorling
Kindersley Limited, 80 Strand, London WC2R 0RL

A Penguin Random House Company

This revised edition published in Great Britain in 2015
by Dorling Kindersley Limited

2 4 6 8 10 9 7 5 3 1
001-274448-May/2015

A CIP catalogue record for this book
is available from The British Library

ISBN 978-0-2411-9866-7

Colour reproduced by BurdaDruck
Printed and bound in China

A WORLD OF IDEAS:
SEE ALL THERE IS TO KNOW

www.dk.com

CONTENTS

Crab in coconut milk • Boatman's prawn masala • King prawn and pumpkin curry • Squid curry Hyderabadi mutton • Kerala lamb • Lamb and plantain curry Tamarind rice • Pork vindaloo • South Indian chicken korma • Sri Lankan chicken curry • Chicken pepper fry • Mixed vegetable curry Spinach and yogurt curry Black-eye beans with spinach and tomato • Okra and aubergine spicy masala • Potato and green bean stew Vegetables with lentils • Mixed vegetable rice Savoury rice breads

G. Sultan Mohideen 135

Chicken in coconut milk curry • Green beans with lentils • Sweet chillies in velvety gravy • Lentils with tomatoes and garlic • Chicken with raw mangoes • Oysters cooked in tomato and coconut Prawns with spicy curry leaves • Fish in raw mango curry • Mutton in lentils curry

PAKISTAN 148

Ingredients • Nihari spice potli • Mustard raita

Mahmood Akbar 158

Spinach and lamb curry • Lamb and tomato curry Minced lamb and kidney curry • Sliced beef curry Special chicken curry • Quails in yogurt curry Prawn curry • Vegetable biryani • Black-eye bean curry • Mixed vegetable curry • Potato curry Leavened roti • Fried roti • Plum chutney • Pickled garlic • Coriander chutney • Apple chutney • Mango pickle • Cumin raita • Mint raita • Onion raita Cucumber raita • Chickpea pilau

G. Sultan Mohideen 181

Balti fish curry • Slow-cooked mutton stew Minced meat and potato curry

MYANMAR & MARITIME SE ASIA 186

Ingredients • Spiced tamarind relish • Chicken stock • Compressed rice • Dried shrimp relish Peanut sauce

Sri Owen 203

MYANMAR 203

Chicken curry with lime and tomatoes • Burmese chicken noodle soup • Pork curry with mango

MALAYSIA 208

Red curry of beef • Laksa with prawns and tofu Beef rendang

SINGAPORE 213

Sour fish curry • Chilli crab • Fish head curry

INDONESIA 217

Duck breasts in Balinese spices • West Sumatran mutton curry • Javanese lamb curry • Hot and sour prawn curry • Rich curry of duck

PHILIPPINES 225

Chicken adobo • Squid adobo • Braised oxtail with peanut sauce

THAILAND 230

Ingredients • Preparing lemongrass • Coconut milk and cream • Green curry paste • Preparing galangal Red chilli paste

David Thompson 246

Cooking Thai curries • Steamed jasmine rice • Coconut and turmeric curry of red snapper • Sour orange curry of brill and Asian greens • Red curry of oyster mushrooms and bean curd • Crab stir-fried with curry powder • Northeastern curry of pork ribs • Fermented fish sauce • Jungle curry of chicken with vegetables and peppercorns • Southern curry of chopped beef Red curry of beef with peanuts • Pineapple curry of mussels • Grilled halibut curry • Steamed scallop curry Green curry of heart of coconut • Green curry of prawns with aubergines and basil • Aromatic curry of pumpkin Cucumber relish • Aromatic curry of chicken and potatoes • Chiang Mai pork curry • Muslim curry of duck with potatoes and onions

MAINLAND SE ASIA 282

Ingredients • Preparing dried chillies

Corinne Trang 294

CAMBODIA 294

Cambodian herbal paste • Cambodian red curry paste Curried fermented fish and pork dip • Steamed snails in curry custard • Catfish curry with rice noodles Cardamom and ginger beef curry with peanuts Chicken curry with young jackfruit

FOREWORD

After writing the recipes for the North Indian chapter, I visited India and decided to ask people in different parts of the country to define 'curry' for me. Most people I asked struggled! It is not that no one in India knows curry, rather it seems that they know it too well to call it something as generic as that. It means different things to different people.

Essentially, any fish, meat or vegetables, cooked in, and with spices and liquid is a curry. The spices and liquid form a sauce that becomes a part of the dish. It is the spices or spice combinations that make each curry different. The cooking method itself varies from simple to sublime – in some cases it could be as simple as simmering in a spiced broth, while in others it may be a complex combination of frying, pot-roasting and braising.

What is amazing is that, with time, this cooking style has travelled the world and exists in varied shapes and forms in so many different parts of the world. This is thanks to a migrant population that carried its traditional way of food and life with it. In fact, the journey of curry is an integral part of its success story. This book takes you on that journey.

Curry is a compilation of curry recipes like no other. What you will find in the pages to follow are some of the best recipes from different parts of the world, contributed by some of the best experts from those regions.

Curry in North India (Chapter one) as it exists today is a combination of techniques, equipments and ingredients that travelled from Persia and the Middle

East through Afghanistan and Pakistan to find their way to North India. North Indian curries today are a unique combination of Middle Eastern techniques brought by Mughal rulers (Muslim invaders who ruled most of India from the 1500s to the 1700s), with local produce. Similarities can be seen in North Indian and Pakistani (Chapter three) dishes – partly because of the proximity of these regions and partly due to similar climates and produce.

The cooking of South India (Chapter two) used to be the cooking of the native Dravidian race. The Dravidians were the original inhabitants of the Indian sub-continent and were pushed southwards and eastwards with the Aryans and Mughals who migrated from the west. This Dravidian influence may explain some of the similarities between South Indian cooking and the cuisine of Maritime Southeast Asia (Chapter four).

In the Thailand chapter (Chapter five) we see that Thai curry cuisine has borrowed a lot from its local surroundings and developed in so many ways that it has taken the level of an art form. The complexity of spices, lightness of touch and depth of flavour are the reasons why Thai curries are now so sought after all over the world.

In the Mainland Southeast Asia chapter (Chapter six) that covers Cambodia, Laos and Vietnam we see how curry has been adapted further to adopt the local flavours and ingredients of these parts of the world.

In the Outposts chapter (Chapter seven) we have included only a few of the many countries that curry has reached – there are many, many more. Here we see the journey of curry to Africa, Britain, the Caribbean and Japan. The migration of Indian labourers from Uttar Pradesh and Bihar to work in sugar fields in the Caribbean resulted in a strong influence of traditional Indian cooking in their new surroundings.

In Britain, curry is a part of the social fabric. During the days of the British Raj, officers returning to Britain from the sub-continent would often bring back recipes to use at home. This desire for a 'curry fix' was the starting point, but the real boom happened in the 1950s when a sizable population of workers migrated from Pakistan, India and Bangladesh to help rebuild London after WWII. What started off as a means to provide food to the migrant community soon made inroads into mainstream society.

In the days of British rule in India, thousands of people also migrated from Gujarat to Kenya. They took their cooking and culture to create a vibrant and colourful combination with African influence. Just after 1971, when the migrant Indian population was forced to leave Africa due to political turmoil, they migrated to the UK and the US and continue to thrive in a culture that is colourful and unique.

I believe it is the combination of simplicity and complexity that has put curry on the map of the world. It is a perfect example of an age-old tradition that has continuously evolved to remain relevant in this age of globalization. As this book shows, curry truly is the food of the world!

Vivek Singh

VIVEK SINGH

CONTRIBUTORS

VIVEK SINGH

As a boy, Vivek spurned family expectations by announcing his intentions to become a chef. After catering college, he joined the Oberoi Hotel group as a specialist in Indian cuisine, first working at their busy flight kitchens in Mumbai. He then moved to the Grand Hotel in Kolkata, before being fast-tracked to Indian chef of the Oberoi's flagship Rajvilas in Jaipur – at the age of just 26. From early on, Vivek read Escoffier and devoured books by Marco Pierre White and Charlie Trotter. When Iqbal Wahhab, the founder of The Cinnamon Club in London, approached him with ideas of marrying Indian flavours with Western culinary styles, Vivek saw his opportunity. Since opening in 2001, The Cinnamon Club has redefined expectations of Indian cooking, by liberating it from the straitjacket of tradition and crafting a brilliant and exotic marriage of Indian and Western cuisines.

G. SULTAN MOHIDEEN

Winner of several awards, which include the Chef De Cuisine Award in 1995, the Chef of the Year Award in 1998, and the Culinary Czar of Indian Cuisine Award in 2006 and 2014, Sultan is no stranger to accolades. After completing his post-graduation from the Oberoi School of Hotel Management, New Delhi, he went on to work in premier 5-star hotels, establishing himself as an institution in Indian cuisine. He has the distinction of having catered for 30 world leaders; including the Clintons and Tony Blair. His research on the gastronomical heritage of the Dravidian Kingdoms of Pandiya, Chera and Tippu Sultan's Kingdom earned him the Dr. Ambedkar Puraskar award from the Karnataka government. He also has a book to his name, Samiyal Sultan, which is a collection of his weekly columns in the Tamil magazine, Ananda Vikatan. He has featured in the New York Times and in The International Who's Who of Chefs 2004–2005, published by IWWC.

DAS SREEDHARAN

Das is the founder chef of Rasa restaurants in London. Since starting up in 1994, he has created a new awareness of regional Indian cuisine. With a humble upbringing, Das learned traditional cooking skills and vegetable gardening from his mother. Now, through his restaurants, he passionately champions the simple, subtle flavours of Keralan food, offering his customers a fresh alternative to typical curry-house dishes. Das has published three cookery books about his native cuisine, and organizes annual festivals promoting Indian food and culture. He conducts weekly classes in London and has a cookery school in India, teaching traditional techniques. Through the school, he aims to encourage healthy home cooking and ethical living. Das lives in London, taking regular trips to Kerala to seek new flavours and spicing for his customers' delight.

MAHMOOD AKBAR

From an early age, Mahmood was exposed to the pleasures of food and cooking by both his father, a great food lover, and his mother, an excellent cook. He obtained his degree in Hotel Management in the US, then joined Hilton International where he spent five years as a Food and Beverage Manager, including time in Hong Kong and the Far East. In 1982, Mahmood decided to start up his own restaurants, including the now famous Salt 'n Pepper Village restaurants in Lahore and Karachi. In his business he is assisted by his wife and, recently, by his daughter, who also graduated in the US with a Hotel Management degree. Mahmood's passion for food is undiminished. The lesson he learnt as a child from his father about using only the freshest ingredients has become his guiding principle in running his own restaurants: all food is purchased fresh every morning and consumed the same day.

SRI OWEN

Sri was born in West Sumatra, and it was there, as a child in her grandmother's kitchen, that she acquired a love of good food. After graduating from university in Yogyakarta, Central Java, she became an English Literature lecturer, and she met and married Roger, an English colleague. Together they came to London, where she made a successful career with the BBC Overseas Service, at the same time writing her first cookery book. This was published in 1976, and has been followed by ten more books as well as other writing on Indonesian and other Southeast Asian food. In 1994 her best seller, The Rice Book, won the André Simon Award for food and cookery book of the year; it was also nominated for a James Beard Award in New York.

DAVID THOMPSON

In the 1980s, David travelled to Thailand from his native Australia and became enamoured of the country, its people and culture. There he met Khun Sombat Janphetchara, whose mother was attached to one of the palaces of Bangkok. From her, David learnt the fundamentals of Thai cuisine. In 1993, he and his partner, Peter Bowyer, opened Darley Street Thai in Sydney, followed in 1995 by Sailors Thai. In 2000, David was approached to start Nahm restaurant in London, which opened in the Halkin Hotel in 2001 and was awarded a Michelin star in 2002. The same year, David published Thai Food, which won numerous awards, including The Guild of Food Writers' book of the year. At the Tio Pepe ITV Awards, David was honoured as London Chef of the Year. He returns to Thailand regularly to continue his research, unearthing long-forgotten recipes that he can draw on for his restaurants.

CORINNE TRANG

Corinne is the New York-based award-winning author of Authentic Vietnamese Cooking, Essentials of Asian Cuisine, and The Asian Grill. Dubbed "the Julia Child of Asian Cuisine" by the media, she is well known in the US for her writing, teaching and radio broadcasts, as well as appearances on television programmes such as Martha Stewart Living and The TV Food Network. Corinne has travelled extensively in Asia and teaches and lectures worldwide on the subject of Asian cookery. She is on the faculty at several universities, including New York University, where she is adjunct professor in the department of Nutrition, Food Studies and Public Health. Corinne is also a food consultant, a published food stylist and accomplished food and travel photographer. She is a member of the International Association of Culinary Professionals, New York Women's Culinary Alliance and Les Dames d'Escoffier.

ROOPA GULATI

Born and raised in Cumbria, Roopa's taste for culinary adventure took her to India, which for 18 years was her home. A Cordon Bleu chef, she blended Western and Asian styles of cooking while working as a consultant chef with the Taj group of hotels, and cooking on a daily live show on the Star TV channel. Roopa returned to Britain in 2001 and now lives in London, where she is Deputy Channel Editor with UKTV Food. She enjoys exploring the tastes of multicultural Britain and has been a judge for BBC Radio 4's Food and Farming Awards, as well as a regular radio broadcaster and a restaurant critic for Time Out magazine. Her recipe-led features have been published in many magazines, including Good Food, Olive and New York-based Gourmet. She's particularly interested in how cooking styles travel – from street stall, to Maharajah's palace, to fine restaurant dining.

JUDY BASTYRA

Judy was born in London and has written about food for more years than she can remember. She prefers eating fruit bat that has feasted on mangoes, but feels that piranha will taste sweet and musty whatever it eats. Many years ago, Judy realised that if you love food and travel, what better job could you have than to be a food and travel writer. She is occasionally torn away from her first love to other meaningful subjects like sex or homelessness, writing books about them too, but then the hunger takes over and she is off again in search of new culinary experiences. Her travels have taken her walking in the High Atlas Mountains in Morocco, climbing the 'stairway to heaven' at Ankor Wat in Cambodia and eating bay scallops in Martha's Vineyard. But her heart remains in the Caribbean where she frequently returns to continue her love affair with Caribbean cuisine.

YASUKO FUKUOKA

As a musician and composer, Yasuko travelled all over Japan in the course of many concert tours. Coupled with her love of good food, this enabled her to gain a deep understanding of Japan's regional specialities and traditional culinary culture. Her curiosity led her to create her own recipes based on Japanese home cooking. Since moving to England, Yasuko has continued to work as a musician while developing her career as a journalist and food writer. Her first cookery book, co-authored with Emi Kazuko, won the Best Asian Cookery Book Award in 2001 at the Gourmand Cookbook Awards. As well as publishing several more Japanese cookery books in English and contributing to Japanese publications, she develops recipes that combine traditional and contemporary Japanese cooking and British products.

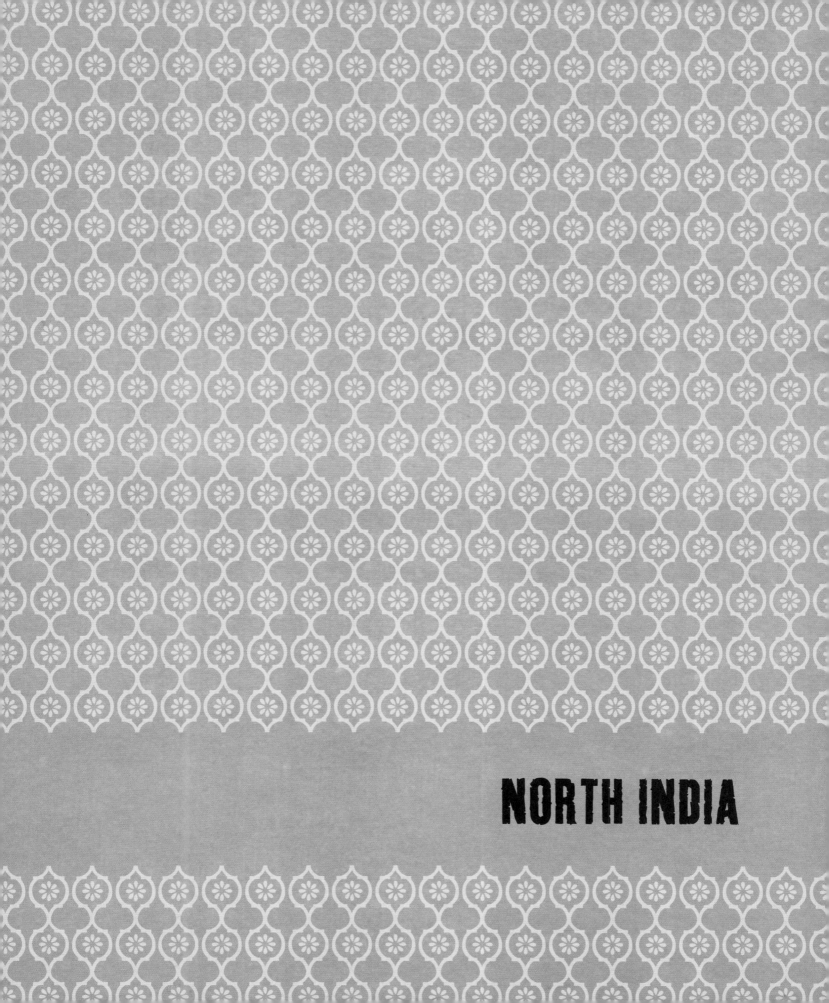

NORTH INDIA

The cooking of northern India has its roots in Persia, where the *tandoor* originated. The *tandoor* was brought to India by the Mughals, Muslim invaders who ruled most of India for almost 200 years, until the early 1700s. With the arrival of the *tandoor* began the great phenomenon of 'tandoori' cooking, which has spread all over the world and, with the curry, come to broadly represent Indian cuisine.

Under some Mughal rulers, great levels of culinary sophistication were achieved. There were periods during which cooking flourished and its practitioners were nurtured like artists, enjoying a status similar to celebrity chefs today. Vast sums of money were spent on kitchens run by skilled master chefs, or *rakabdar*, as they were called. Each ruler aspired to out-do the other, in hospitality and in the dishes his chefs devised.

From this, it might seem as if all of North Indian cooking was influenced by Mughal rulers alone, but this could not be further from the truth. Like every cuisine, the cooking of a country or region is shaped by what grows there, the seasons, the climate and the availability of ingredients, as well as religious and socio-economic factors.

Rulers in some parts of northern India made great efforts to preserve their own culture and identity. One such were the Rajput rulers from Rajasthan, who were keen hunters of deer, wild boar, partridges and sand grouse, which is why this region has a fine tradition of game curries. In this arid desert region little grows, and cooking is earthy and rustic. Dried vegetables, roots, berries and fruiats are more common than fresh. Sangri beans, which need little water to grow, are much eaten. Rather than cattle and buffalo, goat and lamb are reared both for milk and meat. Yogurt is used for cooking and as a drink, as it has a cooling effect on the body. Chickpeas, maize and millet are the staples here, unlike the rest of the country. In such a dry climate this makes sense, because consumption of chickpea flour and cornmeal help the body retain water.

Punjab, Delhi and the rest of the north are relatively much better off in terms of fertile land, kinder climate and better irrigation, as a result of the five rivers that feed the region. This is a land of plenty and plenty of milk, cream, butter and other milk products are used; fresh vegetables, such as spinach, mustard greens and fenugreek, are abundant; wheat is grown; and lamb and chicken are reared. Just about the best of everything is available and is used in the cooking in this region.

The *tandoor* has had a major impact on the way of life here – even today most households have a tandoori oven tucked away in their courtyard. If not, the village has a communal tandoor, where ladies will gather at midday or early evening to make their bread or simply exchange news and gossip. The mighty *tandoor* is so much more than just a means of cooking food – it is an essential part of the fabric of life in this region.

Bengal and the eastern states have very fertile land in the plains, as the river Ganges brings with it the rich soil from the north. The climate is mild and monsoons mean that two crops can be harvested each year. One of them is rice. Local vegetables are plentiful; mustard grows in abundance, so mustard seeds and oil are used in cooking. With the proximity to the sea, fish is frequently used in Bengali curries.

When the British arrived in India, they made Kolkata, or Calcutta as it was formerly known, their headquarters. As a result, British influences can be seen in some Bengali dishes (and vice versa). Kedgeree and Bengali vegetable 'chops' are just two examples of the cross-over of cultures.

Today in northern India, 65 per cent of the population is vegetarian, which explains why there is such a wide variety of vegetarian curries in the Indian culinary repertoire. The majority of North Indians are Hindus and Muslims, followed by Sikhs and those of other religions. Because cows are sacred to Hindus and pork is banned in the Muslim faith, beef and pork are rarely eaten.

While history, geography and religion have all played an important role in shaping North Indian cuisine, there is one other important aspect – without which no cuisine can develop and survive – and that is creativity. And it is creativity that has enabled North Indian curries to travel all round the world, finding new homes wherever Indian migrants have settled. In adapting recipes to what is available locally, new curries have been created, but they are still identifiable as North Indian in their essence.

Vivek Singh

Frying whole spices >
Add them to hot oil so they
crackle and toast

TASTE OF NORTH INDIA

1. fennel seeds
2. broken cashew nuts
3. black cardamom pods
4. gold leaf
5. saffron threads
6. coriander leaves
7. split green lentils
8. split red lentils
9. split black lentils
10. whole black lentils
11. split *gram* lentils
12. split yellow lentils
13. pomegranate seeds
14. sultanas
15. black onion seeds
16. mustard paste
17. ground *garam masala*
18. coriander seeds
19. cumin seeds
20. dried fenugreek leaves
21. chilli powder
22. crushed dried chillies
23. dried red chillies
24. fresh green chillies
25. dried morels
26. fresh root ginger
27. garlic
28. black lentils papadum
29. mustard oil
30. mustard seeds
31. carom seeds

THE RAW MATERIALS

One of the things that makes North Indian cuisine so special is the spectacular variety of ingredients available to the cook. Each of the four regions has its own distinctly different cooking style, based on the climate and crops grown, religious influences and the cooking mediums preferred. Everywhere the cooking is enhanced with fresh aromatics, herbs, spices and other flavouring ingredients.

TURMERIC

One of the most widely used spices in Indian cooking, turmeric flavours most Indian curries, be they meat, vegetable or lentil, and also gives them a rich yellow-orange colour. The roots (or rhizomes) are sold both fresh and dried, or ground to a fine powder. Turmeric has good preservative properties too, so is used in the making of many Indian pickles.

CORIANDER

In its leaf form, this herb is widely used to finish curries and as a garnish. The seeds of the plant are used as a spice, whole or ground. Thought to have been cultivated for over 3000 years, coriander is said to have cooling effect on the body and thus an infusion is a cure for fever.

SAFFRON

The costliest of all spices, saffron is the dried stigmas of a variety of crocus. Just a few saffron threads (stigmas) will give intense golden colour and a unique slightly bitter, perfumed taste to savoury and sweet dishes. Store this precious spice in an airtight jar in a dark place, to retain its colour and fragrance.

ROSE WATER AND SCREWPINE ESSENCE

Essences have been a part of Indian cookery since antiquity. During the time of the Mughal emperors, rare flowers were grown in the royal greenhouses to make attars, or fragrant essential oils, and some of these turned up in the kitchen. Floral essences such as rose water and screwpine essence (*kewra*) are the most popular today, used to flavour *biryanis*, *pulaos*, kebabs, desserts and treats.

GOLD LEAF

This is the ultimate in exotic, luxury cooking. While edible silver leaf is quite commonly used to adorn dishes and decorate sweets in India, gold leaf is not as easy to find. Used as a decoration, it lifts up a dish in every sense.

SULTANAS

These dried grapes are used extensively in Indian curries, desserts and snacks. Their colour vary from light green to dark brown depending on the variety of grapes used to make them. They vary in size and are priced accordingly. They are deliciously moist, have a tender texture and a delicate flavour. They are easily available in any Asian grocery store. Sultanas can be stored for up to 3 months, at room temperature.

CASHEW NUTS

These kidney-shaped dry nuts are creamy white in colour. Known as *kaju* in India, cashew nuts are widely cultivated along the west coast of India. Good quality cashew nuts are about 1cm ($1/2$in) long. They are mildly sweet, nutty and creamy in taste. Since these dry nuts are expensive so broken cashew nuts are used to make a paste, which is then used in making gravies. These nuts are widely used in Indian curries, snacks, desserts and biscuits.

CHAPATTI FLOUR

This finely ground wholewheat flour is used to make unleavened breads (see recipe p40).

CHICKPEA FLOUR

Also known as *besan* and *gram* flour, this is obtained from husking and then grinding split *gram* lentils (*chana dal*) into a powder. It is a very versatile flour, commonly used to make dumplings (p37), in batters for fritters and in bread doughs. Chickpea flour can be kept in an airtight jar for up to 6 months. Another form in which chickpea flour is available is *daria dal*, for which the split *gram* lentils are roasted before grinding. Roasting takes away the raw flavour and increases the flour's ability to absorb water. Roasted chickpea flour is often used as a thickener at the end of cooking.

CHILLIES

Many different chillies, both fresh and dried, are used in North Indian cookery, varying in their fieriness and pungency. Kashmiri chillies, which are large and deep red, have a good flavour and colour but are not too hot, so can be used in larger quantities than the smaller, much hotter green chillies. Whole dried chillies can be stored for up to a year in a cool, dark place (exposure to light will fade their vibrant colour), whereas crushed or ground dried chillies will lose their power and spiciness after a few months.

GINGER AND GARLIC

After salt, these are probably the most used ingredients in the cooking of Delhi and Punjab. They are added to marinades for meats, fish and vegetables when preparing them for the *tandoor*, as well as being a flavouring in many curries. Ginger and garlic are normally made into a paste, which can be done separately or in combination: take about 100g (3½oz) peeled fresh ginger and 75g (2½oz) peeled garlic and blend with 175ml (6fl oz) water, using a food processor. The paste can be kept in an airtight jar in the refrigerator for up to 5 days.

MORELS

These wild mushrooms can be used fresh as well as dried. The upper portion of the mushroom has the appearance of a honeycomb. Morels are first soaked in water for a while before cooking them. This expensive ingredient is used in gravies, curries and sauces and are also cooked with wine.

COCONUT

The hard, brown, hairy fruits of the coconut tree contain 'water', which makes a refreshing drink enjoyed straight from the fruit. The crunchy, sweet white flesh is used to make rich coconut milk (p241), which is an important part of many Indian curries. Freshly grated coconut flesh is used in Bengali cuisine, while desiccated coconut features in Muslim cooking.

Dried Kashmiri chillies

BLACK LENTILS

Also known as *ma* in the Punjab, these lentils are primarily used whole in northern India, most famously in a festive Punjabi dish with red kidney beans. Whole black lentils (*urad*) have a stronger aroma and richer, earthier taste than split black lentils (*urad dal*). Whole black lentils can be kept in an airtight container for up to 4 months.

SPLIT LENTILS

The most common variety of split lentils in India are *toor dal*, also called split yellow peas. They are used all over India to make the dishes known as *dals*. *Chana dal* are split *gram* lentils, a type of chickpea, from which the husk has been removed. A very versatile ingredient, *chana dal* are used in many ways in different parts of the country, and are also ground into a flour (p22). *Masoor* or red lentils are the easiest to cook and digest, and are commonly used to make lentil soups and *dals*, as well as kedgeree, which is essentially food for invalids and children. When whole, *moong dal* (mung beans) have a green skin; it is these whole beans that are sprouted to use in salads and other cold dishes. Split, they are used in northern India for a variety of things, such as in the making of popadums, batters and fritters, but *moong dal* are rarely cooked on their own.

YELLOW CHILLI POWDER

Less spicier than its red variant, yellow chillies, in India are largely grown in Kashmir and Punjab in India. Yellow chilli powder is made out of dried yellow peppers, ground into a fine powder. It lends a mild yellow colour to the dish. It can be stored upto two months in an airtight container.

BLACK CARDAMOM

An essential Indian spice, cardamon is one of the ingredients that is used in *garam masala*. It has a warm flavour. The black cardamom is bigger than the light green variety and has a stronger flavour. It can be stored in an airtight container for up to a year.

FENNEL SEEDS

A very commonly used spice in India, whole or ground fennel seeds add a warm and sweet flavour to all kinds of curries. Fennel seeds are also used in pickles and chutneys and in desserts. Fennel is thought to have digestive properties, so roasted seeds are often served after a rich Indian meal.

NIGELLA SEEDS

Although more commonly known as black onion seeds, this spice has nothing to do with onions and is actually the fruit of a herb related to the garden plant 'love-in-a-mist'. The small black seeds have an unusual, slightly bitter taste. Much used in Bengali cooking, nigella (*kalonji*) also garnishes many Indian breads.

CAROM SEEDS

Closely related to cumin, which it resembles in appearance and fragrance, carom seeds (*ajowan*) have a hot and bitter taste. However, when they are cooked with other ingredients, the flavour mellows. Carom seeds are particularly good in seafood dishes and with root vegetables.

ROYAL CUMIN SEEDS

Also called black cumin, these spice seeds are very dark brown, long and very thin, and smaller than regular cumin. Their aroma is earthy and strong during cooking; the taste is nutty and warm. Royal cumin is used extensively in Kashmiri cuisine, and in Mughal cuisine as a tempering for meats.

FENUGREEK

The fresh leaves of this aromatic plant are eaten as a vegetable; when dried (*kasoori methi*) they are used to flavour all sorts of Indian savouries and curries (the best quality *kasoori methi* comes from Qasoor in Pakistan). The seeds of the plant are used as a spice. Ancient herbalists prescribed fenugreek to aid digestion, a remedy that continues to be used today.

GARAM MASALA

Garam masala, which literally means 'hot spices', is a mixture of roasted spices that is used whole or ground to a fine powder. Each region of India has its standard version of *garam masala*, using the spices available and popular and the cooking of the area, and the recipes change according to individual taste. (See recipe p31.)

POMEGRANATE SEEDS

The fleshy and juicy pomegranate seeds are either used fresh in curries and gravies, or dried and ground and added in spice mixes.

KASUNDI MUSTARD

This ready-made mustard paste is commonly used in Bengali cooking. It is made by soaking mustard seeds in vinegar, then grinding them to a paste with mustard oil and the addition of dried mango. Kasundi mustard adds its characteristic flavour to numerous dishes from the region. If not available, it can be replaced with Dijon or any other prepared grain mustard.

< Grinding spices using mortar and pestle

CiNNAMON LEAVES

Although commonly referred to as 'bay leaf' in Indian recipes, what is meant is actually the dried leaf of the cassia tree. I like to call it cinnamon leaf. Used in most dishes all over northern India, cinnamon leaves have a mild, sweet flavour. They are not edible, so should be removed before serving. Should you find it difficult to obtain them, you can use bay leaves instead.

KACHRi

A sour, tomato-like compound fruit native to Rajasthan, it has a hard skin and seeds inside. Available fresh and dried, it is used to tenderise meat and in the making of certain chutneys

ASAFOETiDA

This essential Indian flavouring, which is a dried resinous gum, has a very unpleasant smell and bitter taste, so is never used alone, but when cooked in a dish it enhances the other flavours. It is sold as powder, granules or lumps, and will keep well for up to a year. In addition to its culinary uses, it is supposed to be a cure for flatulence and to help respiratory problems like asthma.

GHEE

This is clarified butter, the pure butterfat, clear and golden in colour. Traditionally in India, *ghee* is made from buffalo milk, which is higher in fat than cow's milk, and the process involves souring milk to make yogurt and then churning this to yield butter. Unsalted butter made from cow's milk can also be used for *ghee*.

MiLK CHEESE

It is prepared by drying the whey from milk by slow-cooking the milk in a heavy-bottomed *kadhai* or wok.

< Cinnamon leaves

Milk cheese or *Khoya* (as it is known in India) is a rich source of milk protein. It is generally grated and used in Indian cooking, either in curries or to prepare desserts. It can be stored in the refrigerator for up to a week.

PANEER CHEESE

An Indian version of set cottage or pot cheese, *paneer* is made by separating the whey from milk by adding lemon juice to curdle it. The solids are collected in muslin, tied and pressed under a weight for a few hours to set to soft curds or firm for slicing. On its own, *paneer* tastes quite bland. It is widely used as an alternative to meat in vegetarian dishes.

MUSTARD OIL

As the name suggests, this oil is extracted from mustard seeds. It is pungent in taste and smell and deep gold in colour. Mustard oil is greatly favoured in Bengal and eastern parts of India, and certain Rajasthani dishes get their unique flavour from it. When used, the oil is normally heated almost to smoking point, then cooled down and reheated again, which tones down its aroma.

RICE

Rice is grown all along the plains of the Ganges, starting from the foothills of the Himalayas right down to Bengal in the east. Although Basmati is the best known, there are hundreds of other varieties of rice available, Patna being another notable one. In Indian homes, rice is most often cooked by the boiling method; pilau rice and rice cooked by the absorption method are reserved for special occasions as they require more skill.

PICKLING SPICES

This combination of equal quantities of fennel, carom, onion, fenugreek, mustard and cumin, either as whole seeds or ground, is used in pickles as well as to flavour sauces and marinades for meat. You can buy ready-made pickling spices in India; elsewhere you will need to mix the spices together yourself.

ANISEED

These spice seeds are small, oval shaped and light brown in colour. They have a distinctive liquorice flavour very similar to fennel. These seeds are dry-roasted to give maximum flavour and taste. They can be stored in an airtight container, for up to 4 months.

GHEE CLARIFIED BUTTER

The process of 'clarifying' butter to make *ghee*, or pure butter fat, turns it into an excellent cooking medium able to withstand high temperatures and constant reheating. It also prevents it from going rancid, an important consideration in a hot country such as India. *Ghee* has a unique rich, nutty taste and is used in almost all Indian cooking.

Yields about 200g (7oz)

250g (9oz) unsalted butter

< Unsalted butter
Free of salt, this slightly sweet flavoured butter is widely used as a cooking fat and in baking.

1 Place the butter in a heavy saucepan and heat it over a gentle heat.

2 Melt the butter and bring it to a gentle boil.

3 Simmer the melted butter for 20–30 minutes until all the water has evaporated.

4 Skim the froth that appears on the surface and discard.

5 Continue to boil until the butter separates into cooked milk solids, which settle at the bottom of the pan, and a clear, golden *ghee* forms at the top.

6 Carefully strain the *ghee* into a bowl. Discard the solids, and leave the liquid *ghee* to cool.

7 Once cool, the *ghee* will solidify, but it will have a creamy consistency, somewhat like soft tub margarine. If refrigerated it will become hard. *Ghee* can be stored for several years if kept in a tin or glass container in a cool, dark place, free from any moisture or contact with water.

BROWN ONION PASTE

This fried-onion paste is used as a base in many Indian curries. It enhances the taste, adds thickness and colour to the gravy. You could prepare and store this paste in the refrigerator for up to 1 week.

makes 250g (9oz)

500g (1lb 2oz) large onions
250ml (9fl oz) vegetable oil
500ml (16fl oz) yogurt

1 Peel and wash the onions and pat dry with kitchen paper. Using a sharp knife, finely slice the onions.

2 Heat the oil in a heavy-bottomed pan, over a moderate heat. Add the sliced onions and fry until golden brown. Remove the pan from the heat. Take the onions out with a slotted spoon and set aside on a plate to cool.

3 Once cooled, put the onions along with the yogurt in a blender and blend for 2–3 minutes to make a smooth paste.

4 Do not touch the paste with your fingers as it might get spoilt. Instead, use a spatula to remove the paste. Either use immediately or transfer to an airtight container and store in the fridge for up to 1 week.

PANCH PHORAN MASALA

'Panch Phoran' literally translates to 'five spices', and is a staple spice combination used mostly in potato and vegetable curries. The combination adds colour and a distinct taste to dishes and is one of the simplest spice packages used in recipes. These spices are usually added while cooking and are either gently tossed or shallow fried (like *tadka*), giving the recipe a distinct aroma and taste.

serves 5

½ tsp cumin seeds
½ tsp fennel seeds
½ tsp nigella seeds
½ tsp fenugreek seeds
½ tsp mustard seeds

1 Measure out the spices and place them in seperate bowls. Use whole spices for this *masala* mix and make sure all the spices are of the same quantity.

2 Mix together the five spices in a bowl. This panch phoran *masala* is used in a variety of Indian curries. You could either grind, dry roast, or fry the spices depending on the recipe you are preparing.

GARAM MASALA HOT SPICE MIX

This aromatic blend of spices may be used whole or ground to a fine powder, depending on the dish. Whole *garam masala* is often added at the beginning or early in the cooking, whereas ground mixes are used to finish a dish. The basic mixture usually includes coriander seeds, cumin seeds, cardamom, cinnamon, cloves, mace, peppercorns and cinnamon leaf, in varying proportions and with other spices added according to the individual cook's preferences and the dish being prepared.

makes about 150g (5½oz)

50g (1¾oz) coriander seeds
50g (1¾oz) cumin seeds
20 green cardamom pods
10 cinnamon sticks 2.5cm (1in) long
2 tbsp cloves
10 blades mace
10 black cardamom pods
½ nutmeg
1 tbsp black peppercorns
4 cinnamon leaves or bay leaves
1 tbsp dried rose petals
1 tbsp fennel seeds

1 Heat a dry frying pan and add all the spices. Stir them and shake the pan as they start to crackle. When they smell roasted and aromatic, remove the pan from the heat and tip the spices on to a plate. Allow to cool.

2 To grind the spices, use a mortar and pestle or a spice mill (or a clean coffee grinder).

Dried rose petals >
With their floral fragrance and sweet flavour, these petals are used for flavour and decorating dishes.

LAAL MAAS FIERY LAMB CURRY

As the name suggests, this is a very hot dish, not for people with a weak constitution. It is by far the hottest dish in this chapter, and is one of the few Indian dishes that contains heat in every sense – both 'chilli hot' and 'spice hot'. You can decide the amount of heat you'd like in your finished dish – discard most of the seeds from the chillies if you want to reduce the heat, or keep them in if you want it really hot. I think this is perfect for cold winter evenings or even a Friday night 'do'. You can use either lamb or goat – they are interchangeable.

serves 4

chilli hot

25-35 dried red chillies, stalks removed

1½ tsp cloves

150g (5½oz) *ghee* or vegetable oil

250g (9oz) plain yogurt, whisked until smooth

2 tsp cumin seeds, roasted

20g (¾oz) ground coriander

1 tsp red chilli powder

2 tsp salt

3 cinnamon leaves or bay leaves

6 green cardamom pods

5 black cardamom pods

75g (2½oz) garlic cloves, finely chopped

250g (9oz) onions, finely chopped

1kg (2¼lb) leg of lamb or goat with bone, chopped into 2.5cm (1in) cubes

750ml (1¼ pints) lamb stock or water

30g (1oz) coriander leaves, finely chopped

1 Set aside 3 or 4 of the dried chillies to use later; put the remainder to soak in 125ml (4fl oz) water. Also put aside 4–6 of the cloves and 1 tbsp of the *ghee*.

2 Mix the yogurt with the cumin seeds, ground coriander, chilli powder and salt in a bowl. Set aside.

3 Heat the rest of the *ghee* in a heavy-bottomed pan. Add the remaining cloves, the cinnamon leaves and the green and black cardamoms. When they begin to crackle and change colour, add the garlic. Sauté for 2 minutes or until the garlic begins to turn golden. Add the onions and cook for 10 minutes or until golden brown, stirring constantly.

4 Stir in the meat and cook for 2–3 minutes. Drain the soaked red chillies and add to the pan. Continue cooking for 10–12 minutes or until the liquid has evaporated and the meat starts to brown slightly. Now add the spiced yogurt and cook for another 10–12 minutes or until the liquid from the yogurt has evaporated.

5 Add the stock or water and bring to the boil, then cover the pan, reduce the heat and simmer until the meat is tender. Check the seasoning. Remove from the heat and keep warm.

6 To prepare the *tadka*, or tempering, which boosts the flavours, heat up the reserved *ghee* or oil in a large ladle over a flame (or in a small pan) and add the reserved cloves and dried red chillies. Cook for 1–2 minutes or until the *ghee* changes colour and the spice flavours are released. Pour the contents of the ladle over the lamb curry, sprinkle with the chopped coriander and serve.

ACHARI KHARGOSH RABBIT LEG COOKED IN PICKLING SPICES

This is the type of dish that would have been cooked on a *shikaar*, or hunting expedition, when the Rajput princes would go out hunting with their entourage. It would originally have been made with hare but works just as well with rabbit.

serves 4

spicy, tangy and sour

4–6 rabbit legs, about 900g (2lb) in total

1 tsp salt

1 tsp ground turmeric

Sauce

3^1/$_2$ tbsp mustard oil

75ml (2^1/$_2$fl oz) *ghee*

4 dried red chillies

1 tbsp mixed pickling spices (p27)

8 garlic cloves, finely chopped

2 onions, about 150g (5^1/$_2$oz) in total, finely chopped

1 tsp salt

^{1}/$_2$ tsp ground turmeric

2.5cm (1in) piece fresh root ginger, cut into julienne strips

25g (scant 1oz) palm sugar or molasses

300g (10oz) plain full-fat yogurt

2 tsp chickpea flour

juice of 1 lemon

1 tbsp finely chopped coriander leaves

1 Place the rabbit legs in a pan and add the salt and turmeric. Pour in 1.5 litres (2^3/$_4$ pints) water and bring to the boil over a moderate heat. Reduce the heat to low, cover with a lid and simmer for 45 minutes or until tender. Remove the rabbit legs from the liquid and drain; reserve the cooking liquid.

2 In another heavy-bottomed pan, heat the mustard oil to smoking point over a moderate heat. Add the *ghee* and, as it melts, add the whole red chillies and allow them to crackle for a few seconds. Next add the pickling spices and, as they begin to crackle and change colour, add the garlic. Sauté the garlic for a minute or so until golden brown, then add the onions. Sauté for 10 minutes or until the onions are soft and translucent but not brown.

3 Stir in the salt and turmeric and add the cooked rabbit legs. Add the ginger and palm sugar and stir for a few minutes, until the legs start to acquire a light brown colour. Now stir in the reserved cooking liquid and let it simmer for 5 minutes.

4 In a bowl whisk the yogurt with the chickpea flour until well combined. Increase the heat and bring the liquid in the pan back to the boil. Slowly add the yogurt mixture, stirring constantly to prevent it from splitting. When all the yogurt has been incorporated, continue simmering for 2–3 minutes. If the oil starts to separate out at the sides of the pan, that's fine.

5 Check the seasoning and, just before serving, stir in the lemon juice and coriander. Serve with either rice or bread.

PITOD KA SAAG CHiCKPEA FLOUR DUMPLiNGS iN YOGURT SAUCE

This is a very unusual vegetarian dish using yogurt and chickpea flour as the primary ingredients. The texture of the dumplings and complex mix of spices make a very interesting dish. This is good in the summer, served with steamed rice.

serves 6

thin and sour

750g (1lb 10oz) plain
   Greek-style yogurt
100g (3½oz) chickpea flour
1 tsp salt
½ tsp ground turmeric
½ tsp sugar
½ tsp ground *garam masala*
2.5cm (1in) piece fresh root
   ginger, finely chopped
2 tbsp *ghee*
1 tsp fennel seeds
pinch of asafoetida
oil for frying

Yogurt sauce

2 tbsp corn oil
pinch of asafoetida
½ tbsp cumin seeds
4 cloves
1 onion, finely chopped
200g (7oz) plain Greek-style
   yogurt
2 tbsp ground coriander
½ tsp ground turmeric
½ tsp red chilli powder
salt and sugar, as needed
2 green chillies, stalk removed
   and slit into 4
1cm (½in) piece fresh root
   ginger, in julienne
20g (¾oz) coriander leaves,
   chopped
juice of ½ lemon

1 First make the dumplings. Whisk the yogurt and 500ml (16fl oz) water with the chickpea flour, salt, turmeric, sugar, *garam masala* and ginger in a bowl. Set aside.

2 Heat the *ghee* in a heavy pan, add the fennel seeds and sauté briefly, then add the asafoetida and stir for 30 seconds. As the flavours are released, add the yogurt mix and cook, stirring constantly, for 20–25 minutes or until the mixture becomes thick and acquires the consistency of a soft dough. Remove from the heat and transfer to a greased 15cm (6in) square tray or tin. Chill in the fridge for about 30 minutes or until set like a cake.

3 To make the sauce, heat the oil in a saucepan over a moderate heat and add the asafoetida, cumin and cloves. When they begin to crackle, add the onion and cook for 5–8 minutes or until soft.

4 Meanwhile, whisk the yogurt with the ground coriander, turmeric, red chilli powder and salt. Add to the onions, stirring constantly, and keep stirring as the mixture comes to the boil again, to prevent the yogurt from splitting. Once boiling, add the green chillies and 200ml (7fl oz) water. Bring back to the boil, then cook for about 5 minutes. Check the seasoning and add salt and sugar to balance the taste, if required. Finish with the fresh ginger, coriander and lemon juice. Keep hot.

5 Cut the dumpling 'cake' into 2.5cm (1in) squares. Heat some oil in a frying pan and, when hot, add the dumplings, a few at a time. Fry for a couple of minutes, until the dumplings have a crust. Serve on top of the hot sauce, or mix into the sauce and bring to a simmer before serving.

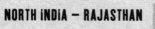

PANCHMAEL DAAL FIVE LENTILS MIX

Panchmael means a mix of five, hence the name of this dish. It can be made with just three types of lentils – those most easily obtainable in larger supermarkets and health food stores are red, *moong* and *chana*. A visit to an Asian grocery store will enable you to find the others but you can even make the dish with just one type.

serves 4

spicy, aromatic and light

2 heaped tbsp split green lentils (*moong dal*)

2 heaped tbsp split yellow lentils (*toor dal*)

2 heaped tbsp split gram lentils (*chana dal*)

2 heaped tbsp split and husked black lentils (*urad dal*)

2 tbsp split red lentils (*masoor dal*)

1¹/₂ tsp salt

¹/₂ tsp ground turmeric

2 tbsp *ghee*

1 large onion, finely chopped

¹/₂ tsp red chilli powder

1 tsp ground *garam masala*

1 tomato, chopped

1 tbsp chopped coriander leaves

squeeze of lemon juice

Tadka

1 tbsp *ghee*

1 dried red chilli

¹/₂ tsp cumin seeds

4 cloves

2 garlic cloves, finely chopped

1 Mix all the lentils together, then wash under running water. Leave to soak in cold water and cover for about 20 minutes.

2 Put the lentils in a saucepan with 600ml (1 pint) water, 1 tsp salt and half of the turmeric. Bring to the boil, skimming off the white scum from the surface whenever necessary. Cover and simmer on a low heat for 20–25 minutes or until all the lentils, except for the *chana dal*, are very soft and broken down.

3 Meanwhile, heat the *ghee* in a frying pan and, when hot, add the onion and cook until golden brown. Add the remaining salt and turmeric, the chilli powder and *garam masala* and sauté for a minute, then add the tomato and cook until soft.

4 Pour the onion and tomato mixture over the lentils and bring to the boil. If the lentils begin to thicken too much, add some boiling water and keep stirring, to ensure that they don't stick to the pan. Finish with the fresh coriander and lemon juice. Remove from the heat and keep hot.

5 For the *tadka*, or tempering, heat the *ghee* in a large ladle (or small pan) until smoking. Add the whole red chilli, cumin seeds, cloves and garlic, in that order and in quick succession as the garlic begins to turn golden, then pour the contents of the ladle over the lentils and cover the pan with a lid. Leave covered for 2 minutes, to let the smoke and flavours be absorbed by the lentils. Remove the lid, stir well and serve immediately.

Split red lentils >
The mildly flavoured split red lentils are the most commonly eaten lentils in an Indian household. They cook very quickly and do not need any pre-soaking.

LAHSUN KI CHUTNEY GARLIC CHUTNEY

This is a fine example of one of the very hot chutneys and pickles that are consumed in the region of Rajasthan. These chutneys and pickles are often made from dried and preserved vegetables or fruit – here, *kachri*, a sour, tomato-like fruit, is used, adding texture as well as acidity and sharpness – and the heavy-handed spicing means that the chutney has a better keeping quality. In the old days, travellers would take these chutneys on their journeys and make a really tasty but simple meal of chutney and bread. This delicious chutney can be stored in the larder for a week as long as it's covered by oil on top. It will keep for up to 2 weeks in the fridge. If you are unable to find *kachri*, you can increase the garlic by the same amount (250g/9oz). The result will be a much hotter chutney. Balance the flavour with 1 tbsp tomato ketchup if it's too hot for your liking.

makes about 500g (1lb 2oz)

hot, spicy and sharp

250ml (9fl oz) vegetable or corn oil

1 tsp cumin seeds

125g (4$\frac{1}{2}$oz) garlic, roughly chopped

75g (2$\frac{1}{2}$oz) dried red chillies, soaked in 250ml (9fl oz) water, drained and made into a paste

75ml (2$\frac{1}{2}$fl oz) malt vinegar

2 tbsp salt

1 tbsp red chilli powder

250g (9oz) *kachri* (see above), coarsely pounded

3 tbsp sugar, or to taste

1 tbsp chopped coriander leaves (optional)

1 Heat the oil in a saucepan, add the cumin seeds and, when they crackle, add the garlic. Fry until it begins to turn golden.

2 Add the chilli paste, vinegar, salt and chilli powder. Cook, stirring constantly, for 5–6 minutes. Add the *kachri* if you have some and cook the chutney for a further 12–15 minutes or until the fat separates out and comes to the top.

3 Check the seasoning and add the sugar, if required. Remove from the heat and allow to cool. This chutney can be eaten cold or hot. If you decide to heat it up before serving, add the fresh coriander to liven it up.

Garlic cloves >

One of the most essential ingredients in Indian curries, garlic's pungency varies in intensity with different cooking techniques. Crushed or pounded garlic cloves are far stronger than whole cloves.

MISSI ROTI CHiCKPEA BREAD

This rustic, spiced bread uses two different flours along with spices and seasoning, which gives it a unique flavour. It was a favourite for travellers, who would carry some of this bread to have with small quantities of very spicy garlic chutney for a light meal during their journey. Chickpea flour increases water retention in the body, which is particularly useful when travelling in the desert. The bread can be served either as an accompaniment to any Rajasthani recipe in this chapter or as a snack with a chutney or pickle of your choice.

makes 8

300g (10oz) chickpea flour
200g (7oz) plain flour
25g (scant 1oz) salt
1 tsp finely chopped fresh root ginger
2 green chillies, deseeded and finely chopped
1 tbsp finely chopped coriander leaves
1 tsp carom seeds
½ tsp red chilli powder
½ tsp ground turmeric
2 tbsp vegetable oil
1 red onion, finely chopped
1 spring onion, finely chopped
3 tbsp melted *ghee* for brushing and basting

1 Mix together the chickpea flour and plain flour in a large bowl. Transfer 3-4 tbsp of the flour mix to a small bowl and set aside to use later if needed. Add the salt, ginger, green chillies, chopped coriander, carom seeds, red chilli powder and turmeric to the large bowl and mix well to combine with the flours.

2 Add the oil and 200ml (7fl oz) water and knead to obtain a stiff dough. If the dough feels slightly soft add some of the reserved flour. Gather the dough into a mound, cover with a damp kitchen cloth and keep aside for 15-20 minutes.

3 Divide the dough into 8 pieces and shape into balls. Top each of the balls with chopped red onion and spring onion, then roll out using a rolling pin into a round 15-20cm (6-8in) in diameter.

4 Place a large frying pan over a low to moderate heat. When hot, cook the breads on the dry pan, one at a time, for 3-4 minutes on each side or until they start to dry out and colour.

5 When both sides are done, brush with some melted *ghee* and turn the bread over, then brush the other side with melted *ghee*. Serve the breads hot.

MAKAI KA SOWETA LAMB AND SWEETCORN CURRY

This is a true example of regional Indian cooking using local ingredients to make a dish that is not only unique but also appropriate for the region. The climate in most of Rajasthan and the Great 'Thar' desert is arid and, while not a lot is produced here, maize is grown and consumed in abundance. Sweetcorn helps water retention in the body and yogurt is also cooling in a hot climate. I've made this recipe with lamb but it would work just as well with goat or mutton, if you can get some.

serves 4–6

warmly spiced

1kg (2¹/₄lb) boned shoulder of lamb, cut into 2.5cm (1in) cubes

100g (3¹/₂oz) *ghee* or corn oil

1¹/₂ tsp cumin seeds

5 green cardamom pods

4 black cardamom pods

10 cloves

2 cinnamon leaves or bay leaves

750ml (1¹/₄ pints) lamb stock or water

450g (1lb) canned sweetcorn, drained and coarsely chopped

juice of ¹/₂ lemon

30g (1oz) coriander leaves, chopped

Marinade

300g (10oz) plain yogurt

2 tsp ground coriander

1 tsp ground turmeric

2 tsp salt

Onion paste

200g (7oz) onions, finely chopped

75g (2¹/₂oz) garlic cloves, finely chopped

12 green chillies

1 Mix together the ingredients for the marinade. Add the cubes of lamb and turn to coat them, then cover and set aside for about 15 minutes.

2 Meanwhile, make the onion paste by blending together the ingredients in a blender until smooth.

3 Heat the *ghee* in a heavy-bottomed pan over a moderate heat, then add all the spices and the cinnamon or bay leaves. As the spices crackle, add the marinated cubes of lamb, with the marinade, and turn up the heat to high. Cook for 12–15 minutes or until all the moisture has evaporated, stirring constantly.

4 Next add the onion paste and cook for a further 10 minutes, still stirring to ensure that the paste does not stick to the pan and burn. Pour over the lamb stock and reduce the heat. Simmer for 30 minutes or until the meat is about 85 per cent cooked.

5 Add the sweetcorn and cook for another 10 minutes, stirring constantly. The dish is ready when the consistency is glossy. Remove from the heat, check the seasoning and transfer to a heated serving dish. Finish with the lemon juice and fresh coriander. Serve with steamed rice or bread.

DAAL MAKHANI BLACK LENTILS

This is an earthy, rich Punjabi dish that is typical of the region, the land of five rivers. It is not for the calorie-conscious, as it requires large amounts of butter and cream. You will need to go to an Asian grocery store to buy the specific type of lentil. The dish normally takes a lot of time to prepare – traditionally it is put on to the embers of the coals in the *tandoor* and left to simmer gently all night.

serves 4

rich, earthy and creamy

250g (9oz) whole black lentils (*urad*), soaked in lukewarm water overnight

1 tsp ginger paste

1 tsp garlic paste

1$^1/_2$ tsp salt

2 tsp red chilli powder

2 tbsp tomato purée

150g (5$^1/_2$oz) slightly salted butter

1 tsp ground *garam masala*

$^1/_2$ tsp ground dried fenugreek leaves

$^1/_2$ tsp sugar

4 tbsp single cream

1 Drain the lentils and transfer them to a saucepan. Pour over 1.5 litres (2$^3/_4$ pints) water and bring to the boil. Simmer for about 1 hour or until the lentils are thoroughly cooked but are not completely broken down and mashed.

2 Add the ginger and garlic pastes, salt and red chilli powder and simmer for a further 10 minutes. Reduce the heat to low and add the tomato purée and butter. Cook for 15 minutes or until the lentils are thick, stirring frequently. Take care that the emulsion does not split – that the butter does not separate from the lentils.

3 Stir in the *garam masala*, fenugreek leaves and sugar, and check the seasoning. Finish with the cream and serve immediately.

Dried fenugreek leaves >
Used as a flavouring herb, dried fenugreek leaves have a slightly bitter taste. When added in the right quantity, they also impart a warm aroma to curries.

MURGH MAKHANI OLD DELHI-STYLE CHICKEN CURRY

In Old Delhi in the 1950s, the legendary Moti Mahal restaurant created the dish that for millions of people around the world (especially, of course, in Britain) defines Indian food. 'Butter Chicken', as Moti Mahal calls it, is the father and mother of Chicken Tikka Masala. In the West, this dish is much interpreted, but in fact it has been enjoyed by Punjabis for decades. This is exactly how it is prepared in Old Delhi. Ideally the chicken should be cooked in a *tandoor* on skewers, to give a smoky flavour, but an oven or barbecue are good enough alternatives. The chicken should be cooked two-thirds of the way through and then simmered in the sauce. Collect the juices from the cooking chicken, strain and add them to the sauce, too.

serves 4–6

rich, smooth and fragrant

1 tsp ginger paste

1 tsp garlic paste

1½ tsp salt

1½ tsp chilli powder

juice of ½ lemon

800g (1¾lb) boned chicken thighs, skinned and cut in half

100g (3½oz) plain Greek-style yogurt

¼ tsp ground *garam masala*

Sauce

1.25kg (2¾lb) tomatoes, cut in half

2.5cm (1in) piece fresh root ginger, crushed

4 garlic cloves, peeled

4 green cardamom pods

2 cloves

1 cinnamon leaf or bay leaf

1½ tbsp Kashmiri chilli powder

60g (2oz) butter, cut into small pieces

2.5cm (1in) piece fresh root ginger, finely chopped

2 green chillies, each slit into 4

75ml (2½fl oz) single cream

1 tsp salt

1 tsp ground dried fenugreek leaves

¼ tsp ground *garam masala*

2 tsp sugar (optional)

1 Prepare the barbecue or preheat the oven to 220°C (450°F/Gas 8).

2 To make the marinade, mix together the ginger paste, garlic paste, salt, chilli powder and lemon juice in a large bowl. Add the chicken and, using your hands, coat the pieces with the mixture. Set aside for 20 minutes. Mix the yogurt with the *garam masala* and apply to the marinated chicken. Set aside for another 10 minutes if you have the time.

3 Thread the chicken on to skewers. Cook on the barbecue or in the oven for 15–18 minutes, turning the skewers after 10 minutes or so, to cook evenly on both sides.

4 While the chicken is cooking make the sauce. Place the tomatoes in a pot with 125ml (4fl oz) water and add the crushed ginger, garlic, cardamom pods, cloves and cinnamon leaf. Cook until the tomatoes are completely broken down and soft.

5 Remove the pan from the heat and, using a hand-held blender, purée the mixture (or do this in a blender or food processor). Press through a sieve to make a very smooth purée.

6 Return the purée to the pan and bring to the boil. Stir in the chilli powder. Cook until the purée starts to thicken, then slowly incorporate the butter, little by little, stirring constantly. The sauce will become glossy.

7 Add the chicken (off the skewers) and the strained juices from roasting. Simmer for 5–6 minutes. As the sauce begins to thicken, add the chopped ginger, slit green chillies and cream. Continue simmering until the sauce is thick enough to coat the chicken.

8 Remove from the heat before the fat separates out and comes to the surface of the dish. (If that does happen, simply stir in 1–2 tbsp water and 1 tbsp more cream and remove immediately from the heat.) Add the salt, ground fenugreek and *garam masala* and mix well. Check the seasoning and add the sugar, if needed.

9 Serve the chicken curry with hot *naan* (p50) or pilau rice.

KADHAI PANEER STiR-FRY OF PANEER CHEESE WiTH PEPPERS

A *kadhai*, or *karahi*, is the Indian wok, and this is the Indian answer to a stir-fry. The recipe here is probably the most popular of all *kadhai* dishes in India, by far the easiest, tastiest and most colourful of the various different versions. This style of cooking is very versatile and quick if you've done some of the basic preparation – prepare a basic sauce in advance, then it's simply a question of choosing your meat, fish or vegetables and degree of spiciness. You may want to keep a jar of this basic *kadhai* sauce in your fridge. The *kadhai* method is getting particularly popular with youngsters and people who are learning to cook and want to try out different things without spending a lot of time in the kitchen.

serves 4–6

colourful, sweet and sour

1 tbsp *ghee* or corn oil

½ tsp crushed dried chillies

2 red or yellow peppers, deseeded and cut into strips 1 x 3cm (½ x 1¼in)

1 red onion, sliced 1cm (½in) thick

600g (1lb 5oz) *paneer*, cut into batons 1 x 3cm (½ x 1¼in)

20g (¾oz) coriander leaves, finely chopped

½ tsp dried fenugreek leaves, crumbled

juice of 1 lemon

5cm (2in) piece fresh root ginger, cut into juliennes

Basic kadhai sauce

80g (scant 3oz) *ghee* or corn oil

30g (1oz) garlic cloves, finely chopped

15g (½oz) coriander seeds, coarsely pounded

8 red chillies, coarsely pounded in a mortar

2 onions, finely chopped

5cm (2in) piece fresh root ginger, finely chopped

3 green chillies, finely chopped

750g (1lb 10oz) fresh ripe tomatoes, finely chopped

2 tsp salt

1 tsp ground *garam masala*

1½ tsp dried fenugreek leaves, crumbled

1 tsp sugar (optional)

1 To make the sauce, heat the *ghee* in a pan, add the garlic and let it colour. Stir, then add the coriander seeds and red chillies. When they release their aromas, add the onions and cook until they start changing to light golden. Stir in the ginger, green chillies and tomatoes. Reduce the heat to low and cook until all excess moisture has evaporated and the fat starts to separate out. Add the salt, *garam masala* and fenugreek leaves and stir. Taste and add some sugar, if needed.

2 For the stir-fry, heat the *ghee* in a *kadhai*, wok or large frying pan. Add the crushed chillies, pepper strips and red onion. Stir and sauté on a high heat for under a minute, then add the *paneer* and stir for another minute. Add the sauce and mix well. Once everything is heated through, check for seasoning, adding a touch of salt if required. Finish with the fresh coriander, fenugreek leaves and lemon juice. Garnish with the ginger and serve with *naan* (p50).

SUBZ SAAG GOSHT LAMB COOKED WITH WINTER VEGETABLES AND SPINACH

This recipe has its origins in Kashmir, the northernmost state of India, on the border of Pakistan, where the winters are severe. It is a simple yet warming everyday dish using turnips, carrots, spinach and dill with lamb. It could have been the starting point of what the Western world knows as Saag Gosht minus the root vegetables, but try it with the vegetables and see the difference for yourself.

serves 4

rich, spicy and rustic

80g (scant 3oz) *ghee* or corn oil

2 tsp cumin seeds

2 tsp cloves

2 large onions, finely chopped

50g (1³/₄oz) garlic, finely chopped

40g (1¹/₂oz) fresh root ginger, finely chopped

2 tsp red chilli powder

1 tsp ground turmeric

2 tsp salt

1kg (2¹/₄lb) boned leg of lamb, cut into 2.5cm (1in) cubes

4 green chillies, slit lengthways

150g (5¹/₂oz) each turnips and carrots, cut into 1cm (¹/₂n) cubes

300ml (10fl oz) lamb stock or water

200g (7oz) tomatoes, finely chopped

400g (14oz) spinach leaves, finely chopped

1¹/₂ tsp ground mixed spices (equal parts cloves, nutmeg, mace and green cardamom)

30g (1oz) dill leaves, finely chopped

1 Heat the *ghee* or oil in a heavy pot and add the cumin seeds and cloves. When they crackle, add the onions and sauté until they become light golden in colour. Add the garlic and ginger and sauté for a further 2–3 minutes or until the garlic begins to change colour.

2 Sprinkle in the red chilli powder, turmeric and salt and stir for another couple of minutes until the spices begin to release their aromas and the fat starts to separate out. Now add the cubes of lamb and cook for 5–6 minutes, stirring constantly, until the lamb begins to brown around the edges.

3 When most of the liquid has evaporated and the lamb is getting browned, add the green chillies, turnips and carrots and stir. Pour in the lamb stock. Reduce the heat to low, cover with a lid and cook until the lamb is three-quarters done.

4 Remove the lid, add the tomatoes and cook for a further 10–12 minutes or until the lamb is nearly cooked and the tomatoes are incorporated with the *masala*. Stir in the spinach and increase the heat again. Cook for 2–3 minutes. (You can cover with a lid if you wish, to speed up the cooking of the spinach.)

5 The lamb and spinach should be cooked by now, so check for seasoning and correct if required. To finish the dish, sprinkle with the ground mixed spices and dill, then cover the pan with the lid and remove from the heat.

6 Remove the lid from the pan at the table and serve immediately, with *chapatti* or tandoori *roti*.

NAAN NAAN BREAD

This humble bread from Delhi and Punjab is probably one of the best gifts from the *tandoor* to mankind. It is widely available and popular the world over, and makes an excellent accompaniment for any curry. *Naan* is traditionally cooked in a charcoal-fired clay oven but will work as well in a regular oven or under the grill. Use your imagination and you could soon be making *naan* sandwiches and wraps or even using it as a base for canapés.

makes 16

35g (generous 1oz) caster sugar
2 eggs
400ml (14fl oz) full-fat milk
750g (1lb 10oz) plain flour
1½ tsp baking powder
1 tbsp salt
3½ tbsp vegetable oil

1 Preheat the oven to 220°C (425°F/Gas 7). Place two non-stick baking trays in the oven to heat up. Alternatively, preheat your grill to maximum heat.

2 Mix the sugar and eggs with the milk in a large jug, stirring until the sugar has dissolved. Put the flour in a large mixing bowl and mix in the baking powder and salt. Gradually pour the milk mixture into the flour, mixing with your hand, and knead lightly just to make a soft dough. Take care not to knead too much or the dough will become too stretchy. Cover the bowl with a damp cloth and leave to rest for 15 minutes.

3 Add the oil and mix lightly to incorporate it into the dough. Divide the dough into 16 small pieces. Roll out each piece into a round about 10cm (4in) in diameter. To form into the traditional 'tear' shape, lay a round over one palm and gently pull one edge down until it stretches a bit. Place the breads on the hot trays and bake for 4–5 minutes.

4 If you are using the grill, heat a grill pan on the hob. When it's hot, place one naan bread on the pan and cook on the hob for a couple of minutes or until the bread starts to colour slightly and cook underneath. Transfer the pan to the grill and cook for a minute or so, until the bread puffs up and becomes slightly coloured on top. Serve warm (if not serving immediately, reheat in a 180°C/350°F/Gas 4 oven for 1–2 minutes).

DAHI WALI MACHLI CATFISH IN YOGURT SAUCE

The north of India is not known for its fish dishes, but every region seems to have at least one standard recipe. Most of the fish used in northern India are river fish or are caught from lakes or ponds. Local fish include *rohu* or *katla* but elsewhere can be replaced by perch, barramundi or prized varieties like halibut or monkfish.

serves 4

light, fresh and slightly sour

1kg (2¼lb) fillet of catfish, perch or carp, cut into 4cm (1½in) cubes
1 tsp salt
juice of 1 lemon
1½ tsp ground turmeric
1½ tsp red chilli powder
1 tbsp carom seeds (optional)
2 tbsp chickpea flour
oil for deep frying

Sauce

3 tbsp *ghee* or corn oil
1 onion, finely chopped
1 tsp ground cumin
1 tsp ground turmeric
1 tsp red chilli powder
1 tsp salt
2.5cm (1in) piece fresh root ginger, finely chopped
2 green chillies, slit
450g (1lb) plain yogurt
40g (1½oz) chickpea flour
250ml (8fl oz) fish stock or water
½ tsp dried fenugreek leaves, crumbled
½ tsp ground *garam masala*

1 Turn on the oven to low before you begin to cook. Place the fish in a large bowl and rub with the salt, lemon juice and turmeric. Set aside to marinate for 20 minutes.

2 Sprinkle the fish with the chilli powder, carom seeds and chickpea flour. Using your hands, mix and rub well to ensure all the cubes of fish are coated with the mixture.

3 Heat oil in a deep saucepan. When hot, add the fish and deep fry for 2–3 minutes or until golden brown. Drain on kitchen paper, transfer to an ovenproof dish and place in the oven to keep warm while you make the sauce.

4 Heat the *ghee* in a saucepan, add the chopped onion and sauté until golden brown. Add the cumin, turmeric, chilli powder and salt and sauté until the spices begin to release their flavour. Stir in the ginger and green chillies and cook for a further 2 minutes.

5 Whisk the yogurt and chickpea flour together in a bowl, making sure there are no lumps. Slowly add the yogurt mixture to the pan, stirring constantly to prevent the yogurt from splitting. When all the yogurt has been incorporated, increase the heat and bring to the boil. Pour in the stock and bring back to the boil, then simmer for 3–5 minutes.

6 Add the pieces of fried fish and continue to cook over a low heat for another few minutes. Check the seasoning, then stir in the fenugreek and *garam masala*. Cover with a lid to retain the aromas of fenugreek and spices and remove from the heat. Serve immediately, with steamed rice.

NALLI GOSHT SLOW-BRAISED LAMB SHANK IN SAFFRON SAUCE

This is a very simple dish to make but is a great indicator of the level of finesse and sophistication in cooking that was reached during the reign of certain Mughal rulers in Lucknow. Slow cooking allows for maximum extraction of gelatine from the shanks, giving a shine and smoothness to the sauce that is unique.

serves 4

smooth and warmly spiced

4 lamb shanks

3 tbsp corn oil

2 black cardamom pods, crushed

2 cinnamon sticks

2 large onions, finely chopped

1 tsp ginger paste

1 tsp garlic paste

1½ tsp chilli powder

½ tsp ground fennel seeds

½ tsp ground coriander

1 tsp ground ginger

2 tbsp plain yogurt

5 tomatoes, puréed

1½ tsp salt

600ml (1 pint) lamb stock or water

To finish

¼ tsp ground *garam masala*

generous pinch of saffron threads

3 drops of rose water (optional)

2 tbsp single cream

1 First blanch the lamb shanks: place them in a large saucepan of boiling water, cover and cook for 20 minutes. Drain. When cool enough to handle, cut away all the gristle from the meat.

2 Heat the oil in a pan large enough to hold the shanks. Add the cardamoms and cinnamon sticks and, when they crackle, add the onions. Cook until golden brown. Add the ginger and garlic pastes and cook for 2 minutes, stirring constantly. Add the ground spices and cook for 3 more minutes.

3 Slowly whisk in the yogurt and stir until the sauce reaches simmering point. Stir in the fresh tomato purée and bring the sauce to the boil. Season with the salt.

4 Add the lamb shanks to the simmering sauce. Cover with a tight-fitting lid and cook over a low heat for 1½–2 hours or until the lamb is very tender and the meat is almost falling off the bone. Add some stock from time to time: you will need the extra liquid to cook the shanks completely.

5 Alternatively, you can cook the lamb shanks in the oven. Put them in a braising tray, cover with the sauce and stock, and braise in a preheated 180°C (350°F/Gas 4) oven for 2½–3 hours. Keep checking the shanks after 2 hours.

6 Remove the shanks and arrange them on a serving tray or plate. Cover and keep warm in a low oven while you finish the sauce.

7 Skim any excess fat or oil from the sauce, then strain the sauce into a smaller saucepan and return to the heat. Add the *garam masala* powder, saffron and rose water, if you have any. Bring to the boil again, check the seasoning and stir in the cream. Remove the shanks from the oven and pour over the sauce. Serve immediately.

< Black cardamom pods
Also known as the 'queen of spices', black cardamoms add a deep, smoky flavour to curry *masalas*.

KACHHI MIRCH KA GOSHT LAMB SHOULDER WITH GREEN CHILLIES, MINT AND YOGURT

Shoulder of lamb is very good for braising, which is one of the cooking techniques used to make this dish. It is similar to a North Indian *korma*, but it has a sharp kick or bite and freshness from the green chillies and mint as well as great texture and mouthfeel resulting from adding onions and more chillies at the end.

serves 4

sharp, hot and fresh

1kg (2¼lb) boned shoulder of lamb, cut into 3.5cm (1½in) cubes

300g (10oz) plain yogurt

1½ tsp black peppercorns, coarsely crushed

10g (¼oz) coriander seeds, roasted and coarsely pounded

10g (¼oz) cumin seeds, roasted and coarsely pounded

2 tsp salt

80g (scant 3oz) *ghee* or corn oil

1 blade mace

5 black cardamom pods

250g (9oz) white onions, finely chopped

20g (¾oz) fresh root ginger, finely chopped

6 green chillies, slit lengthways

750ml (1¼ pints) lamb stock or water

40g (1½oz) cashew nut paste

2½ tbsp single cream

1 red onion, cut into 1cm (½in) cubes

1 tbsp finely chopped mint leaves

juice of 1 lemon

1 tsp ground roasted fennel seeds

1 Wash the diced lamb in running cold water for 10 minutes to remove any blood. Dry using kitchen paper. Put the lamb in a bowl with the yogurt, peppercorns, roasted pounded coriander and cumin, and salt. Toss to mix, then set aside to marinate.

2 Reserve 1 tbsp of the *ghee* for later use and heat the rest in a heavy-bottomed pot. Add the mace and black cardamoms and stir for a few seconds. Add the white onions and cook them over a moderate heat until soft and translucent but not brown. As they begin to turn slightly golden, add the ginger and 4 of the green chillies.

3 Add the marinated lamb and stir. Cook for 12–15 minutes, stirring constantly, making sure that the lamb does not brown in the process. Pour in the stock, reduce the heat to a low and cook, covered, until the lamb is almost done.

4 Stir in the cashew nut paste and cook for a further 5–7 minutes. Add the cream and correct the seasoning, if required. Leave to simmer gently.

5 In a separate pan, heat the remaining *ghee* and briskly sauté the red onion and the remaining green chillies until the onion is soft and translucent. Add to the simmering lamb, sprinkle with the mint and lemon juice, and stir in the fennel powder. Serve immediately, with *paratha* (p64) or pilau.

REZALA BHOPAL-STYLE GOAT CURRY

This is a fascinating recipe that comes from the kitchens of a very wealthy *maharani* in central India. I like it as it's very easy to remember and very simple to make. It strangely resembles a pound cake recipe from the medieval era, where you put in equal quantities of everything, mix and bang it into the oven. In this case, just mix together all the ingredients and seal the pot. Cook either in the oven or on the hob over a very slow flame. The recipe here uses goat but feel free to replace it with lamb or mutton as both work just as well.

serves 4

hot, spicy and rich

1kg (2¼lb) boned leg of goat, cut into 2.5cm (1in) cubes

200ml (7fl oz) corn oil or *ghee*

200g (7oz) green chillies, slit lengthways and deseeded

200g (7oz) crisp-fried onions, crushed coarsely

25g (scant 1oz) pineapple, blended to a paste

200g (7oz) plain Greek-style yogurt

2 tbsp finely chopped fresh root ginger

1 tbsp garlic paste

25g (scant 1oz) roasted chickpea flour

25g (scant 1oz) salt

1 tsp whole allspice

2 tsp royal cumin or black cumin seeds

2 tsp red chilli powder

2 tsp ground cumin

2 tsp ground *garam masala*

Layered *paratha* dough (p64), or a flour and water dough, to seal

To finish

100ml (3½fl oz) single cream

50g (1¾oz) fried cashew nuts, pounded or blended to a paste

120g (4¼oz) coriander leaves, chopped

20g (¾oz) mint leaves, chopped

1 If cooking in the oven, preheat it to 180°C (350°F/Gas 4).

2 Mix the meat with all the other ingredients (except the *paratha* dough) and set aside to marinate for 10–15 minutes.

3 Transfer the marinated meat to an ovenproof earthenware casserole or flameproof pot with a tight-fitting lid. Seal the lid using the *paratha* dough. If need be, place a weight on the lid to prevent steam from escaping during cooking.

4 Put the casserole in the oven or the pot over a low flame. Cook for 2 hours or until the meat is tender. If cooking in the oven, reduce the heat to 110°C (230°F/Gas ¼) after 25–30 minutes.

5 Stir the sauce, then finish by adding the cream and cashew nut paste. Bring back to the boil. Taste and correct the seasoning, if required. Sprinkle with the chopped coriander and mint, and serve.

Mint leaves >
Used mainly as a garnish, the cool minty notes of these leaves are a welcome addition to spicy curries.

SUBZ MILONI SEASONAL VEGETABLES IN SPINACH AND GARLIC SAUCE

Vegetables such as mushrooms and baby corn were not available in the past, but are now more widely seen. As this is a dish of mixed vegetables, feel free to use whatever you like. Just remember to cut all of the vegetables to more or less the same shape and size. Also, parboil hard vegetables beforehand and add the delicate and green vegetables later in the cooking.

serves 4–6

fresh, light and aromatic

150g (5¹/₂oz) carrots, cut into 1cm (¹/₂in) cubes

150g (5¹/₂oz) cauliflower, trimmed into 1cm (¹/₂in) florets

100g (3¹/₂oz) fine green beans, cut into 1cm (¹/₂in) lengths

1kg (2¹/₄lb) young spinach leaves

75g (2¹/₂oz) *ghee* or vegetable oil

2 tsp cumin seeds

40g (1¹/₂oz) garlic, finely chopped

1 large onion, finely chopped

2.5cm (1in) piece fresh root ginger, finely chopped

6 green chillies, finely chopped

1¹/₂ tsp ground coriander

2 tsp salt

100g (3¹/₂oz) button or chestnut mushrooms, cut into 1cm (¹/₂in) cubes

50g (1³/₄oz) baby corn, cut into 1cm (¹/₂n) lengths, or canned sweetcorn (optional)

50g (1³/₄oz) broccoli florets, trimmed into 1cm (¹/₂in) pieces (optional)

50g (1³/₄oz) frozen peas or petit pois, thawed

1 tbsp chickpea flour

25g (scant 1oz) butter

4 tbsp single cream

1 tsp dried fenugreek leaves, crumbled

1 tsp ground *garam masala*

1 Parboil the carrots, cauliflower and green beans until al dente (3 minutes for the cauliflower and green beans, 4 minutes for the carrots). Drain well and refresh in iced water; drain again.

2 Blanch the spinach in boiling salted water until wilted, then drain and cool quickly in iced water. Squeeze dry. Blend in a food processor to make a smooth paste, adding a little water as required.

3 In a heavy-bottomed pan, heat the *ghee* over a moderate heat. Stir in the cumin seeds and, when they start to crackle, add the garlic and sauté until golden. Add the onion, reduce the heat to low and cook until soft and golden brown. Add the ginger and chillies and sauté for 2–3 minutes.

4 Stir in the carrots and cauliflower and cook for 2–4 minutes. Add the coriander and salt, then the mushrooms and sauté, stirring, for 2–3 minutes or until they soften up. Add the baby corn and sauté for 1–2 minutes. Next add the broccoli, beans and peas. Mix together well. Add the chickpea flour and stir for 2–3 minutes, to cook off the flour. Add the spinach paste, then bring to the boil, stirring in the butter and cream.

5 As soon as the vegetables are boiling, check for seasoning and correct if necessary. Finish with the fenugreek leaves and *garam masala*. Do not cook for too long after adding the spinach paste as it will discolour and render the dish unappetizing in appearance. Serve with *paratha* (p64) or *chapatti*.

Button mushrooms >
One of the most readily available mushrooms, sauté them in *ghee* or butter to enhance their mild flavour.

BATEYR MASALA QUAILS IN SPICY CURRY

In the 1750s, when *bawarchis* (cooks) supplied prepared dishes to their wealthy patrons, the food was delivered in covered and sealed trays, to prevent any tampering. A dish such as this would have been cooked for special occasions. Served with a pilau, it could be the centrepiece of your dinner table. Other game birds such as partridge, pheasant or grouse will also work well.

serves 6

slightly fatty and aromatic

6 quails, about 300g (10oz) each, skinned

25g (scant 1oz) ginger paste

25g (scant 1oz) garlic paste

2 1/2 tsp red chilli powder

1 tsp ground turmeric

2 1/2 tsp salt

200ml (7fl oz) vegetable oil or *ghee*

2.5cm (1in) cinnamon stick

1 blade mace

2 black cardamom pods

1 tbsp black peppercorns

5 cloves

5 green cardamom pods

250g (9oz) onions, blended to a fine paste

2 tbsp ground coriander

450g (1lb) plain yogurt

1 1/2 tbsp chickpea flour

1 tsp ground *garam masala*

50g (1 3/4oz) coriander leaves, finely chopped

1 Clean the quails inside and out by washing under running cold water; drain and pat dry using kitchen paper. Season them by rubbing with a mixture of 1 tbsp of the ginger paste, 1 tbsp garlic paste, 1 tsp red chilli powder, 1/2 tsp turmeric and 1 tsp salt. Set aside to marinate for 10–15 minutes.

2 Take a shallow but wide pot or pan that can hold the quails in it comfortably and which has a tight-fitting lid. Set it over a moderate heat and pour in the oil. When hot, place the quails in the pot, a few at a time, and cook until they are golden brown on all sides. Using a slotted spoon, transfer the quails to a dish and set aside.

3 Heat the juices and oil left in the pot and add the whole spices, stirring to release their aromas. Add the onion paste and the remainder of the ginger and garlic pastes and cook, stirring constantly to prevent the pastes from sticking to the bottom of the pan. After 5–6 minutes add the remainder of the chilli powder, turmeric and salt and the ground coriander. Cook until the fat begins to separate out from the pastes.

4 Return the seared quails to the pot and spoon the sauce over them carefully, taking care not to break the birds. Whisk the yogurt with the chickpea flour, then pour over the birds and mix into the sauce. Cover with the lid, reduce the heat to low and cook for 15–20 minutes.

5 Remove the lid and transfer the quails to a serving dish; keep warm. Whisk the sauce for a few minutes using a hand whisk or fork to emulsify the mixture. It will still separate a little but should have a coating consistency. Taste and correct the seasoning if required and finish with the *garam masala* and fresh coriander. Spoon over the quails and serve immediately.

GUCCHI AUR MURGH KALIA CHiCKEN AND MOREL CURRY

In the mid-18th century, competition between *rakabdars* (chefs) in Lucknow was at its peak. Each tried to out-do the others by creating ever more sophisticated dishes. Addition of gold leaf was, and still is, the ultimate luxurious adornment.

serves 4–6

aromatic and spicy

50g (1³/₄oz) large dried morels
500g (1lb 2oz) onions, finely sliced
oil for deep-frying
300g (10oz) plain yogurt
100g (3¹/₂oz) *ghee* or vegetable oil
1 tsp royal cumin seeds
1 tsp whole allspice
¹/₂ nutmeg
1 blade mace
4 green cardamom pods
¹/₂ tsp black peppercorns
1kg (2¹/₄lb) boned chicken thighs, excess fat removed and each cut lengthways in half
2 tbsp ginger paste
2 tbsp garlic paste
2 tbsp Kashmiri red chilli powder
2 tsp salt
250ml (9fl oz) chicken stock
100ml (3¹/₂fl oz) single cream
pinch of saffron threads
¹/₂ tsp ground *garam masala*
few drops of rose water (optional)
2 sheets of gold leaf (completely optional)

1 Wash the morels thoroughly to get rid of any grit. Soak in 200ml (7fl oz) water for 30 minutes to rehydrate. Drain the morels, reserving the liquid, and pat dry with kitchen paper.

2 While the morels are soaking, deep-fry the onions until golden. Drain, then blend with 50g (1³/₄oz) of the yogurt and a little water to make a paste.

3 Heat 1 tbsp of the *ghee* in a heavy-bottomed pan and add ¹/₂ tsp of the royal cumin. When it crackles, add the morels and sauté for a couple of minutes over a moderate heat. Using a slotted spoon remove the morels from the pan and set aside.

4 Heat the rest of the *ghee* in the pan and add the whole spices, together with the remaining royal cumin. Stir for 1–2 minutes, then add the chicken pieces. Saute for 2–3 minutes on a high heat, then add the onion, ginger and garlic pastes and mix together. Stir for another 2–3 minutes. Add the red chilli powder and salt and cook for 2–3 minutes. Stir in the remaining yogurt, little by little. Cook for 5 minutes, then add the stock and the reserved morel soaking liquid. Reduce the heat, cover the pan and simmer gently until the chicken is cooked.

5 Remove the chicken pieces with a slotted spoon and set aside. Pass the sauce through a sieve, then return to the pan and bring back to the boil. Boil until reduced to a sauce-like consistency.

6 Reduce the heat to low and stir in the cream, saffron and *garam masala*. Add the chicken pieces and simmer briefly to heat up. Lastly, just before serving, add the morels and finish with the rose water, if using. Transfer to a shallow dish and garnish with the optional gold leaf.

MUTTER PULAO GREEN PEAS PILAU

This is one of the simplest pilau rice preparations that you will ever come across. Traditionally in Lucknow and central states, pilaus were of many varieties and often used several ingredients together. In fact, pilaus were considered to be more exotic and special than *biryanis*, which were thought to be 'rough and ready'. The basic difference between boiled rice and pilau rice is not the use of spices but the method of cooking. Boiled rice may well be cooked with spices, but the cooking liquid is drained away at the end, similar to when cooking pasta. For pilau rice it is important to use just the right quantity of water, as all should be absorbed when the rice is done. Rice has more flavour and nutrients when cooked by the pilau method.

serves 4

deliciously perfumed

400g (14oz) Basmati rice

75g (2^1/$_2$oz) *ghee*

1 tsp cumin seeds

^{1}/$_2$ tsp cloves

1 cinnamon leaf or bay leaf

4 green cardamom pods

1 cinnamon stick

2 red onions, finely sliced

100g (3^1/$_2$oz) frozen petit pois or peas, thawed

1 tbsp salt

10g (^{1}/$_4$oz) mint leaves, shredded

10g (^{1}/$_4$oz) coriander leaves, chopped

1 Wash the rice in cold running water, then soak in cold water to cover for 20–25 minutes. Soaking the rice reduces the cooking time and prevents the grains from breaking while cooking.

2 Heat the *ghee* in a thick-bottomed casserole over a moderate heat and add the whole spices. When they crackle, add the sliced onions and sauté until they are golden brown. Add the peas and sauté for 2–3 minutes. Pour in 800ml (1^1/$_3$ pints) water. Add the salt, cover and bring to the boil.

3 Drain the soaked rice and add to the casserole. Cover again and bring back to the boil. Cook, covered, for 8–10 minutes over a moderately high heat. From time to time remove the lid and gently stir the rice, keeping in mind that too much handling can break the rice grains.

4 When the water is nearly all absorbed and you can see small holes on the surface of the rice, sprinkle over the mint and the coriander. Cover the casserole tightly and reduce the heat to low. Cook for a further 10 minutes. Alternatively, finish cooking the rice in a preheated 130°C (250°F/Gas ^{1}/$_2$) oven for 10 minutes.

NOTE To make the pilau in a microwave, follow the recipe up to the stage of adding the peas. Then add the salt and the soaked rice and mix lightly for a couple of minutes, until the grains of rice are coated with oil. Transfer to a microwave container. Pour the measured quantity of water over the rice, cover with cling film and prick it to make a few holes. Place in the microwave (800W) and cook for 18–20 minutes. Allow the rice to rest for 5 minutes, then transfer to a serving dish.

TAWA PARATHA LAYERED PARATHA

These triangular breads are prepared in thousands of households across northern India almost every morning, to eat for breakfast, lunch and dinner. You can add different spices, chillies, pastes, and so on to create your own unique *paratha*.

makes 8

500g (1lb 2oz) *chapatti* flour

2 tsp salt

1 tbsp vegetable oil

50g (1³/₄oz) *chapatti* flour to dust

3 tbsp melted *ghee* or vegetable oil

1 tbsp carom seeds or black onion seeds (optional)

1 Mix the *chapatti* flour with the salt, oil and 275ml (9fl oz) water in a large bowl, to make a smooth dough.

2 Cover with a damp cloth or cling film and leave to rest for 15 minutes.

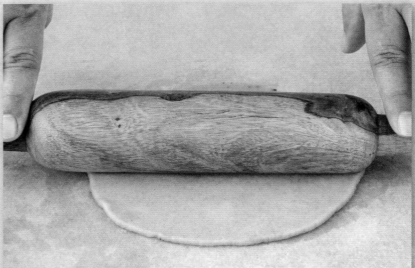

3 Divide the dough into 8 equal portions and shape each into a smooth round ball. Take one ball at a time and flatten it. Dust with some of the extra flour and, using a rolling pin, roll it out into a disc 6–8cm (2¹/₂–3in) in diameter.

4 Spread a little *ghee* on the surface of the disc, sprinkle with some seeds (if using) and dust with a little flour. Fold the disc in half to form a half moon.

5 Repeat the same process of *ghee*, seeds and flour on the surface of the half moon, then fold into a triangle. Now flatten the triangle carefully, using the rolling pin, until it is about 3mm (1/8in) thick.

6 Heat a dry *tawa*, griddle or frying pan and fry each bread for a couple of minutes, until the surface is dry and it starts to get specks of brown colour. Turn it over and cook for a further 2 minutes.

7 While the second side is cooking, brush the first side lightly with *ghee*. Turn the bread over again and brush the other side with *ghee*. You should see the steam opening up the layers as the bread cooks.

8 Remove from the heat once both sides are golden and crisp. Serve the breads hot from the pan.

CHINGRI MALAI CURRY KiNG PRAWNS iN COCONUT CURRY SAUCE

This is one of the all-time favourite Bengali dishes, reserved for very special guests, big celebratory buffets and weddings. I still have memories of the curry being served inside a green coconut. As a child I was told the term *malai* referred to the creamy flesh inside the coconut. It made sense then and it makes sense now, as this is how most people think of the dish. While travelling and working as a chef, it surprised me no end to see the similarity between Chingri Malai Curry and a Malaysian *laksa*. I often wonder if the Bengali name that we use has its origins in the 'Malaya', which is how Malaysia is known in India.

serves 4

rich, creamy, sweet and spicy

5cm (2in) piece fresh root ginger, roughly chopped

10 garlic cloves, roughly chopped

6 onions, roughly chopped

225ml (7½fl oz) vegetable oil

800g (1¾lb) freshwater prawns, the largest you can find, peeled and deveined

1 tbsp ground turmeric

1 tbsp salt

3 cinnamon leaves or bay leaves

2 tbsp ground cumin

4 green chillies, slit lengthways

200ml (7fl oz) thick coconut milk (p241)

1 tsp sugar (optional)

5 green cardamom pods, seeds removed and finely ground in a mortar

2 tbsp *ghee*

1 Blend the ginger and garlic together in a food processor to make a fine paste. Remove and set aside. Blend the onions to a fine paste with 100ml (3½fl oz) of the oil.

2 Season the prawns with ½ tsp each of turmeric and salt. Heat 2 tbsp of the oil in a non-stick frying pan and sear the prawns briefly, then remove and set aside.

3 Heat the remaining oil in a heavy frying pan and add the onion paste with the cinnamon leaves. Sauté over a moderate heat for 10 minutes or until light brown, stirring occasionally. Mix together the cumin, remaining turmeric, ginger-garlic paste and 150ml (5fl oz) water, then add to the onions. Reduce the heat to low and cook for a further 5–8 minutes, stirring regularly. Stir in the remaining salt, the green chillies and prawns and cook for 2–3 minutes.

4 Mix in the coconut milk and simmer for 2–3 minutes or until the prawns are just cooked, adding a little more water if necessary. Correct the seasoning with salt and sugar, sprinkle over the cardamom powder and stir in the *ghee*. Serve immediately, with steamed rice.

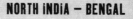

BHAPA LOBSTER STEAMED LOBSTER WiTH COCONUT, GiNGER AND CHiLLi

This would make a great party dish, one sure to impress your guests. In India it is reserved for special occasions and intimate gatherings, when important guests and relations arrive. The use of coconut, mustard, chilli and ginger creates an interesting play of flavours. The sweetness of lobster and coconut is balanced by the heat from chilli and ginger and the pungency of the mustard oil.

serves 4–6

sweet, hot and creamy

75g (2½oz) yellow mustard seeds

scant 2 tbsp white vinegar

6 raw lobsters, about 450g (1lb) each

250ml (9fl oz) thick coconut milk (p241)

100g (3½oz) plain Greek-style yogurt

6 green chillies, slit lengthways

5cm (2in) piece fresh root ginger, cut into julienne strips

5 garlic cloves, blended to a paste with a 1cm (½in) piece fresh root ginger

2 tsp salt

1½ tsp caster sugar

75ml (2½fl oz) mustard oil

1 tsp black mustard seeds

To finish

50g (1¾oz) coriander leaves, finely chopped

1 tsp ground *garam masala*

1 tbsp shredded fresh root ginger

1 Soak the yellow mustard seeds overnight in the white vinegar, then drain and blend to a paste.

2 Preheat the oven to 180°C (350°F/Gas 4). Slit each lobster lengthways in half, leaving the head and shell on. Clean the lobster halves and dry on kitchen paper. Arrange the lobsters, shell side down, side by side in a casserole or roasting tin.

3 Whisk together the coconut milk, yogurt, chillies, ginger julienne, garlic and ginger paste, yellow mustard paste, salt and sugar.

4 Heat the mustard oil in a pan to smoking point, then remove from the heat and allow to cool. Reheat the oil and add the black mustard seeds. Once the seeds crackle, add the coconut-spice paste and bring to the boil over a low heat, whisking constantly. Take care not to let the mixture split. Simmer gently for 2–3 minutes, then remove from the heat.

5 Pour the sauce over the lobster and cover with foil. Cook in the oven for 15–18 minutes. Remove from the oven, sprinkle with the chopped coriander, *garam masala* and shredded ginger, and serve immediately, with steamed rice.

BEKTI JHAL DEYA PERCH IN BENGALI MUSTARD AND ONION SAUCE

Bekti is a freshwater fish commonly eaten in India. There are two varieties. The Kolkata fish is smaller and has beautiful white flesh with a delicate flavour. It is considered far superior to its Bombay counterpart, which is much larger, fattier and considerably cheaper. Lake Victoria perch is a very good alternative to Kolkata *bekti*, but any meaty white fish such as halibut or cod could work just as well. If you wish, you can substitute 100g (3½oz) English wholegrain mustard for the mustard paste.

serves 6

sharp, hot and crunchy

1kg (2¼lb) white fish fillet, cut into 4cm (1½in) cubes

1 tsp salt

1 tsp red chilli powder

1 tsp ground turmeric

vegetable or corn oil for deep frying

50g (1¾oz) coriander leaves, finely chopped

Mustard paste

75g (2½oz) yellow mustard seeds

100ml (3½fl oz) white vinegar

1 tsp salt

1 tsp caster sugar

1 tsp ground turmeric

Curry

75ml (2½fl oz) mustard oil

1 tsp black mustard seeds

3 red onions, finely sliced

2 tsp ground cumin

1 tbsp red chilli powder

1½ tsp salt

400ml (14fl oz) fish stock or water

3 tomatoes, cut into quarters and deseeded

6 green chillies, slit lengthways

pinch of caster sugar (optional)

4 tbsp coconut cream (p241)

1 To make the mustard paste, soak the mustard seeds in the vinegar overnight. Drain, then grind to a fine paste. Mix together the salt, sugar and turmeric and stir into the paste.

2 Rinse the fish under cold running water, then dry with kitchen paper. Season with the salt, chilli powder and turmeric. Deep-fry the fish in hot oil for 1–2 minutes or until golden brown, then drain on kitchen paper and keep aside.

3 To make the curry, heat the mustard oil in a deep pan or flameproof casserole over a moderate heat. When it starts to smoke remove from the heat and set aside to cool. Reheat the oil, then add the mustard seeds and allow them to crackle. Add the onions and sauté over a moderate heat for 5–8 minutes or until translucent.

4 Add the mustard paste and sauté for a further 5 minutes. Stir in the cumin, chilli powder and salt. Add the fish stock and bring to the boil. Reduce the heat to low and simmer for 2–3 minutes. Now add the fried fish, tomatoes and green chillies, and simmer for a further 6–8 minutes. Correct the seasoning with salt (and sugar) if required and gently stir in the coconut cream. Garnish with the chopped coriander and serve with steamed rice.

Yellow mustard seeds >
Used as a condiment in many curries, whole yellow mustard seeds have virtually no aroma. They release a strong earthy aroma only when crushed and sautéed.

KOSHA MANGSHO LAMB COOKED IN RICH ONION SAUCE

This is a lamb curry from West Bengal and is quite popular in Bihar and neighbouring areas as well. The term *kosha* literally translated means 'tightened', which refers to the thickening of the spices and sauce to give a rich finish. The curry is often served on a cold day with a soft *khichri*, the original kedgeree, the combination being both comforting and invigorating.

serves 4

rich, spicy and slightly sweet

3¹/₂ tbsp mustard oil

3¹/₂ tbsp *ghee* or vegetable oil

3 cinnamon leaves or bay leaves

5 black peppercorns

3 black cardamom pods

4 dried red chillies

3 blades mace

6 large red onions, blended to a paste

35g (generous 1oz) ginger paste

35g (generous 1oz) garlic paste

70g (2¹/₄oz) red chilli powder

30g (1oz) ground cumin

30g (1oz) ground coriander

1kg (2¹/₄lb) boned leg of lamb, cut into 2.5cm (1in) cubes

5 large tomatoes, puréed

1¹/₂ tbsp salt

400ml (14fl oz) lamb stock or water

1 tsp caster sugar

To finish

10g (¹/₄oz) each cinnamon stick, green cardamom pods and coriander seeds, roasted and ground to a powder (p354)

finely chopped coriander leaves

1 Heat the mustard oil in a deep pan and bring to smoking point, then add the *ghee*, followed by the whole spices. When they start to crackle, stir in the onion paste and fry until it is light brown, stirring constantly to prevent it from sticking to the bottom of the pan and burning.

2 Add the ginger and garlic pastes and mix into the onions along with the chilli powder and ground cumin and coriander. Fry for 2–3 minutes, then add the cubes of lamb. Cook on a moderate heat for 15–20 minutes, stirring frequently.

3 Add the puréed tomatoes and salt and cook for a further 15 minutes. Pour in the stock, reduce the heat to low and cover the pan. Simmer until the lamb is tender. Uncover the pan, increase the heat and reduce the sauce until it becomes thick and coats the lamb.

4 Correct the seasoning with salt, if required, and stir in the sugar to balance the spiciness of the dish. Finally, stir in the ground roasted spices and sprinkle generously with chopped coriander. Serve immediately with *paratha*, or even with a kedgeree.

Mace blades >
Add this spice at the beginning of the cooking process for its delicate yet warm flavour to release completely.

PORK CHOP BHOONI MASALA PORK CHOPS

Until the late 18th century pork was not used much in Indian cooking. Although most of the country was Hindu, and consumption of pork was not barred, a large proportion of the population was vegetarian. It was only in Anglo-Indian cooking and in the hills in the eastern part of the country that pork was consumed. This recipe originates from Darjeeling, a hill-station very popular with the British when they lived in India. The term *bhooni*, refers to the dry, almost coating consistency of the spices that remain on the pork chops when the dish is finished.

serves 4

hot and fatty

8 pork chops, about 100g (3½oz) each, excess fat trimmed

1 tsp salt

1 tsp red chilli powder

1 tbsp corn oil

Masala

1½ tbsp mild chilli powder

1 tsp ground turmeric

1 tbsp ginger paste

1 tsp garlic paste

3 tomatoes, finely chopped

4 tbsp corn oil

½ tsp fenugreek seeds

20 curry leaves

2 large onions, finely sliced

2 tbsp tomato ketchup

1 tsp salt

1 tsp caster sugar

1 tsp ground *garam masala*

To garnish

2 large potatoes, peeled and cut lengthways

½ tsp salt

½ tsp ground turmeric

2 tbsp corn oil

2 tbsp chopped coriander leaves

1 Sprinkle the pork chops with the salt and chilli powder and rub on well. Heat the oil in a large heavy pan and sear the pork chops for 2 minutes on each side or until they are coloured. Remove from the pan and set aside.

2 For the *masala*, mix together the chilli powder, turmeric, ginger and garlic pastes and tomatoes in a bowl. Set aside.

3 Heat the 4 tbsp oil in the pan, add the fenugreek seeds and stir for a minute. As the seeds begin to brown, add the curry leaves and onions and sauté for 6–8 minutes or until the onions begin to turn golden brown. Add the tomato mixture to the pan and sauté for a further 3–5 minutes or until the spices are fragrant.

4 Return the seared chops to the pan, and stir in the tomato ketchup, salt and sugar. Spoon the spice mixture over the chops to coat them evenly. Reduce the heat to low and add 200ml (7fl oz) water. Simmer, covered, for 15–20 minutes or until the chops are cooked through and tender.

5 While the chops are cooking, prepare the garnish. Cook the potatoes in boiling water seasoned with the salt and turmeric for 6–8 minutes or until they are just tender but still firm. Drain. Heat the oil in a frying pan, add the potatoes and cook until crisp and golden. Keep hot.

6 Remove the chops from the pan, transfer to a serving platter and keep warm. Continue to cook the sauce, uncovered, for a few more minutes, until it has a thick coating consistency. Finish by stirring in the *garam masala*.

7 Pour the sauce over the pork chops. Arrange the crisp potatoes around the edge and sprinkle with the chopped coriander. If you like, serve with *chapatti*, rice or even some crusty bread.

MURGIR JHOL HOME-STYLE CHICKEN CURRY

The basic chicken curry differs from household to household. Every cook has his or her own recipe and each swears by theirs. *Jhol* refers to the thin curry – or 'gravy', as it's called in India – that makes it so special. This is quite a simple and rustic method of cooking – true home-style. You could use boneless chicken if you prefer, or even a whole bird cut up into small pieces. Or you could use quails, partridges or even pheasants for this recipe; just adjust the cooking times.

serves 4–6

rustic, fresh and spicy

75ml (2¹/₂fl oz) corn or vegetable oil

¹/₂ tsp cumin seeds

2 cinnamon leaves or bay leaves

3 green cardamom pods

4 black peppercorns

4 large red onions, finely chopped

4 medium potatoes, peeled and cut into quarters (optional)

2 tsp salt

1kg (2¹/₄lb) chicken thighs with bone, skinned and cut in half

1 tbsp ginger paste

1 tbsp garlic paste

2 tbsp ground coriander

2 tbsp ground cumin

1 tbsp chilli powder

1 tbsp ground turmeric

4 tomatoes, chopped or blended to a purée

400ml (14fl oz) chicken stock or water

3 green cardamom pods, roasted and ground

5cm (2in) cinnamon stick, roasted and ground

1 tbsp finely chopped coriander leaves

1 Heat the oil in a large pan and add the whole spices. When they crackle, add the onions and fry over a moderate heat until golden brown. Stir in the potatoes, if using, and cook for 5 minutes. Add 1 tsp of the salt, then add the chicken and cook for 5–8 minutes or until lightly browned.

2 Add the ginger and garlic pastes, the ground coriander and cumin, the remaining salt, chilli powder and turmeric. Cook for a further 10 minutes, stirring constantly, until the spices begin to release their aromas. Stir in the tomatoes and cook for 5 minutes, then pour in the stock. Bring to the boil. Reduce the heat to low and simmer until the chicken is cooked.

3 Taste and correct the seasoning, if required. Sprinkle over the roasted cardamom and cinnamon powder and finish with the chopped coriander. Serve with steamed rice.

Green cardamom pods >

Used in most spice mixes in India, green cardamom pods have a smoky aroma and a sweet-spicy taste. Crush the pods to get most of their fragrance and flavour before adding them to gravies.

GHEE BHAAT GHEE RICE

This is a basic dish of boiled Basmati rice enriched with the addition of *ghee*. The nuttiness of *ghee* combined with the texture of sea salt is simple cooking at its very best. Normally you will find cooking times on the packaging of Basmati rice, so follow these if they are given.

serves 8-10

500g (1lb 2oz) Basmati rice

3 tbsp *ghee*

1 tbsp flaked sea salt

1 Wash the rice in running cold water, then leave to soak in cold water to cover for 20-25 minutes. Soaking the rice reduces the cooking time and prevents the grains from breaking while cooking.

2 Meanwhile, bring 2 litres (3½ pints) water to the boil in a large saucepan. When the water is boiling, add the drained rice. Bring back to the boil, then cook, uncovered, over a moderately high heat for 10-14 minutes or until the rice is just cooked. It should not be al dente, like pasta, but nor should it be over-boiled so that it disintegrates.

3 Drain the rice in a colander and, while the rice is still hot, add the ghee and sea salt and mix well. Serve immediately. If the rice goes cold, you can reheat it in a microwave (650W) for 1-2 minutes.

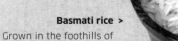

Basmati rice >

Grown in the foothills of the Himalayas, this long-grain rice has a unique aroma and acquires a smooth, glossy texture when cooked.

POORIES DEEP-FRiED PUFFED BREADS

Poories, or *luchis* as they are called in Bengal, are an excellent accompaniment to dry curries, as well as being very popular with children as a snack or even as picnic bread. In Bengal they sometimes use a tad more oil or *ghee* when making their dough, which produces a shorter and crisper bread, and they also use refined white flour more than wholewheat flour, which is the norm in the rest of India. In addition, the Bengalis like to add some onion and carom seeds, which makes the bread dramatic in appearance, more flavoursome and easier to digest.

makes 20

500g (1lb 2oz) *chapatti* flour, plain flour or a mixture of the two (half of each)

2 tsp salt

1 tsp caster sugar

1 tsp carom seeds

1 tsp black onion seeds

1 tbsp *ghee* or oil

oil for deep frying

2 tbsp vegetable oil for rolling

1 Mix together the flour, salt, sugar and seeds in a bowl. Rub in the *ghee* with your fingers until it is thoroughly blended with the flour.

2 Make a well in the centre of the flour and pour in 250ml (9fl oz) water little by little, mixing to make a stiff dough. Work the dough well with your hands.

3 Cover with a damp cloth and set aside for 15 minutes.

4 Divide the dough into 20 pieces and cover once more with the damp cloth. Work with one piece at a time, keeping the rest covered.

5 While oil is heating in your deep-fryer or wok to about 180°C (350°F), roll each piece of dough into a smooth ball: apply a little oil to each dough ball, then, using a rolling pin, roll out into a disc about 10cm (4in) in diameter.

6 Deep fry the breads in the hot oil for 1–2 minutes or until they have puffed up and are crisp and golden on both sides.

7 Drain on kitchen paper and serve hot.

JHINGA DUM ANARI QUALIYA PRAWNS iN POMEGRANATE AND CREAM CURRY

In this recipe, prawns are cooked in a sumptuous and velvety gravy with a touch of saffron and cream. The pomegranate marinade is the perfect tangy complement to the creaminess of the curry. I had the pleasure of serving this dish to the late M.F. Hussain, the legendary artist, who loved and appreciated it.

serves 5

mildly spiced and creamy

1kg (2¹/₄lb) large prawns, peeled and deveined, set aside the shells, tails and heads for the stock

3 tbsp clarified butter or *ghee*

1 tsp fenugreek seeds

1 tbsp ginger and garlic paste

1 tsp ground turmeric

1 large onion, ground

1 tbsp yellow chilli powder

¹/₂ tsp ground *garam masala*

salt

250ml (9fl oz) plain yogurt, whisked until smooth

1 tsp ground fennel seeds

5 green chillies, each slit into half

4 tbsp fresh cream

pinch of saffron threads

100g (3¹/₂oz) fresh pomegranate seeds, to garnish

1 tbsp finely chopped coriander leaves, to garnish

Stock

1 tsp black peppercorns

1 onion, roughly chopped

2 bay leaves

3.8cm (1¹/₂in) ginger, crushed

20g (³/₄oz) coriander roots

Marinade

500g (1lb 2oz) fresh pomegranate juice

pinch of salt

2 tbsp lemon juice

1 tbsp red chilli powder

Onion and cashew nut paste

2 medium-sized onions

25g (scant 1oz) cashew nuts

1 To prepare the stock, take a large saucepan and boil 1 litre (1³/₄ pints) water. Crush the prawn heads, shells and tails and add to the boiling water. Add the rest of the ingredients for the stock and boil for 20 minutes. Using a muslin cloth, strain the stock in a jug and set aside.

2 Mix together the ingredients for the marinade. Add the prawns and turn to coat them. Cover and set aside for 1 hour.

3 To make the onion and cashew nut paste, boil the onions with the cashew nuts in 250ml (9fl oz) water for 5 minutes. Leave to cool, then transfer the boiled onions and cashew nuts along with the water to a food processor and grind to make a fine paste.

4 Heat the butter or *ghee* in a large frying pan over a moderate heat. Add the fenugreek seeds and sauté for 30 seconds. Add the ginger and garlic paste, turmeric and ground onion. Sauté for 2–3 minutes or until the onion is translucent.

5 Add the yellow chilli powder, *garam masala* and salt and cook over a moderate heat for 1–2 minutes, stirring continuously. Stir in the yogurt and cook for 1 minute. Now add the onion and cashew nut paste, mix well and cook for another 2 minutes.

6 Add the prawns along with the marinade to the pan, cover and cook over a moderate heat for 5–7 minutes or until the prawns turn pink. Uncover and add the ground fennel seeds and green chillies, mix well, cover and cook for 30 seconds.

7 Remove the cover and pour in the stock, mix well and cook for 3 minutes. Add the cream and saffron and mix well.

8 Transfer to a serving dish and garnish with the pomegranate seeds and coriander leaves.

MURGH KE MUKUL CREAMY CHICKEN CURRY

Mukul in Hindi refers to a flower bud. In this Rajasthani recipe, chicken pieces are cooked in special spices that render the pieces as soft as flower buds. It was traditionally cooked with game meat, such as rabbit, by the royalty, but works equally well with chicken. I learnt this recipe from the chef who worked for the Raja Bhawani Singh of Jaipur.

serves 5

mildly spiced and nutty

3 medium-sized onions, peeled

4 tbsp *ghee*

6 green cardamom pods

5 cloves

3 bay leaves

1 tbsp ginger and garlic paste

$^1/_2$ tsp black peppercorns

$^1/_2$ tsp ground turmeric

1 tsp ground coriander

1 tsp red chilli powder

1 tsp ground cumin

600g (1lb 5oz) boneless chicken, julienned

250ml (9fl oz) yogurt, whisked until smooth

$^1/_2$ tsp nutmeg powder

$^1/_2$ tsp ground mace

salt

2 tbsp cashew nuts paste

3 tbsp fresh cream

1 First prepare the onion paste. Roughly chop 2 onions and boil them in 100ml (3$^1/_2$fl oz) water for 5 minutes. Drain and leave to cool, then blend in a food processor to make a paste. Leave aside.

2 Heat the *ghee* in a heavy-bottomed pan over a moderate heat. Add the cardamoms, cloves and bay leaves and sauté for 30 seconds or until they release their flavour.

3 Finely chop the remaining onion and add to the spices. Sauté until golden. Stir in the ginger and garlic paste and sauté for another 30 seconds. Add in the peppercorns, turmeric, coriander, chilli and cumin powder and sauté for another 30 seconds. Reduce the heat to low, sprinkle a tablespoon or two of water and cook, stirring frequently, until the oil separates.

4 Increase the temperate to moderately high, add the chicken and sauté for 2 minutes. Now mix in the onion paste and cook for 5 minutes, stirring frequently.

5 Fold in the yogurt and cook for another 5 minutes, stirring frequently. Now add the nutmeg and mace and spinkle in the salt. Reduce the heat to low, cover and simmer for 7–9 minutes.

6 Uncover the pan and stir in the cashew nut paste along with 400ml (14fl oz) water. Cover and allow it to simmer for another 3 minutes or until the chicken is almost done.

7 Uncover the pan and fold in the cream. Add salt if necessary. Discard the whole spices and serve this creamy chicken curry with rice or *roti*.

< Black peppercorns
Used for their spicy heat, black peppercorns not only retain their flavour during cooking but also bring out the flavour of other spices.

CHICKEN SHAHJAHANI

The term *shahjahani* suggests that this is a Mughlai preparation preferred by none other than Shah Jahan, the Mughal Emperor who built the Taj Mahal. However, over time with various adaptations it became a popular dish in Awadhi cuisine. A garnish of saffron and omelette adds strength to this aromatic and rich curry.

serves 5

rich and aromatic

1kg (2¼lb), boneless chicken breasts and legs, cleaned and cut into 20 pieces

2 tbsp *ghee*

5 green cardamom pods, crushed open

2 cinnamon sticks

5 cloves

3 bay leaves

2 medium-sized onions, chopped

150g (5½oz) plain yogurt, whisked

4 green chillies, finely chopped

¼ tsp grated nutmeg

¼ tsp ground mace

salt

¼ tsp ground cardamom

1 tbsp grated milk cheese

1 tbsp roasted and finely chopped sultanas or raisins, to garnish

1 tbsp chopped cashew nuts, to garnish

Marinade

1 tbsp ginger and garlic paste

5 green chillies

½ tbsp lemon juice

100g (3½oz) plain yogurt, whisked

salt

Paste

1 tbsp poppy seeds

50g (1¾oz) cashew nuts

45g (1½oz) freshly grated coconut

Omelette

3 eggs

2 tbsp fresh cream

salt and freshly ground black peppercorns

pinch of saffron

1 tbsp vegetable oil

1 Mix together the ingredients for the marinade. Add the chicken pieces and toss to coat with the marinade, then cover and set aside for 30 minutes.

2 Meanwhile, blend the poppy seeds, cashew nuts and grated coconut with 5 tablespoons of water in a food processor to make a paste.

3 Heat the *ghee* in a heavy-bottomed saucepan. Add the cardamoms, cinnamon stcks, cloves and bay leaves and sauté for 10 seconds over a moderate heat. Add the onions and fry for 30 seconds or until translucent. Add the chicken along with the marinade and cook for 5 minutes, stirring occasionally. Cover the saucepan and let the chicken cook in its own juices. When almost dry, add the yogurt and mix well. Add the chillies and cover. Leave the chicken to cook for another 4–5 minutes or until almost tender.

4 Meanwhile, for the garnish, prepare the omelette by whisking together the eggs and cream. Season, add the saffron and mix well. Heat the oil in a non-stick frying pan over a moderate heat. Pour the beaten egg into the pan and swirl to make a thin omelette. Cook for 3 minutes or until set. Transfer to a plate and cut into small pieces.

5 When the chicken is tender, add the paste and mix well. Sprinkle in the nutmeg and mace and cook for 2 minutes over a moderate heat. Add 150ml (5fl oz) water and stir. Add salt and cook for 5 minutes or until the chicken is cooked through. Now sprinkle in the ground cardamom and milk cheese, mix well and cook for another 30 seconds.

6 Transfer to a serving plate, remove the whole spices and garnish with the omelette pieces, sultanas and cashew nuts.

DUM KI GUCCHI STUFFED MORELS

Morels or *gucchis* are rare mushrooms found in the Himalayan region. Loved by food connoisseurs for their flavour, these are mostly used in rice preparations and non-vegetarian dishes. However, they are also prepared as a vegetable, as in this recipe, and eaten with Indian breads or steamed rice.

serves 5

mildly spiced and nutty

10 large dried morels

1 tbsp unsalted butter

salt

juice of 1 lemon

1 tbsp pomegranate seeds, for garnishing

Filling

15g (1/2oz) unsalted butter

2 tbsp broken cashew nuts

1 tbsp sultanas

1/4 tsp cumin seed

1/2 tsp finely chopped green chillies

1/2 tsp finely chopped ginger

1/2 tsp yellow chilli powder

1 tsp chopped coriander leaves

1 tsp chopped mint leaves

1 tbsp grated milk cheese

4 tbsp grated Cheddar cheese

salt

1/4 tbsp lemon juice

Sauce

3 green cardamom pods

3 cloves

3 cinnamon sticks

2 bay leaves

1 tsp ginger and garlic paste

1 tsp ground coriander

1/2 tsp Kashmiri red chilli powder

1/2 tsp yellow chilli powder

1/2 tsp ground *garam masala*

2 pinches of nutmeg and mace powder, each

1/2 tsp crushed white peppercorns

1 tbsp brown onion paste (p30)

150g (51/2oz) plain yogurt, whisked

2 tbsp almond paste

100g (31/2oz) tomato paste

10g (1/4oz) grated milk cheese

2 tbsp single cream, plus extra for garnishing

few drops of rose water

pinch of saffron threads, soaked in water

1 Soak the morels in warm water for 30 minutes. Clean them thoroughly to get rid of any grits and trim off the stems.

2 Heat 1/2 tablespoon of the butter in a pan over a moderate heat. Add the morels and sauté. Sprinkle in the salt and lemon juice and cook, tossing occasionally (the morels will burn fast if tossed too much), until the morels are soft. Do not overcook, as the morels will loose their flavour. Using a slotted spoon, transfer the morels to a dish and set aside to cool.

3 To make the filling, in the same pan, melt the butter over a low heat. Add the cashew nuts and sultanas and sauté until the nuts are golden brown. Add the cumin seeds, green chillies, ginger, yellow chilli powder, coriander and mint leaves and toss for a minute. Add the milk cheese and sauté well, then add the Cheddar cheese. Sprinkle salt and lemon juice and mix well. Transfer the filling to a plate and set aside to cool. Once cooled, stuff the morels with the filling.

4 To make the sauce, melt the remaining 1/2 tablespoon butter in the same pan over a moderate heat. Add the whole spices. When they release their flavour, add the ginger and garlic paste and sauté for a minute, stirring frequently. Sprinkle a little water to prevent the *masala* from sticking to the base of the pan.

5 Mix in the rest of the dry spices along with three tablespoons of water and cook, stirring occasionally. Add the brown onion paste along with 100ml (31/2fl oz) water. Cook for 30 seconds. Fold in the yogurt and cook for another 2–3 minutes. Add the almond paste, this will thicken the gravy.

6 Add the milk cheese and stir. As the gravy reaches a semi-thick consistency, fold in the cream and add salt if necessary. Sprinkle a few drops of rose water and the saffron threads, reserving the saffron-flavoured water. Reduce the heat to low and slowly add the stuffed morels to the sauce. Cover the pan and simmer for 3 minutes.

7 Sprinkle the saffron-flavoured water and garnish with a few drops of cream and pomegranate seeds. Serve hot with Indian bread or rice.

PAPAD KI SUBZI PAPADUM CURRY

This recipe comes from the desert state of Rajasthan, famous for its dry vegetables, *ghee*, yogurt and red chilli based curries. Papadum curry is a simple but flavourful dish, which could be prepared any time of the year with ingredients that are readily available in most of our kitchens. Several varieties of papadums, such as potato, *urad*, *jeera* or plain, are available in the market. Prepare the dish with the one that suits your taste.

serves 3-4

hot and sour

1 tbsp *ghee*
1/4 tsp mustard seeds
3 whole red chillies
1/4 tsp cumin seeds
2 sprigs of curry leaves
1/2 tbsp ginger and garlic paste
1/2 tsp ground turmeric
1/2 tsp red chilli powder
1/2 tsp ground cumin
2 pinches of asafoetida
250g (9oz) mildly sour yogurt
15g (1/2oz) chickpea flour
salt
6 split and husked black lentils
   (*urad dal*) papadums

To garnish

1/2 tsp finely chopped
   coriander leaves
1/2 tsp finely chopped mint leaves
1/2 tsp finely chopped green chillies

1 Heat the *ghee* in a heavy-bottomed saucepan over a moderate heat. Add the mustard seeds and whole red chillies and fry until the seeds crackle. Cover the pan with a lid if the crackling sputters out. Add the cumin seeds and toss until brown, then add the curry leaves, ginger and garlic paste and sauté for 2–3 minutes.

2 Mix in the turmeric, chilli powder and ground cumin and cook for another 2–3 minutes or until the spices begin to release their aroma. If necessary, add 2 tbsp water to prevent the *masala* from sticking to the pan. Sprinkle in the asafoetida and cook for a minute. This will help enhance the flavour of the spices.

3 Meanwhile, whisk the yogurt in a bowl until it is well combined and thick. Add the chickpea flour and mix well. Add 250ml (9fl oz) water to dilute the yogurt mixture.

4 Slowly add the yogurt mixture to the saucepan, stirring constantly to prevent it from splitting. When all the yogurt has been incorporated, reduce the heat to a low and simmer for 6-7 minutes, stirring occasionally. Add about 120ml (4fl oz) water and simmer until the gravy thickens slightly. Season to taste. The gravy should retain the sourness of the yogurt.

5 Roast the papadums, one at a time, over a moderate heat or in an oven. Break the roasted papadums into quarter and add to the gravy. Simmer for just 3 minutes. Do not overcook or the papadums will loose their crunchiness.

6 Transfer to a serving dish, sprinkle over the coriander, mint and green chillies and serve with rice or any Indian bread.

GOSHT YAKHNI MUTTON iN YOGURT CURRY

Yakhni is a traditional dish of the Kashmiri Wazwan. This is an exotic yet simple, authentic Indian lamb or goat curry cooked in yogurt and milk gravy with aniseed and ginger powder. This aromatic curry is generally served with steamed rice or pilau.

serves 5

mildly spiced and aromatic

1kg (2¼lb) mutton, bones reserved, washed, dried and cut into 4cm (1½in) cubes.

1 tsp ginger and garlic paste

3 cinnamon sticks, each 5cm (2in) long

7 black cardamom pods

1 tbsp ground aniseed

1½ tsp ground cumin

300g (10oz) plain yogurt

30g (1oz) milk cheese (*khoya*), grated

½ tbsp sugar

12 green cardamom pods, crushed

1 tbsp ground dried ginger

salt

250ml (9fl oz) whole milk

3 tbsp *ghee*

1 tsp chopped coriander leaves (optional)

1 tsp chopped mint leaves (optional)

1 Place the mutton in a heavy-bottomed casserole and add the ginger and garlic paste, cinnamon sticks, black cardamoms, ground aniseed and cumin along with 750ml (1¼ pints) water.

2 Place the casserole over a moderate heat, cover and cook for 30 minutes, stirring occasionally. If you feel the water is drying up, add another 100ml (3½fl oz) water. Once the meat is three-fourth done, reduce the heat and allow it to simmer. (Check to see if the meat is cooked by piercing a fork into a mutton piece. If the piece starts to break but does not fall apart, it is three-fourth done.)

3 Meanwhile, in a separate bowl, mix together the yogurt, milk cheese, sugar, green cardamoms, ground dried ginger and salt. Add the mixture to the meat, stir for 2 minutes, cover and simmer for another 10 minutes. As the gravy starts acquiring a slighly thick consistency, add the milk, stirring continuously to prevent it from curdling. Simmer for another 8–10 minutes and check the seasoning.

4 Add the *ghee*, stir and cook for another 2–3 minutes. Garnish with coriander and mint leaves, if using, and serve hot.

BHINDI KADHI OKRA IN YOGURT CURRY

Most vegetarian meals in India often have a *kadhi* preparation, especially in the absence of *dal*. *Kadhi*, which is a yogurt based gravy, is simple to make and has a balanced nutrition while being spicy. This is a Rajasthani preparation, made with okra that is easily available in India.

serves 5

slightly tangy and mildly spicy

250g (9oz) plain yogurt

30g (1oz) chickpea flour

3 tbsp vegetable oil

1/2 tsp mustard seeds

3 sprigs of curry leaves, plus extra for garnishing

1 tsp ginger and garlic paste

3 whole red chillies

1 tsp ground turmeric

1/2 tsp roughly crushed red chillies

1 medium-sized onion, finely chopped

15 okra, washed, dried and cut into 2.5cm (1in) thick pieces

1/2 tsp red chilli powder

salt

1 tsp lemon juice

1/4 tsp asafoetida

1 Whisk the yogurt in a bowl until smooth. Add the chickpea flour along with 100ml (3½fl oz) water and mix well to avoid lumps.

2 Heat 2 tbsp of the oil in a heavy-bottomed saucepan over a moderate heat. Add the mustard seeds and sauté. When they crackle, add the curry leaves, ginger and garlic paste, whole red chillies and sauté for 20 more seconds or until the ginger and garlic paste start to release flavour. Remove the red chillies from the saucepan and set aside for garnishing. Mix in half the turmeric along with the crushed red chillies and onion and sauté for 2–3 minutes or until the onion turns light golden brown. Sprinkle 2 tbsp water and stir constantly to prevent the *masala* from sticking to the base of the pan.

3 Fold in the yogurt mixture and cook for 6–7 minutes, stirring frequently. Reduce the heat to low and simmer for another 5 minutes. Set aside.

4 Meanwhile, take another saucepan and smear it with the remaining oil. Add the okra pieces along with the remaining turmeric, red chilli powder, salt and sauté for 2 minutes over a moderate heat. Sprinkle lemon juice, mix well and cook, stirring frequently, until the okra pieces are tender.

5 Add the yogurt gravy to the okra and cook for 2 minutes, stirring occasionally. If the okra pieces are not tender enough, simmer for a couple more minutes.

6 Sprinkle asafoetida and check the seasoning. Garnish with the curry leaves and the sautéed red chillies.

< Okra

This tropical vegetable has a slippery texture and a mild flavour and is widely used in vegetarian dishes in India.

PANEER FIRDOUSI PANEER CHEESE IN NUT GRAVY

Firdousi, a common item in most Indian restaurants specializing in Mughlai cuisine, literally means 'heavenly' in Urdu. Any kind of meat cooked in this rich gravy tastes heavenly, and the erstwhile rulers often had it garnished with gold or silver leaves to signify its specialness. Here I have used *paneer* cheese, the vegetarian substitute for meat in most Indian preparations.

serves 5

rich, nutty and creamy

3 tbsp vegetable oil

1 bay leaf

4 green cardamom pods

4 cloves

2 cinnamon sticks, each 2.5cm (1in) long

½ tbsp ginger and garlic paste

100g (3½oz) tomato purée

½ tsp red chilli powder

½ tsp ground cumin

½ tsp ground coriander

¼ tsp chopped green chillies

50g (1¾oz) brown onion paste (p30)

50g (1¾oz) cashew nuts, ground with a little water to make a paste

100ml (3½fl oz) single cream

salt

3 pinches of green cardamom powder

1 tbsp chopped coriander leaves

generous pinch of saffron threads, soaked in warm milk

500g (1lb 2oz) *paneer*, cut into bite-sized pieces

To garnish

10 cashew nuts, finely julienned

10 sultanas, finely julienned

10 almonds, finely julienned

10 pistachio nuts, finely chopped and sautéed in butter until golden brown

1 tbsp chopped coriander leaves (optional)

gold or silver leaf (optional)

1 Heat the oil in a heavy-bottomed pan over a moderate heat and add the whole spices. When they start to crackle, stir in the ginger and garlic paste and fry for a minute or until light golden brown. Add the tomato purée and stir for another 2 minutes.

2 Mix in the chilli powder along with the ground cumin and coriander. Add 4 tbsp water and cook over a moderate heat, stirring occasionally, for 5 minutes or until the oil separates out. Sprinkle a little more water if you think the *masala* is sticking to the base of the pan. Add the green chillies and stir for 2–3 minutes or until the *masala* begins to release a spicy aroma.

3 Add 100ml (3½fl oz) water and stir for 1 minute. Mix in the brown onion paste, cashew paste and cream and cook for 3 minutes. The onion and cashew paste should blend with the gravy giving it a thick consistency. Sprinkle in some salt to taste.

4 Add the cardamom powder, coriander leaves and the saffron along with the soaking milk to the gravy. Slowly add the *paneer* to the gravy and cook for 1 minute.

5 Remove the whole spices and transfer to a serving dish. Garnish with the dry fruits and serve with *naan* (p50) or *roti*. You could also garnish the dish with chopped coriander leaves and a gold or silver leaf.

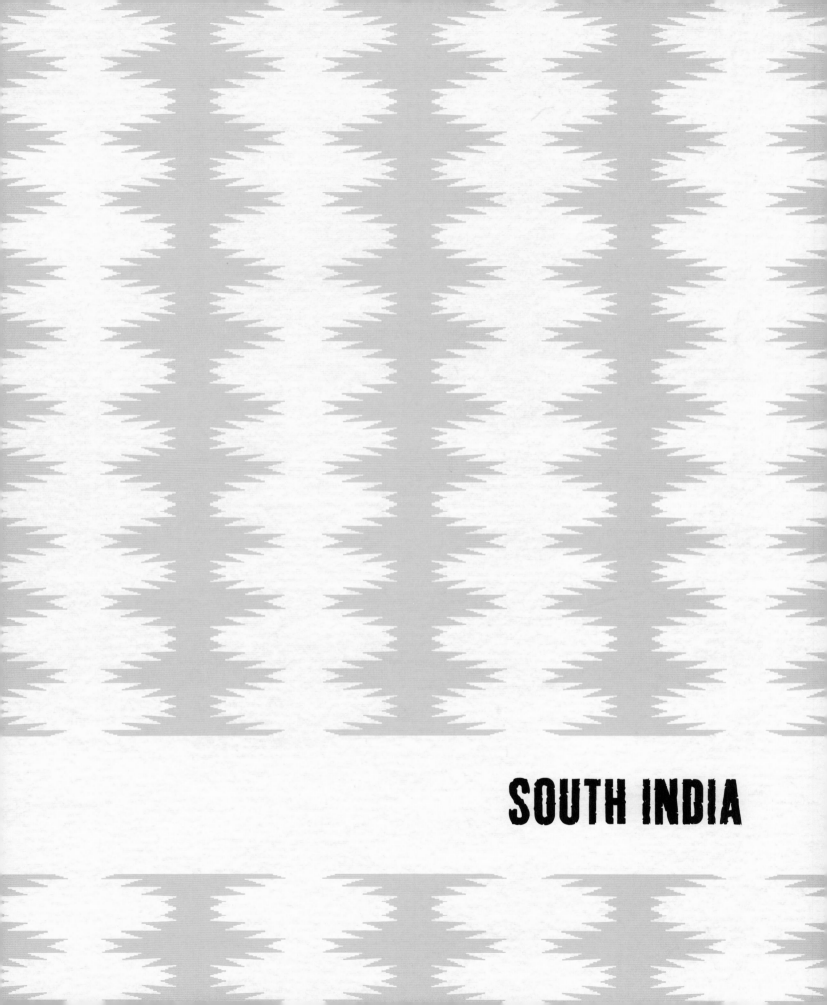

SOUTH INDIA

Southern India's ancient and deep-rooted cultural essence has been retained despite invasions, traders, religious conversions and modernization. Like the rest of India, it originally consisted of many kingdoms whose Hindu and Muslim rulers fought wars to control the land and its resources. Many foreigners first touched Indian soil in the south, starting with the early Christians, and continuing over the centuries with the Portuguese, Dutch, Arabs, French and, finally, the British towards the end of the 17th century. After independence from Britain, southern India was divided on a linguistic basis into four different states: Andhra Pradesh, Tamil Nadu, Karnataka and Kerala. The population was and is predominantly Hindu, just as in other parts of India, and as a result the cooking tradition is primarily vegetarian. Ayurveda (the ancient Indian medical system and way of life) has also had a great influence on the cooking culture. South Indians have great respect for the therapeutic value of food and people follow Ayurvedic principles in their everyday eating. A traditional meal is more or less the same in most of the region: a large heap of rice on a banana leaf, with a variety of colourful vegetarian or meat dishes and pickles around it, arranged to balance flavours and provide nutritional richness.

New cultures and religions brought new dimensions to South Indian cooking. For example, meat cookery was introduced by the Muslims in northern Kerala and Hyderabad and in the Christian communities in Mangalore, Kochi and central Kerala. Hyderabadi Muslim *biryani* is still the favourite *biryani* for the majority of Indian people.

The cuisine in each of the four states has its own unique characteristics. Andhra food is considered to be the spiciest. Hot and spicy Andhra lamb and chicken curries are hugely popular with lovers of traditional Indian food.

The temple state of Tamil Nadu is renowned for its traditional vegetarian food and its huge variety of delicious snacks. The rice pancakes called *dosas*, steamed rice and lentil cakes called *idlis*, and popular train snacks like *vadais* and *bondas* are all contributions of the rich Brahmin (the upper class Hindu caste) community of Tamil Nadu. In the southern areas like Chettinad, meat and spicy-hot chicken curries are very popular, even though the majority of the people still keep to a strict vegetarian diet. The tangy flavour of *sambar*, spicy, peppery soups like *rasam*, and wonderful rice preparations with yogurt and sour tamarind are all examples of fine Tamil cooking. Karnataka, home to the garden city of Bangalore, has a distinct culinary identity of its own. It is predominantly vegetarian, except for its border areas like Mangalore, where the Christian and Anglo-Indian communities enjoy meat, just like people in the neighbouring state of Kerala. Udupi, on the coast near Mangalore, is known for the cooking of its Hindu community, particularly famous for their dosas and other crispy pancakes. They also make tasty rice dishes like Bissi Bela Bhath (p132) and Chitra Anna, which are finished with fresh colourful garnishes and savoury tempering.

Kerala, on the southwest coast, is the most beautiful part of southern India. This lush, fascinating state is known as the spice capital of the country and has a strong tradition of Ayurvedic practice. It's no surprise that Keralan cooking is so healthy, colourful and light. Kerala has a solid base of Christians and Muslims in addition to Hindus, plus a small community of Jewish families, and all these faiths add to the culinary diversity. In the north of Kerala, you find excellent Muslim meat cooking, whereas Travancore, in central Kerala, has wonderful Christian chicken and lamb curries. Delicious seafood delicacies are prepared in the fishing communities along the coast, and the ancient Nair community is renowned for its vegetarian cooking.

In almost all the South Indian states, people prefer to use fresh ingredients like ginger, curry leaves and coconut in their cooking, and these, as well as many spices, are grown in home gardens, as well as commercially to be exported to other parts of the world. Unlike northern India, where breads are often eaten with curries, people in this region like rice, preferring the local red rice to Basmati for everyday meals.

In the villages, food is cooked in clay and earthenware pots, whereas affluent families use brass and silver utensils for everyday cooking (these metals are deemed to be auspicious and to offer medicinal value). Most of the dishes are stir-fried or boiled first and then cooked in coconut-based *masala* pastes. The final touch is to 'temper' the dish with aromatic curry leaves, fragrant mustard seeds and the sexy flavour of dried red chillies. The combination of these magical flavours is what makes South Indian curries so special.

Das Sreedharan

Roasting fresh coconut >
Brown it with ginger, garlic
and whole spices

TASTE OF SOUTH INDIA

1. sambar onion
2. coconut
3. *gram* lentils
4. fenugreek seeds
5. cumin seeds
6. black mustard seeds
7. basmati rice
8. yellow *gram* lentils
9. black peppercorns
10. poppy seeds
11. split black lentils
12. coriander seeds
13. fennel seeds
14. cashew nuts
15. peanuts
16. fresh green chillies
17. dried red chillies
18. tamarind pulp
19. curry leaves
20. limes
21. fresh root ginger

THE RAW MATERIALS

Indian cooking is often thought to use a lot of spices and combinations of very intense flavours. But South Indian cuisine employs a much simpler collection of spices and flavourings. More than in the cooking of the north of the country, in southern India great importance is given to the balancing of flavours. Subtle variations are created and layering of spices makes the food lighter.

CASHEW NUTS

Cashews are cultivated in South India and are often added to savoury dishes, as well as being used in many snacks and almost all sweets.

CURRY LEAVES

This is the most widely used herb in South Indian cuisine. As the name suggests, it smells and tastes like curry. While the flavour is spicy, it is also nutty, a quality brought out when the leaves are lightly fried in oil until crisp. Curry leaves can also be added to a dish just like any other fresh herb, whole or torn. Buy them whenever you find them fresh, as they can be stored in the freezer wrapped in foil or sealed in a plastic bag.

GINGER

This rhizome (underground stem) is used extensively in Indian cooking, and many people grow their own ginger so they will have it fresh whenever it is needed. Dried ground ginger is sometimes acceptable, but the fresh root is always preferred.

LIMES

Lime juice (and lemon juice) is used all over India to give an instant sour flavour to stir-fries and other dishes. The Indian lime is small and very aromatic with a strong citrus flavour.

CHILLIES

In the traditional cooking of this region, there are several kinds of chillies used, including fresh green ones about 7cm (scant 3in) long and dried red chillies, which can range in size from tiny and very hot to those that are larger and less hot. Chillies are famously known for their fiery power and people feel wary of using them, but you can control their heat by using them whole so they don't lose their seeds in the sauce. Or, if chopping chillies, split them and remove the seeds first.

COCONUT

Coconut is a very important ingredient all over the world, but most particularly in South Indian cooking. Freshly grated coconut is often ground with spices or dry-roasted for curries, as well as being used in savoury snacks and many sweets. Unsweetened desiccated coconut can be used as a replacement, although it is drier in texture. Coconut milk and cream (p241) are also much used in South Indian curries, adding creaminess and sweetness.

BLACK MUSTARD SEEDS

Black or brown mustard seeds are used in most savoury dishes, providing a flavour that is typical of South Indian cooking. When the mustard seeds are fried in oil, often with curry leaves and dried red chillies, they release a most delicious aroma. Most recipes can be made without them, but they bring a special magic.

CUMIN SEEDS

This popular spice has a delicate character. Its mild pungency makes it a perfect component of many spice mixtures, including *garam masala* (p31). Cumin seeds are also dry-roasted to sprinkle over rice dishes.

CORIANDER SEEDS

Coriander seeds are part of most of the *masala* preparations in southern India, either dry-roasted or fried in oil. They have a very distinctive, strong flavour. Usually combined with fenugreek seeds, black peppercorns and dried red chillies, they flavour many vegetarian and seafood dishes.

Curry leaves

< **Whole and chopped red chillies**

POPPY SEEDS

Obtained from the dry pods of the poppy plant, these tiny, light ivory colour seeds are and then ground into paste, or are lightly fried and made into a paste and used in curries and gravies. Poppy seeds lend a nutty flavour and a lovely creamy texture to dishes they are used in.

FENNEL SEEDS

In flavour fennel seeds are similar to anise, and they look like slightly plumper, greener cumin seeds. They have a very strong flavour, so use them carefully and in small quantities or they will overpower lighter spices.

FENUGREEK SEEDS

This very bitter spice provides the earthy, musky curry aroma in many South Indian dishes, both meat and vegetarian. The seeds, which are angular in shape and yellowish in colour, are added to pickles and chutneys too. Use them in small quantities.

RICE

The traditional rice in South India is a red variety with a short, thick grain. It is not often found outside India. Fragrant Basmati rice is considered to be the supreme variety and is reserved for special dishes. Mild-flavoured rice flour is the main ingredient for making batters and doughs.

SAMBAR ONIONS

Generally small in size, these onions have a sharp taste and strong aroma. They are used extensively in South Indian cooking.

SPLIT BLACK LENTILS

Black lentils are very popular in many parts of India. In the north, they are used whole to make rich dishes, whereas in South India, the lentils are usually skinned and split (*urad dal*). In many recipes, split black lentils are used as a spice, giving the dish a nutty flavour and crunchy texture. Their name is a bit confusing since they are, in fact, creamy in colour.

TAMARIND

This sweet and sour fruit is commonly used in South Indian cooking as a souring agent and it brings a tangy contrast to mild coconut sauces. It's also used for chutneys and drinks. Tamarind pulp is sold in dried blocks and needs to be soaked in hot water to soften, then strained to yield tamarind water (p355).

BLACK PEPPER

Known as 'black gold', pepper is one of the most widely used spices all over the world. Kerala is considered to be its birthplace, because the plant from which the spice comes (*Piper nigrum*) is native to Tranvancore. Black peppercorns are the dried, almost ripe berries of the plant. Keralan pepper markets are attractive places to visit – the spicy aroma of the crowded markets is carried a long way. Black peppercorns can be used whole or ground for garnishing dishes.

Cracked coconut shell and grated coconut >

DAKSHIN CURRY PASTE

This paste is used in various South Indian curries and gravies. Though the paste is on the spicier side, the tamarind gives it a refreshing tanginess. Depending on the recipe you are preparing, you could also add yogurt, tomato paste or grated coconut to this paste.

makes 750g (1lb 10oz)

1 tsp mustard seeds

2 tbsp cumin seeds

2 tbsp black peppercorn

100g (3¹/₂oz) dry red chillies

50g (1³/₄oz) coriander seeds

25g (scant 1 oz) tamarind

400g (14oz) sambar onions, peeled

250ml (9fl oz) vegetable oil

4 sprigs of curry leaves

3 tbsp ginger and garlic paste

1 tsp ground turmeric

salt

2 tbsp chopped coriander leaves

1 Heat a small, heavy-bottomed frying pan or griddle over a moderate heat. Add the whole spices and roast for about 1 minute, stirring constantly. As soon as they start to release their flavour, the smoky smell of the spices will indicate this, remove from the heat and transfer to a plate. Set aside.

2 Meanwhile, soak the tamarind in 250ml (9fl oz) water for 15 minutes or until the pulp has softened. Strain the softened tamarind through a seive into a bowl and set aside (p355). Using a blender, grind the onions into a fine paste. Transfer the roasted spice mix to a mortar and grind to a fine powder using the pestle (p354). Alternatively, use a blender or a small food processor.

3 Heat the oil in a frying pan, add the curry leaves and ginger and garlic paste, and sauté for 30 seconds. Now add the onion paste and sauté until the onions turn light brown.

4 Add the turmeric and sauté for 20 seconds. Mix in the tamarind water and cook for 2 minutes over a low heat.

5 Add the dry spice mix and sauté for 30 seconds, stirring frequently.

6 Season to taste and sprinkle over the coriander leaves, and stir. Remove from the heat, cool and store or use immediately.

MEEN KARI SRi LANKAN FiSH STEW

In Sri Lanka, as along the South Indian coast, fish is more popular than meat or chicken, and many of the dishes and cooking techniques on this beautiful island are similar to those in southern India. A wide variety of fresh seafood can be found in the markets. This tasty curry is common to many communities in Sri Lanka. It goes well with tamarind rice (p117) or a simple bread like Akki Rotti (p134).

serves 4

deliciously spiced

1 tbsp *ghee* or butter

12 shallots, cut into wedges

1¹/₂ tsp plain flour

3 tbsp tomato purée

¹/₂ tsp chilli powder

¹/₂ tsp ground coriander

¹/₄ tsp ground turmeric

salt

400g (14oz) kingfish or salmon fillet, skinned and cut into small pieces

250ml (9fl oz) thick coconut milk (p241)

1 tbsp wine or cider vinegar

pinch of crushed black peppercorns

1 Heat the ghee or butter in a large saucepan, add the shallots and fry for 5 minutes or until brown. Remove the pan from the heat and sprinkle the flour over the shallots. Mix well, then return the pan to a low heat.

2 Slowly add 450ml (15fl oz) water, mixing well to avoid lumps. Stir in the tomato purée, chilli powder, coriander, turmeric and some salt. Bring to the boil, stirring well, then add the fish. Simmer gently, covered, for 20 minutes or until the fish is cooked, stirring occasionally.

3 Remove the pan from the heat. Pour in the coconut milk and stir for 2 minutes. Add the vinegar and sprinkle with the crushed black pepper. Serve immediately.

MADRAS MEEN KOLAMBU TAMARiND FiSH CURRY

Giant tamarind trees grow everywhere in southern India, offering shade from the sun and their fruits for cooking. The sweet and sour flavour of tamarind is found in all kinds of dishes, from the fruity sweets loved by schoolchildren to curries such as this one. Fish cooked in terracotta pots with red chillies and tamarind is eaten by millions of people in the fishing communities. Serve this curry with plain rice.

serves 6

sweet and sour

2 tbsp vegetable oil

1 tsp mustard seeds

10 curry leaves

pinch of fenugreek seeds

2 garlic cloves, chopped

2 onions, chopped

¹/₄ tsp ground turmeric

¹/₂ tsp chilli powder

3 tomatoes, chopped

1 tsp tomato purée

sea salt

100ml (3¹/₂fl oz) tamarind water, made with 50g (1³/₄oz) pulp and 100ml (3¹/₂fl oz) water (p355)

500g (1lb 2oz) lemon sole fillets

1 Heat the oil in a large saucepan. Add the mustard seeds and, when they begin to pop, add the curry leaves, fenugreek seeds and garlic. Sauté for 1–2 minutes or until the garlic turns brown. Stir in the onions and cook over a moderate heat, stirring occasionally, for 10 minutes or until the onions are golden.

2 Add the turmeric and chilli powder and mix well, then add the chopped tomatoes, tomato purée and some salt and cook for a further 2 minutes. Pour in the tamarind water and 200ml (7fl oz) water. Bring the mixture to the boil and simmer for 12 minutes, stirring occasionally, until the sauce thickens.

3 Cut the fish fillets into pieces and carefully mix into the sauce. Lower the heat and cook gently for 4–5 minutes or until the fish is just cooked through. Serve immediately.

Madras meen kolambu >

ARACHU VECHA CURRY COCONUT FISH CURRY

This is a traditional fish curry from the region of Travancore, in southern Kerala, one of the most beautiful parts of southern India, where the coastal lowlands on the Arabian Sea are surrounded by lagoons. This is a fantastic dish for people who like mild curries. The creamy smooth flavour will balance spicier dishes. Serve with plain rice or any Indian bread.

serves 6

mild, creamy, nutty and aromatic

2 tbsp vegetable oil

200g (7oz) shallots, chopped

10 curry leaves

500g (1lb 2oz) tilapia or other white fish fillets, skinned

1 tbsp lemon juice

Spice paste

100g (3½oz) freshly grated coconut

1 tsp ground coriander

½ tsp chilli powder

large pinch of ground turmeric

1 To make the spice paste, put the coconut, ground coriander, chilli powder and turmeric in a blender. Pour in 200ml (7fl oz) water and process for 2–3 minutes to make a smooth paste. Set aside.

2 Heat the oil in a large frying pan, *karahi* or wok. Add the shallots and curry leaves and cook over a moderately low heat for 5 minutes or until the shallots are soft. Stir in the coconut spice paste together with 100ml (3½fl oz) water and bring the mixture to the boil. Cook for about 5 minutes, stirring occasionally, until the sauce has thickened.

3 Cut the fish fillets into 2.5cm (1in) pieces and add to the sauce. Pour in the lemon juice and mix carefully. Cook gently for 4–5 minutes or until the fish is cooked through. Remove the pan from the heat and serve immediately.

< Shallots
Juicier than regular onions, shallots provide a sweet, subtle flavour to curries and stews.

NADAN MEEN KOOTAN KiNGFISH CURRY

Eating a fish curry at least once a day is a must for the majority of South Indians who live on the coast. Kingfish is very popular and versatile. Its rich flavour works well with the tamarind and coconut milk combination here, which is typical of the region. Many of the fish dishes are simple, prepared for daily meals, whereas this curry would be made for a festival or other special occasion.

serves 4–6

sour and spicy

2 tbsp vegetable oil

1/2 tsp mustard seeds

10 curry leaves

pinch of fenugreek seeds

1 large onion, chopped

2.5cm (1in) piece fresh root ginger, thinly sliced

1/2 tsp ground turmeric

1/2 tsp chilli powder

1 tsp ground coriander

2 tomatoes, chopped

sea salt

3 tbsp tamarind water, made with 1 tbsp pulp and 3 tbsp water (p355)

500g (1lb 2oz) kingfish fillet, skinned and cut into 4cm (1¹/₂in) pieces 200ml (7fl oz) thick coconut milk (p241)

pinch of crushed black peppercorns

1 Heat the oil in a large saucepan, *karahi* or wok. Add the mustard seeds and, when they start to pop, add the curry leaves and fenugreek seeds. Sauté for 1 minute or until the fenugreek seeds turn golden, then add the onion and cook for 5 minutes on a moderate heat, stirring occasionally.

2 Add the ginger, turmeric, chilli powder and ground coriander. Mix well, then add the tomatoes and salt to taste. Cook for 5 minutes, stirring constantly. Stir in the tamarind water and 300ml (10fl oz) water and slowly bring to the boil.

3 Lower the heat under the pan, then add the fish cubes and simmer for 5–6 minutes or until the fish is just cooked through.

4 Turn the heat as low as possible and pour in the coconut milk. Add the pepper. Simmer gently for 2 minutes, then remove the pan from the heat. Serve immediately with boiled rice or potatoes.

Ground coriander >
Generally combined with ground cumin in spice mixes, ground coriander has a nutty flavour that deepens with cooking.

MEEN PORICHATHU SHALLOW-FRIED MASALA SARDINES

For a feast, this dry curried fish makes a fantastic combination with wetter chicken and meat dishes. It's crunchy and has a delicious spicy flavour. Serve it as a dry side dish or with plain rice or a green salad as a main dish. Pomfret or any flat fish can be used instead of sardines.

serves 2-4

fragrant, spicy and dry

4 sardines, about 300g (10oz) in total

5 tbsp vegetable oil

1 small onion, finely sliced

small handful of chopped coriander leaves

wedges of lemon

Spice paste

1 onion, chopped

2 green chillies, chopped

1cm (1/2in) piece fresh root ginger, finely chopped

10 curry leaves

10 black peppercorns

1/2 tsp chilli powder

1/2 tsp ground turmeric

2 tbsp wine or cider vinegar

1 tsp lemon juice

salt

1 Place all the ingredients for the spice paste in a food processor or blender. Process for 2-3 minutes to make a fine paste. Set aside.

2 Wash the fish under cold running water, then pat dry with kitchen paper. With a very sharp knife, make some slashes about 2.5cm (1in) apart along the whole length of the fish, on both sides. Don't cut too deeply, just enough to break the skin and cut slightly into the flesh.

3 Place the fish on a baking tray and spread the spice paste all over the fish, ensuring that it penetrates well into the cuts. Leave to marinate for 15-20 minutes.

4 Heat 2 tbsp of the oil in a large frying pan. Add the onion and cook for 5-6 minutes over a very high heat until the onion is well browned and crisp. Remove the onion from the pan and drain on kitchen paper.

5 Heat the remaining oil in the same pan over a low heat. Carefully place the fish in the pan, cover and cook for about 6 minutes on each side. Turn the fish once only during cooking to avoid breaking it up. Cook until the skin is brown and the flesh is cooked thoroughly.

6 Carefully remove the fish and place on a large serving dish. Sprinkle the crisp onions over the fish and garnish with coriander and lemon wedges.

NJANDU THENGAPAL CRAB IN COCONUT MILK

In most of southern India, crabs are not often cooked at home, mainly because it is hard for women to handle them. Crab would more likely be prepared in homes in fishing communities or in the traditional toddy bars. Unlike the usual spicy dry preparation, for this curry the crabs are cooked in a nicely spiced coconut milk sauce. Eat this with tamarind rice (p117) or a bread such as *chapatti* or *paratha*.

serves 4

creamy and refreshing

3 tbsp vegetable oil

200g (7oz) shallots, finely sliced

10 curry leaves

3 garlic cloves, chopped

2.5cm (1in) piece fresh root ginger, finely sliced

1/2 tsp chilli powder

1/2 tsp ground turmeric

1 fresh, uncooked crab, about 400g (14oz), cleaned and quartered

300ml (10fl oz) coconut milk (p241)

2 tomatoes, quartered

salt

1 tsp lemon juice

1/2 tsp black pepper

1 Heat the oil in a large frying pan and fry the shallots for 5 minutes or until they are soft. Add the curry leaves, garlic and ginger and cook for a further 5 minutes over a moderate heat.

2 Add the chilli powder and turmeric, then slowly pour in 250ml (9fl oz) of water, stirring. Bring the mixture to the boil, then lower the heat and simmer for 10 minutes, stirring occasionally.

3 Add the crab pieces and continue simmering the curry over a moderate heat for 10 minutes or until the crab is cooked.

4 Stir in the coconut milk and tomatoes and heat through gently for 2-3 minutes. Add salt to taste. Remove the pan from the heat, cover and set aside for a few minutes, then add the lemon juice and sprinkle with the black pepper. Serve immediately.

< Curry leaves

An essential ingredient in most South Indian recipes, these intensely aromatic leaves impart a spicy, citrussy note to curries. They are either used at the start of the cooking process or at the end in tempering or *tadka*.

KOYILANDI KONJU MASALA BOATMAN'S PRAWN MASALA

King prawn dishes are a treat in coastal southern India, as prawns are not easily affordable for ordinary people unless they live near beaches or areas where you can source fresh catch. Kerala has its own distinctive ways of cooking prawns and lobsters. This is a very popular dish in the local bars, which are well known for excellent spicy dishes. Eat this with breads like *paratha* or plain rice.

serves 4–6

vibrant and spicy

3 tbsp vegetable oil

pinch of cumin seeds

10 curry leaves

3 onions, sliced

1/2 tsp ground turmeric

1 tsp chilli powder

1 tsp tomato purée

4 tomatoes, sliced

2.5cm (1in) piece fresh root ginger, thinly sliced

sea salt

500g (1lb 2oz) raw king prawns, peeled but last tail section left on

chopped coriander leaves to garnish

1 Heat the oil in a large frying pan, *karahi* or wok. Add the cumin seeds, curry leaves and onions and cook over a moderately low heat for 10 minutes, stirring occasionally, until the onions are golden.

2 Add the turmeric, chilli powder, tomato purée, tomatoes, sliced ginger and a little salt to taste. Cook for 5 minutes, stirring occasionally.

3 Add the prawns and simmer for a further 5–6 minutes or until they turn pink and are just cooked.

4 Serve scattered with chopped coriander leaves.

Chilli powder >
Another important spice in Indian cuisine, chilli powder infuses a red hue and a sharp, spicy flavour to curries.

KONJU PULUNGARI KING PRAWN AND PUMPKIN CURRY

Pumpkins are festival vegetables in most of the states in southern India. They are grown abundantly in almost every household garden and cooked in all kinds of ways. There are many varieties, with a range of colours, flavours, sizes and seasons. White pumpkin has a particularly delicious and refreshing flavour, which goes amazingly well with coconut and prawns in this subtle curry. Serve with tamarind rice (p117) or breads such as *paratha*.

serves 4–6

subtle and light

2 tbsp vegetable oil

1/2 tsp mustard seeds

pinch of cumin seeds

10 curry leaves

2.5cm (1in) piece fresh root ginger, cut into strips

2 green chillies, slit lengthways

2 onions, sliced

150g (51/2oz) peeled pumpkin flesh, thinly sliced

1/2 tsp ground turmeric

salt

400ml (14fl oz) thick coconut milk (p241)

500g (1lb 2oz) raw king prawns, peeled but last tail section left on

1 tsp white vinegar

1 Heat the oil in a large frying pan. Add the mustard and cumin seeds and, when they start to pop, add the curry leaves, ginger, chillies and onions. Cook over a moderately low heat for 10 minutes, stirring occasionally, until the onions are golden.

2 Add the pumpkin, turmeric and a little salt and mix well for 1 minute, then pour in the coconut milk and 200ml (7fl oz) water. Bring the mixture to the boil, stirring constantly.

3 Add the prawns to the pan and cook, stirring, for 5 minutes or until the prawns and pumpkin are cooked. Add the vinegar and mix well. Serve hot, with rice or bread.

KOONTHAL ULLATHIYATHU SQUID CURRY

Squid is enjoyed in both southern India and Sri Lanka, cooked as a curry, stuffed or fried. If you go out on a boat to fish, the fishermen cook the freshly caught squid onboard with the minimum of spices and offer them as a special treat. Squid must be cooked for a short time or long simmered, otherwise it will be rubbery. Try this with breads such as *paratha* or *chapatti* or any flavoured rice.

serves 4

warm and colourful

3 tbsp vegetable oil

1/2 tsp mustard seeds

2 large onions, sliced

3 green chillies, slit lengthways

2.5cm (1in) piece fresh root ginger, finely sliced

1/2 tsp chilli powder

1/2 tsp ground coriander

2 large tomatoes, sliced

400g (14oz) cleaned squid, cut into 1cm (1/2in) pieces and tentacles reserved

1 tbsp chopped coriander leaves

1 Heat the oil in a large frying pan and add the mustard seeds. When they begin to pop, add the onions and cook for 5 minutes or until they are golden brown.

2 Stir in the green chillies and ginger, then add the chilli powder and ground coriander. Mix well and add the tomatoes. Cook over a moderate heat for 5–10 minutes or until the tomatoes break down to give a thick sauce.

3 Add the squid pieces and tentacles and mix thoroughly. Cover and continue cooking over a low heat for 15 minutes, stirring occasionally to prevent burning and sticking. If the dish becomes dry very quickly, stir in a few spoonfuls of water. Serve hot, garnished with the coriander.

< Green chillies
The heart and soul of most Indian curries, green chillies have a sharp, fresh flavour and their heat varies according to the cooking technique.

ATTIRACHI KOOT HYDERABADI MUTTON

Hyderabad is known for its spicy meat and chicken dishes, and even more for its meat *biryanis*. The traditional Islamic community there has introduced lots of new cooking combinations and delicacies to modern Indian cuisine. Mutton is the favourite meat. This dish was once called a royal dish and relished only by rich people, but today it is found on Indian restaurant menus all over the world. Serve with tamarind rice (p117) or *chapattis*.

serves 4

spicy

500g (1lb 2oz) boned mutton, cut into 1cm (½in) cubes
4 tbsp vegetable oil
2 cloves
2 cardamom pods
1cm (½in) cinnamon stick
1 bay leaf
1 onion, finely chopped
salt
coriander leaves to garnish

Marinade

1 tsp ginger paste
1 tsp garlic paste
2 tomatoes, finely chopped
1 onion, finely chopped
½ tsp ground turmeric
½ tsp chilli powder
1 tsp ground coriander
2 tbsp coriander leaves

1 Mix together the ingredients for the marinade in a bowl. Add the cubes of mutton and toss to coat with the marinade. Set aside for 20 minutes.

2 Heat the oil in a large saucepan and add the cloves, cardamom pods, cinnamon stick and bay leaf. Sauté for 1 minute, then add the onion and cook until it is golden.

3 Add the marinated mutton to the pan with salt to taste and mix well. Cover and cook on a low heat for about 30 minutes or until the mutton is tender. Garnish with coriander leaves and serve.

Bay leaves >
Bay leaves have a sweet, almost floral flavour. Add them at the start of the cooking process as they yield their flavour slowly.

KERALA LAMB

This is a restaurant speciality, famously known as Malabar Mutton Curry, cooked all over southern India in Malabari Restaurants. Muslims in Calicut are very fond of this dish, as it is easy to cook and has an extraordinary taste. The roasted coconut base and peppercorn flavour are typical of Keralan cooking. Plain rice or *paratha* are the best accompaniments.

serves 4

exquisite and aromatic

3 tbsp vegetable oil

200g (7oz) shallots, chopped

1 tbsp ground coriander

$\frac{1}{2}$ tsp ground turmeric

$\frac{1}{2}$ tsp chilli powder

salt

500g (1lb 2oz) boned lamb, cut into cubes

Spice paste

100g (3$\frac{1}{2}$oz) freshly grated coconut or desiccated coconut

2.5cm (1in) piece fresh root ginger, sliced

3 garlic cloves, chopped

2.5cm (1in) cinnamon stick

3 cloves

2 bay leaves

10 curry leaves

5 black peppercorns

For tempering

2 tbsp vegetable oil

$\frac{1}{2}$ tsp mustard seeds

10 curry leaves

2 green chillies, slit lengthways

1 First make the spice paste. Roast the coconut with the ginger, garlic, cinnamon stick, cloves, bay leaves, curry leaves and peppercorns in a dry pan until the coconut is browned. Allow to cool, then grind in a food processor, gradually adding about 250ml (9fl oz) water to make a fine paste.

2 Heat the 3 tbsp of oil in a frying pan, add the shallots and fry for 5 minutes or until soft. Add the spice paste, the ground coriander, turmeric, chilli powder, some salt and 400ml (14fl oz) of water. Bring to the boil. Add the lamb, then reduce the heat and cook, covered, for 30 minutes or until the lamb is well cooked.

3 Now prepare the tempering mixture. In a separate frying pan, heat the oil and add the mustard seeds. Once they start popping, add the curry leaves and green chillies. Stir-fry for 1 minute.

4 Pour the tempering mixture over the lamb curry and continue cooking for about 10 minutes or until the curry is very dry and thick. Serve hot.

ETHAKKA ATTIRACHI CURRY LAMB AND PLANTAIN CURRY

A contribution from my head chef Prasad, this is a speciality from his home village. Lamb dishes are very popular with Keralans, and they like to experiment by adding unusual ingredients like plantain. Lamb is an expensive meat for home cooks, so this is a special occasion dish. Breads like *chapatti* and *paratha* are good with it.

serves 4

spicy and rich

4 tbsp vegetable oil

1 tsp mustard seeds

10 curry leaves

2.5cm (1in) fresh root ginger, chopped

5 garlic cloves, chopped

2 green chillies, chopped

2 onions, sliced

2 tsp ground coriander

1/2 tsp ground turmeric

1/2 tsp chilli powder

3 tomatoes, sliced

400g (14oz) boned lamb, cut into cubes

1 plantain, peeled and cut into small pieces

salt

1 Heat the oil in a large frying pan. Add the mustard seeds and, when they start to pop, add the curry leaves. Then add the ginger, garlic and green chillies and sauté for 3 minutes. Add the onions and cook for a further 10 minutes or until the onions are brown.

2 Stir in the ground coriander, turmeric, chilli powder and tomatoes, mixing well, then add the lamb and 400ml (14fl oz) water. Bring to the boil, then cover and cook over a low heat for 15 minutes.

3 Now stir in the plantain pieces together with some salt. Leave to cook for another 15 minutes or until the lamb is cooked through and the plantain is tender, stirring occasionally. Serve hot.

< **Mustard seeds**
These seeds have a strong, earthy aroma, which is released once they are dry-roasted or heated in oil.

PULI CHORU TAMARIND RICE

Rice preparations are very common in Tamil Nadu and Karnataka. The addition of nuts and lentils and careful spicing make this rice dish very savoury and colourful. It goes well with all kinds of curries, be they meat, fish, poultry or vegetable.

serves 4

fragrant, rich and savoury

50g (1³/₄oz) tamarind pulp

250g (9oz) long-grain or Basmati rice

salt

2 tbsp vegetable oil

1 tsp mustard seeds

1 onion, finely chopped

20g (³/₄oz) raw peanuts

1 tbsp split *gram* lentils (*chana dal*) or split yellow lentils (*toor dal*)

10 curry leaves

3 dried red chillies

1 tsp fenugreek seeds

1 tsp asafoetida

1 tsp chilli powder

1 tsp ground coriander

1 tsp ground turmeric

1 tbsp chopped coriander leaves

1 Bring 100ml (3¹/₂fl oz) water to the boil in a small saucepan. Add the tamarind pulp and simmer for 10 minutes, stirring occasionally. Sieve the thick tamarind water into a bowl and set aside.

2 In a large saucepan, bring 500ml (16fl oz) of water to the boil. Add the rice and a little salt to taste. Allow to cook for 20–25 minutes or until the rice is tender. Drain and keep warm.

3 Rinse the saucepan, then heat it and pour in the oil. When the oil is hot, add the mustard seeds. As they begin to pop, add the onion, peanuts, lentils, curry leaves, dried chillies and fenugreek seeds. Cook, stirring frequently, until the onions are soft.

4 Add the asafoetida, chilli powder, ground coriander, turmeric and some salt. Cook over a moderate heat, stirring, for 2–3 minutes. Pour in the tamarind water. Mix well and cook for 15 minutes.

5 Add the rice and stir to combine, then transfer to a bowl. Garnish with the chopped coriander.

Split gram lentils >
These lentils with a mild sweet flavour have the ability to absorb the *masala* it is cooked in very well.

PORK VINDALOO

Vindaloo (from the Portuguese vindalho) originates from Goa, where the cooking combines Portuguese influences with fiery Indian flavours. *Vindaloo* dishes are made by families in Goa for their Christmas celebrations. What makes a *vindaloo* dish unusual is the combination of curry spices and vinegar. This is an elaborate dish but worth the effort. If you can handle spicy food be more generous with the chilli. This is traditionally eaten with red rice, although plain rice is good too.

serves 4

fiery hot
and sour

900g (2lb) boned pork, cut
   into 5cm (2in) cubes

4 tbsp vegetable oil

5 garlic cloves, finely chopped

2 onions, chopped

1 tsp ground turmeric

1/2 tsp chilli powder

1/2 tsp tomato purée

3 tomatoes, chopped

3 tbsp wine or cider vinegar

salt

pinch of crushed black peppercorns

1 tbsp chopped coriander leaves

Spice paste

1 tsp cumin seeds

4 cardamom pods

4 cloves

2.5cm (1in) cinnamon stick

5 black peppercorns

1 green chilli, chopped

2.5cm (1in) piece fresh root
   ginger, chopped

4 garlic cloves, peeled

3 tbsp lemon juice

1 To make the spice paste, grind the cumin seeds, cardamom pods, cloves, cinnamon stick and peppercorns in a clean coffee grinder or spice mill into a fine powder. Blend the spice powder with the green chilli, ginger, garlic and lemon juice in a food processor to make a fine paste.

2 Mix the pork with the spice paste in a large bowl. Cover it with cling film, then leave to marinate in a cool place for 1 1/2 hours.

3 Heat the oil in a frying pan, add the garlic and sauté for 1 minute. Add the onions and cook until they are golden, stirring occasionally. Add the turmeric, chilli powder, tomato purée, chopped tomatoes and vinegar and stir well.

4 Add the marinated pork and salt to taste. Cook for 10 minutes, stirring occasionally. Pour in 275ml (9fl oz) water and bring to the boil, then reduce the heat and simmer for 30 minutes or until the meat is cooked through and the sauce is thick.

5 Add the black pepper, then serve hot, garnished with the chopped coriander.

KOZHY KURUMA SOUTH INDIAN CHICKEN KORMA

Simple, mild chicken curries are typical of home cooking in the region, and in the Christian communities chicken dishes are prepared for celebrations and special occasions, to be eaten with popular breads like *appams*. Home-grown chickens are preferred for their outstanding flavour.

serves 4

aromatic, nutty and mild

3 tbsp vegetable oil

2.5cm (1in) cinnamon stick

3 cloves

2 bay leaves

3 cardamom pods, crushed

2 onions, chopped

1 tsp ground coriander

1/2 tsp ground turmeric

1/2 tsp chilli powder

2 tsp tomato purée

500g (1lb 2oz) boneless chicken breast, cut into cubes

pinch of black pepper

salt

40g (1 1/4oz) cashew nuts, ground with a little water to make a paste

coriander leaves to garnish

Ginger-garlic paste

2.5cm (1in) fresh root ginger, chopped

4 garlic cloves, peeled

1 For the ginger-garlic paste, put the ginger, garlic and a little water in a small food processor or blender and grind to make a fine paste. Keep it aside.

2 Heat the oil in a large frying pan. Add the cinnamon stick, cloves, bay leaves and crushed cardamom pods and sauté for 2 minutes. Add the onions and stir well, then cook for 5 minutes or until the onions are soft.

3 Add the ginger-garlic paste, ground coriander, turmeric, chilli powder and tomato purée. Mix well, then cook over a low heat for 5 minutes, stirring occasionally. Stir in the chicken, black pepper, salt to taste and 150ml (5fl oz) water. Bring to the boil, then cover and simmer for 15–20 minutes or until the chicken is well cooked.

4 When the chicken is cooked, add the cashew paste and blend well. Simmer for a further 3 minutes. Serve hot, garnished with coriander leaves.

< Cinnamon sticks

Cinnamon sticks have an intensely warm, woody aroma. Break the sticks to release this aroma before adding them to curry *masalas*.

KUKUL MUS KARI SRI LANKAN CHICKEN CURRY

Chicken curry is one of the highlights of weekend lunches in Sri Lanka. As in Keralan cooking, a special aroma is imparted with the use of coconut, and the layering of the spices makes it very easy to distinguish their various flavours. This dish comes from our friend Raj from Colombo. It is his favourite recipe from his grandmother. In return I had to teach him some traditional vegetarian cooking from Kerala. Serve this with rice or bread.

serves 4

very creamy and lightly spiced

3 tbsp vegetable oil

2 onions, finely sliced

2.5cm (1in) piece fresh root ginger, chopped

2 garlic cloves, chopped

1/2 tsp ground turmeric

1 tsp chilli powder

2 tsp ground *garam masala*

400g (14oz) boneless chicken breast, cut into bite-sized pieces

200ml (7fl oz) coconut milk (p241)

2 tomatoes, quartered

salt

1 Heat the oil in a medium saucepan, add the onions and cook until golden brown. Add the ginger, garlic and ground spices. Mix well for 1 minute, then add the chicken. Cook, stirring, over a moderate heat for 5 minutes.

2 Pour in 300ml (10fl oz) water. Bring to the boil, then reduce the heat, cover the pan and cook for 10 minutes.

3 Reduce the heat to very low and add the coconut milk. Cook for a further 10 minutes or until the chicken is throughly cooked. Stir in the tomatoes and salt to taste. Cook for a final 5 minutes to blend the *masala* well. Serve hot.

Root ginger >

Extensively used in Indian cuisine, root ginger is available year round in any Asian market. It has a fresh, lemony aroma and adds slight spiciness to curries.

KOLI ERACHI MOLAGU CHiCKEN PEPPER FRY

This dish comes from Tamil Nadu, where it is cooked for festivals like Diwali and other special occasions. In some of the villages, the dish is prepared as an offering to the goddess as part of worship. The spice combination and abundance of black pepper make this dish different from other Tamil chicken recipes. Enjoy its fiery savouriness and thick texture with Indian breads and a cold glass of beer.

serves 4

peppery and thick

3 tbsp vegetable oil

1/2 tsp mustard seeds

10 curry leaves

2.5cm (1in) piece fresh root ginger, finely sliced

3 garlic cloves, chopped

3 green chillies, sliced

2 onions, chopped

2 tomatoes, diced

salt

500g (1lb 2oz) boneless chicken breasts, cut into 1cm (1/2in) cubes

large pinch of crushed black peppercorns

Spice paste

1 tbsp vegetable oil

100g (3 1/2oz) freshly grated coconut or desiccated coconut

2 cloves

2 cardamom pods

3 black peppercorns

1cm (1/2in) cinnamon stick

1/2 tsp chilli powder

1/2 tsp ground turmeric

1 tsp ground coriander

1 To make the spice paste, heat the oil in a frying pan and roast the coconut with the cloves, cardamom pods, peppercorns and cinnamon stick until the coconut is brown. Add the ground spices and sauté for 1 minute. Leave to cool, then transfer to a food processor or blender. Add 200ml (7fl oz) water and grind to make a fine paste. Keep aside.

2 Heat the oil in a large saucepan and add the mustard seeds. As they begin to pop, add the curry leaves, ginger, garlic and green chillies. Cook for 3 minutes. Add the onions and cook until they are golden brown. Add the tomatoes and cook for another minute, then pour in the spice paste and add some salt. Stir well.

3 Add the chicken cubes and 250ml (9fl oz) of water. Bring to the boil, then cover the pan and cook for 20 minutes or until the chicken is cooked. Serve hot, sprinkled with the black pepper.

RASA KAYI MIXED VEGETABLE CURRY

A common preparation in Karnataka, mixed vegetables are beautifully cooked in a tomato *masala* that is flavoured – unusually – with fennel seeds. It's much spicier than a lot of other South Indian vegetarian dishes, although coconut milk makes it creamy and slightly sweet. Serve this with *paratha* or *chapatti*, or as a side dish with meat and poultry curries.

serves 4

quite spicy and slightly sweet

100g (3½oz) carrots, peeled

100g (3½oz) potatoes, peeled

100g (3½oz) green beans (fresh or frozen)

3 tbsp vegetable oil

2 onions, cut into small pieces

1 green chilli, slit lengthways

½ tsp chilli powder

½ tsp ground coriander

½ tsp ground turmeric

salt

100g (3½oz) cauliflower, separated into florets

100ml (3½fl oz) coconut milk (p241)

Spice paste

2 garlic cloves, peeled

2cm (¾in) piece fresh root ginger, finely chopped

1 green chilli, finely chopped

½ tsp fennel seeds

100g (3½oz) tomatoes, chopped

1 Grind all the ingredients for the spice paste in a mortar and pestle, or a blender or small food processor, until fine. Set aside. Cut the carrots, potatoes and green beans into 2.5cm (1in) pieces and keep aside.

2 Heat the oil in a large pan, add the onions and green chilli and cook until the onions are soft. Add the carrots, chilli powder, ground coriander, turmeric and salt to taste. Mix well. Lower the heat and add the potatoes. Cover and cook for 10 minutes.

3 Add the cauliflower and green beans together with the spice paste and mix well. Cook, covered, for a further 10–15 minutes.

4 Remove the pan from the heat and slowly add the coconut milk, stirring to blend well. Serve hot.

< Carrots
Carrots have a refreshing aroma and add a natural sweetness to mixed vegetables and curries.

CHEERA MORU CURRY SPINACH AND YOGURT CURRY

Every Keralan meal has two things in common: a yogurt curry and a *thoran* (dry stir-fried vegetable). A yogurt curry is a dish we look forward to and it's one of the easiest to make, adding vegetables in season. Spinach is my favourite, while the red leaves in the beet family are very popular in our village. This is a mild dish, but can be made spicier if you prefer. Remember, though, not to heat it too much once you add the yogurt. A yogurt curry is always eaten with rice.

serves 4

lightly spiced and creamy

2 tbsp vegetable oil

1/2 tsp mustard seeds

pinch of fenugreek seeds

2 garlic cloves, finely chopped

3 dried red chillies

10 curry leaves

100g (3½oz) shallots, chopped

3 fresh green chillies, slit lengthways

2.5cm (1in) piece fresh root ginger, finely chopped

2 tomatoes, finely chopped

1/2 tsp ground turmeric

salt

100g (3½oz) spinach, chopped

300g (10oz) plain yogurt

1 Heat the oil in a large saucepan and add the mustard seeds. As they begin to pop add the fenugreek seeds, then add the garlic, dried chillies and curry leaves and sauté for 1 minute. Add the shallots, green chillies and ginger and cook, stirring occasionally, until the shallots turn brown.

2 Add the tomatoes, turmeric and salt to taste. Mix thoroughly, then add the spinach and cook for 5 minutes, stirring occasionally.

3 Remove the pan from the heat and gradually add the yogurt, stirring slowly and constantly. Set the pan on a low heat and warm gently for 3 minutes, stirring constantly. Serve warm.

Spinach >
Use this juicy, earthy flavoured leafy vegetable in the right quantity as it drastically reduces in volume once cooked.

THAKKALI PAYARU CURRY BLACK-EYE BEANS WITH SPINACH AND TOMATO

A refreshing and light tomato dish, this is easy to make and it's very versatile in that you can make it with other pulses. I like to use my all-time favourite, black-eye beans. Be sure not to overcook the tomatoes, so that they retain their freshness. You can serve this with plain rice or *chapatti* to make a meal.

serves 4

fresh, light and creamy

3 tbsp vegetable oil

$1/2$ tsp mustard seeds

2 garlic cloves, finely chopped

10 curry leaves

100g ($3^1/_2$oz) chopped onion

2 green chillies, slit lengthways

$1/2$ tsp chilli powder

1 tsp ground coriander

$1/2$ tsp ground turmeric

200g (7oz) tomatoes, cut into small pieces

50g ($1^3/_4$oz) spinach, chopped

100g ($3^1/_2$oz) cooked or canned black-eye beans

salt

300g (10oz) plain yogurt

1 Heat the oil in a large saucepan and add the mustard seeds. When they start to pop, add the garlic, curry leaves and onion. Cook over a moderate heat for 5 minutes or until the onion is soft.

2 Add the green chillies, chilli powder, coriander and turmeric. Mix well, then add the tomato pieces. Give a nice stir, then add the spinach. Cook over a low heat for 5 minutes.

3 Now add the black-eye beans with salt to taste. Cook for a further 1 minute or until everything is hot. Remove the pan from the heat and slowly add the yogurt, stirring well. Serve warm.

VENDAKKA VAZHUTHANANGA MASALA OKRA AND AUBERGINE SPICY MASALA

Okra and aubergine are the favourite vegetables for many South Indians, but in this versatile dish you can replace them with your choice. I like the way the crunchy okra and juicy aubergine blend with the aromatic spices. This can be eaten as a main dish with *paratha* or as a fantastic side dish with meat and fish curries.

serves 4

nicely spiced and dry

3 tbsp vegetable oil

pinch of fenugreek seeds

pinch of fennel seeds

2–3 cardamom pods

2cm (³⁄₄in) cinnamon stick

1 bay leaf

3 garlic cloves, chopped

2 onions, finely chopped

¹⁄₂ tsp ground turmeric

¹⁄₂ tsp chilli powder

1 tsp ground coriander

1 tbsp tomato purée

2 tomatoes, finely chopped

150g (5¹⁄₂oz) okra, cut into pieces

150g (5¹⁄₂oz) aubergine, cut into pieces

salt

2 tbsp chopped coriander leaves

1 Heat the oil in a saucepan and add the fenugreek seeds, fennel seeds, cardamom pods, cinnamon stick, bay leaf, garlic and onions. Cook, stirring occasionally, until the onions are golden brown.

2 Add the turmeric, chilli powder, ground coriander and tomato purée and stir well, then cook for a further 1 minute. Stir in the chopped tomatoes and 500ml (16fl oz) of water. Bring to the boil, then reduce the heat and simmer for about 10 minutes or until the sauce is thick.

3 Add the okra and aubergine to the sauce with salt to taste and stir thoroughly. Cover and cook on a low heat for 5 minutes or until the aubergine and okra become tender.

4 Garnish with chopped coriander and serve hot.

< Aubergines
Native to tropical Asia, aubergines have a very tender texture that easily absorbs other flavours.

KIZHANGU PAYARU STEW POTATO AND GREEN BEAN STEW

This is a wonderful dish, so easy to make and with a divine flavour. At home, we always relished simple stews with potatoes, but my mother liked to experiment by adding seasonal vegetables. This one was my favourite. You can replace the vegetables according to availability and to make the dish more colourful. Stew dishes are traditionally eaten with *dosas* and *paratha*.

serves 4

slightly sweet and very light

2 tbsp vegetable oil

1 tsp mustard seeds

2 dried red chillies

a few curry leaves

2 onions, chopped

1/2 tsp ground coriander

1/2 tsp ground *garam masala*

1/2 tsp ground turmeric

1/4 tsp chilli powder

2 tomatoes, quartered

300g (10oz) potatoes, peeled and cut into wedges or cubes

100g (3¹/₂oz) green beans (fresh or frozen), cut into 2.5cm (1in) pieces

salt

200ml (7fl oz) coconut milk (p241)

pinch of crushed black peppercorns

1 Heat the oil in a large saucepan and add the mustard seeds. When they begin to pop, add the dried chillies and curry leaves and sauté for 2 minutes. Stir in the onions and cook over a moderate heat for 5 minutes or until the onions are soft.

2 Stir in the coriander, *garam masala*, turmeric and chilli powder. Add the tomatoes and cook for 5 minutes. Add the potatoes and mix well, then cook over a gentle heat for a further 5 minutes.

3 Add the green beans and salt to taste. Cook for another minute, then reduce the heat to very low. Pour in the coconut milk and 100ml (3¹/₂fl oz) water. Stir well to combine. Cook for 15–20 minutes or until all the vegetables are tender. Garnish with the black pepper and serve hot.

< Green beans
These fleshy beans have a crunchy texture that pairs perfectly with soft, fluffy potatoes, as in the above recipe.

KOOTU SAMBAR VEGETABLES WITH LENTILS

Sambar is the most famous accompaniment for the traditional pancake-like breads called dosas, and it is the curry always served first at any feast in southern India. Sambar is made in hundreds of ways in the different regions, using a variety of vegetables and different roasted spices. It is a dish of the common man. Enjoy it with rice, *dosas* or Akki Rotti (p134).

serves 4

hot and tangy

100g (3¹/₂oz) split yellow lentils (*toor dal*)

1 tsp ground turmeric

1 tsp chilli powder

2 onions, cut into small pieces

100g (3¹/₂oz) carrots, peeled and cut into 2.5cm (1in) pieces

100g (3¹/₂oz) green beans (frozen or fresh), cut into 2.5cm (1in) pieces

3 tomatoes, quartered

100g (3¹/₂oz) potatoes, peeled and cut into cubes

4 tbsp tamarind water, made with 1 tbsp pulp and 4 tbsp water (p355)

salt

Spice paste

100g (3¹/₂oz) freshly grated coconut or desiccated coconut

2 tsp coriander seeds

1 dried red chilli

For tempering

1 tbsp vegetable oil

1 tsp mustard seeds

10 curry leaves

3 dried red chillies

1 For the spice paste, roast the coconut and spices until brown. Leave to cool, then grind in a food processor, gradually adding about 250ml (9fl oz) water to make a fine paste.

2 Bring 300ml (10fl oz) of water to the boil in a saucepan and add the lentils, turmeric, chilli powder and onions. Simmer until the lentils are well cooked.

3 Add the carrots, beans, tomatoes and potatoes and stir well. Cover and cook for 10 minutes or until the vegetables are tender. Add the tamarind water and salt to taste. Cover and cook for a further 5 minutes.

4 Stir in the spice paste. Bring to the boil, then reduce the heat to moderate and cook, uncovered, for 5 minutes, stirring occasionally.

5 For tempering, heat the oil in a frying pan and add the mustard seeds. As they begin to pop, add the curry leaves and dried red chilies. Pour this over the curry and gently stir through. Serve hot.

BISSI BELA BHATH MiXED VEGETABLE RiCE

In this typical dish of the Brahmin community of southern India, mixed lentils are cooked with Basmati rice to introduce a nutty aromatic flavour. It's a rich dish and can be eaten as a complete meal.

serves 4

nutty, aromatic and rich

150g (5½oz) split yellow lentils (*toor dal*)

2 tbsp vegetable oil

75g (2½oz) freshly grated coconut

7 dried red chillies

2 tsp coriander seeds

1 tsp split gram lentils (*chana dal*)

1 tsp split black lentils (*urad dal*)

1 tsp ground turmeric

½ tsp fenugreek seeds

pinch of asafoetida

500g (1lb 2oz) Basmati rice

salt

120ml (4fl oz) tamarind water, made with 50g (1¾oz) pulp and 120ml (4fl oz) water (p355)

For tempering

2 tbsp vegetable oil

1 tsp mustard seeds

10 curry leaves

1 tbsp chopped raw cashew nuts

1 Bring 450ml (15fl oz) water to the boil in a large saucepan. Add the yellow lentils and simmer until tender. Drain and keep aside.

2 Heat the oil in a frying pan and add the coconut, red chillies, coriander seeds, split gram and black lentils, turmeric, fenugreek seeds and asafoetida. Fry until fragrant. Allow to cool, then grind to a fine powder in a clean coffee grinder or spice mill.

3 Clean the rice in cold running water, then place it in a large saucepan. Add 1 litre (1¾ pints) water and a little salt. Bring to the boil, then simmer for about 20 minutes.

4 Add the yellow lentils, tamarind water and spiced coconut powder. Cook for a further 5 minutes. Add just a little more water if the mixture becomes very dry too quickly.

5 Meanwhile, for the tempering, heat the oil in a frying pan and add the mustard seeds. As they begin to pop, add the curry leaves and cashew nuts and cook, stirring, until the nuts turn golden brown. Pour the mixture over the cooked rice, mix together and serve hot.

AKKI ROTTI SAVOURY RICE BREADS

Unlike in northern India, where wheat flour is used, breads in the south of the country are made with rice flour. This is my friend Vidya's recipe, which she made for me many times. It's a very light bread, spiced for a delightful change. Unlike many other breads, this can be made very quickly.

serves 4

300g (10oz) rice flour

50g (1³/₄oz) freshly grated
  coconut or desiccated coconut

2 tbsp chopped coriander leaves

10 curry leaves, chopped

2 green chillies, chopped

75g (2¹/₂oz) shallots, finely sliced

10 cashew nuts, roasted and ground

salt

vegetable oil for frying

1 Put all the ingredients in a large bowl and mix well. Make a well in the centre and gradually stir in about 450ml (15fl oz) water to make a soft dough. With floured hands, knead the dough to mix and shape it into small balls.

2 Roll out the balls on a surface dusted with rice flour to make discs as thin as possible. Leave to rest for 10 minutes.

3 Heat a large frying pan and coat the bottom with oil. Place one disc of dough in the pan and cook for 2–3 minutes or until golden brown. Turn over and brown the other side. Remove from the pan and keep hot while you cook the remaining breads. Serve hot.

< Grated coconut
One of the essential ingredients in South Indian cuisine, grated coconut adds a sweet flavour and a crunchy texture to dishes.

CHICKEN ISTEW CHiCKEN iN COCONUT MiLK CURRY

Istew, the famous dish from South India, is generally prepared with vegetables or meat along with coconut milk, southern spices and potatoes. Despite the distinctive flavour of the spices, the natural flavour of the main ingredients is not overpowered. The mild sweetness of the curry is from the freshly made coconut milk, which gives the dish its delicate flavour. *Istew* is often eaten with *appam*, *puttu* or Malabar *paratha* for breakfast or brunch and is extremely light and healthy.

serves 5

mildly sweet, delicately flavoured

500g (1lb 2oz) coconut, grated

2 tbsp coconut oil

1/2 tsp mustard seeds

5 green cardamom pods, roughly crushed

3 cloves

3 cinnamon sticks, each 2.5cm (1in) long

1 medium-sized onion, sliced

1 tsp roughly crushed ginger

1/2 tsp ground turmeric

2 sprigs of curry leaves

750–800g (1lb 10oz–1 3/4lb) skinless, with bone chicken, cut into 18–20 pieces

1 medium-sized carrot, peeled and cut into 1cm (1/2in) cubes

6 French beans, topped, tailed and cut into 1cm (1/2in) pieces

2 medium-sized potatoes, peeled and cut in 1cm (1/2in) cubes

2 tbsp green peas

4 green chillies, slit open

salt

10 black peppercorns, roughly crushed

5–6 cashew nuts, ground with a little water to make a paste

1 To make the coconut milk, the grated coconut along with 120ml (4fl oz) lukewarm water in a blender and process for 1–2 minutes to make a paste. Strain the paste through a fine strainer to extract the liquid, which will be thick coconut milk. Add another 250ml (9fl oz) water to the residue and grind into a fine paste. Once again strain the paste through a fine strainer. You will now have thinner coconut milk.

2 In a heavy-bottomed saucepan, heat the oil over a moderate heat. Add the mustard seeds and allow them to crackle. Add the cardamoms, cloves and cinnamon sticks and sauté for a minute or until they become slightly brown amd roasted. Stir in the onion and ginger and fry for 1–2 minutes or until the onions turn soft and translucent but not brown. Add the turmeric, half of the curry leaves and sauté for 2 minutes.

3 Add the chicken pieces and cook for another 5 minutes or until the pieces start to acquire a light brown colour. Pour in 150ml (5fl oz) water and the thin coconut milk. Cover the saucepan and cook for 17–20 minutes, stirring occasionally.

4 Remove the cover and add all the chopped vegetables along with 200ml (7fl oz) water. Add the chillies and salt. Place back the cover and cook for another 3–4 minutes. Once the chicken and vegetables are tender, add the thick coconut milk and crushed peppercorns. Mix the cashew nuts paste with the remaining curry leaves and add to the gravy. Cook for a minute, stirring constantly.

5 Remove the whole spices from the gravy and serve hot with *puttu*, *appam* or steamed rice.

BEANS USSILI GREEN BEANS WITH LENTILS

This recipe from the Iyengar community of Tamil Nadu is a must in any vegetarian spread during festivities and important dinners in South India. I discovered this recipe when researching for a vegetarian menu for a South Indian restaurant. The dish is a tasty combination of green tender beans with spicy and slightly crispy lentils, cooked in a simple combination of spices.

serves 5

nutty and aromatic

100ml (3½fl oz) coconut oil

1 tsp ground turmeric

salt

200g (7oz) French beans, cut in 5mm (¼in) cubes

1 tsp mustard seeds

3 sprigs of curry leaves, plus extra for garnishing

6 green chillies, slit lengthways

1 tsp split black lentils (urad dal)

50g (1¾oz) freshly grated coconut

6 pinches of asafoetida

Lentil paste

50g (1¾oz) split black lentils (urad dal)

50g (1¾oz) split yellow lentils (toor dal)

50g (1¾oz) split gram lentils (chana dal)

5 red chillies

5 pinches of asafoetida

1 To make the lentil paste, mix all the lentils together and wash under running water. Leave to soak in cold water for 1 hour.

2 Strain the excess water and put the lentils in a blender. Add the red chillies and grind to a coarse paste. Add 6 pinches of asafoetida, mix well and set aside.

3 Heat the oil in a kadhai or wok over a moderate heat. Add the lentil paste and sauté, stirring frequently, for 7–8 minutes or until the lentils turn crispy and crumbly. Separate the excess oil and transfer the lentils to a bowl.

4 Heat 500ml (16fl oz) water in a separate pan, add half the turmeric, along with the salt and beans. Increase the heat and bring to the boil. Remove from the heat, strain the beans and set aside.

5 Place the saucepan with the excess oil over a moderate heat. Add the mustard seeds and allow them to crackle for a few seconds. Add the curry leaves, green chillies and split black lentils and cook for 2–3 minutes or until the lentils turn brown.

6 Mix in the grated coconut and sauté for 1 minute or until light brown. Stir in the rest of the turmeric and cook for another minute. Now add the boiled beans and the sautéed lentil paste and mix well. Reduce the heat to low, add the asafoetida and simmer for 3–4 minutes.

7 Pour 200ml (7fl oz) water and simmer for another 3–4 minutes, stirring frequently, until it starts to sizzle. Garnish with curry leaves and serve hot with steamed rice or roti.

MIRCH KA SALAN SWEET CHILLIES IN VELVETY GRAVY

This curry originated in Hyderabad, the seat of the Nizams, where food is judged not just by its *swaad* (taste), but also its aroma. Prince Tusi, the great grandson of the last Mughal Emperor of India, Bahadur Shah Zafar, introduced this dish to me. Mirch ka Salan is a classic Hyderabadi preparation, with its characteristic tangy and mildly spiced *salan* or rich velvety gravy. The sharpness depends on the type of chillies you use. It is advisable to use deseeded green chillies to avoid a very hot dish. Interestingly, the use of sesame seeds, grated coconut and peanut paste balances the sharpness of the chillies very well.

serves 5

mildly spicy and tangy

10–15 thick green chillies, each with 1cm (1/2in) stem

3 tbsp peanut oil

4 sprigs of curry leaves

1/2 tsp mustard seeds

1/4 tsp cumin seeds

1/2 tsp nigella seeds

1 tbsp ginger and garlic paste

2 medium-sized onions, finely chopped

5 medium-sized tomatoes, puréed

1/2 tbsp red chilli powder

1/2 tsp ground turmeric

30g (1oz) tamarind, soaked in 120ml (4fl oz) water to make tamarind water

salt

2 tbsp finely chopped coriander

Nut paste

50g (1 3/4oz) skinless, roasted peanuts

30g (1oz) white sesame seeds

100g (3 1/2oz) coconut, grated and roasted

15g (1/2oz) poppy seeds

1 Soak all the ingredients for the nut paste in 250ml (9fl oz) water for 1 hour. Transfer the soaked nuts along with the water to a blender and blend to a paste.

2 Clean and wash the green chillies. Slit open each chilli lengthways on one side and remove the seeds.

3 Heat the oil in a saucepan and slowly add the chillies. Sauté over a moderate heat until they change colour and blisters form on the surface. Using a slotted spoon remove the chillies from the saucepan and set aside.

4 In the same oil, add the curry leaves, mustard seeds, cumin seeds and nigella seeds and sauté for 1 minute over a moderate heat. Once they begin to crackle add the ginger and garlic paste and sauté for 30 seconds. Add the onions and sauté for 2–3 minutes or until golden brown. Mix in the tomato purée and stir for a few seconds. Cover the saucepan, so that the flavours remain intact in the gravy, and cook for 3 minutes or until the purée is well cooked, stirring occasionally. Now mix in the red chilli powder and turmeric and stir for 1 minute. Pour 150ml (5fl oz) water and cook for 1–2 minutes, stirring constantly. Alter the quantity of water depending on how thick you like the gravy.

5 Stir in the nut paste and cook for 4–5 minutes. Add 5–6 tablespoons of water if the *masala* begins to thicken too much. Now mix in the tamarind water and stir for 5 minutes.

6 Sprinkle in salt to taste. Reduce the heat to low, add the sautéed green chillies and slowly fold them into the gravy. Simmer for 10–12 minutes, stirring occasionally.

7 Transfer to a serving dish, garnish with coriander leaves and serve with plain rice.

TOMATO PAPPU LENTILS WITH TOMATOES AND GARLIC

This curry comes from the southern state of Andhra Pradesh. *Pappu* refers to *dal* or lentils in this region, which is prepared with tomatoes and mild spices. While most recipes from this region are extremely spicy, this lentil preparation is an exception with its full and comforting taste. You could alter the quantity of chillies as per your taste.

serves 4

slightly tangy and mildly spicy

150g (5½oz) split yellow lentils (*toor dal*)

75g (2½oz) shallots, each cut in half

½ tsp ground turmeric

2 medium-sized tomatoes, quartered

salt

2 tbsp vegetable oil

Tadka or tempering

3 tbsp *ghee*

½ tsp mustard seeds

½ tsp cumin seeds

2 sprigs of curry leaves

1 tbsp ginger and garlic paste

50g (1¾oz) shallots, chopped

5 garlic cloves, sliced

6 green chillies, roughly chopped

4 red chillies, roughly chopped

2 tomatoes, chopped

¼ tsp asafoetida

1 Wash the lentils under running water. Put them in a pressure cooker along with the shallots, turmeric, tomatoes, salt and oil. Add 200ml (7fl oz) water. Put the lid on and pressure cook on a high heat until it gives out 8–9 whistles. Remove the cooker from the heat and set aside.

2 Alternately, leave the lentils to soak in cold water for about 20 minutes. Transfer them to a saucepan along with 200ml (7fl oz) water, shallots, turmeric, tomatoes, salt and oil. Bring to a boil, skimming off the white scum from the surface whenever necessary. Reduce the heat to low and simmer, covered, for 20–25 minutes or until the lentils are very soft and almost broken down.

3 For the *tadka*, or tempering, heat the *ghee* in a large ladle over a moderate heat. Add the mustard and cumin seeds and curry leaves and allow them to crackle. Mix in the ginger and garlic paste and sauté for 30 seconds. Add the shallots and stir-fry until golden brown, then add the garlic and sauté until brown. Throw in the chillies and fry for another 30 seconds. Mix in the tomatoes and stir for 3 minutes. You could sprinkle a tablespoon or two of water to prevent the *masala* from sticking to the base of the ladle. Add the asafoetida and stir. Now pour the boiled lentils in the tempering and mix well.

4 Add 100ml (3½fl oz) water, cover and simmer for 5–7 minutes. If the lentils have not already broken down, cook for another 15–20 minutes over a moderate heat. Check the seasoning and add salt, if necessary.

5 Serve hot with steamed rice or any Indian bread.

< Split yellow lentils
Widely used in India, split yellow lentils have a mild and nutty flavour. They take longer to cook than other lentils.

KAIRE MURGH KORMA CHICKEN WITH RAW MANGOES

Cuisine from Andhra Pradesh has a lot of variations due to the diversity of the region. Hyderabad has excellent Nizami cuisine with mellow flavours, and the Guntur and Nellore regions have very spicy food. In this recipe, the spiciness is balanced out with the help of summer ingredients, which are souring and cooling agents, such as raw mango, tender tamarind leaves, mint leaves and lemon.

serves 5

mildly sour and spicy

100ml (3½fl oz) vegetable oil

2 medium-sized onions, sliced

30g (1oz) cashew nuts

20g (¾oz) poppy seeds

20g (¾oz) almonds

20g (¾oz) mixed melon seeds

5 green cardamom pods

5 cloves

3 cinnamon sticks, each 5cm (2in) long

3 bay leaves

1 tbsp ginger and garlic paste

½ tsp ground turmeric

1 tbsp red chilli powder

1 tbsp ground coriander

½ tsp ground *garam masala*

1kg (2¼lb) boned chicken, washed and cut into cubes

200ml (7fl oz) yogurt, whisked until smooth

2 raw mangoes, sliced

200ml (7fl oz) tomato purée

5 green chillies, slit open

1 tbsp finely chopped coriander leaves

1 tbsp chopped mint leaves

4 tbsp single cream

salt

1 Heat the oil in a heavy-bottomed saucepan over a moderate heat. Add the onions and fry until light brown. Add the cashew nuts, poppy seeds, almonds, mixed melon seeds and fry until the cashew nuts are light golden. Strain the excess oil in a bowl. Set aside the fried onions and dry nuts and allow to cool, then grind in a food processor or a mortar and pestle gradually adding 5–6 tablespoons of water to make a paste.

2 In a separate pan, heat the excess oil over a moderate heat. Add the cardamoms, cloves, cinnamon sticks and bay leaves and sauté for 10 seconds. Add the ginger and garlic paste and sauté for 25 seconds or until golden. Mix in the turmeric, red chilli powder, coriander and *garam masala* and sauté for another 20 seconds. Sprinkle a tablespoon or two of water to prevent the *masala* from sticking to the base of the pan.

3 Add the chicken and sauté for 3–5 minutes or until golden. Reduce the heat to low, mix in the yogurt and raw mangoes and simmer for 4 minutes. Uncover, add 500ml (16fl oz) water, cover and simmer for another 5–7 minutes.

4 Increase the heat, mix in the tomato purée and cook for 2 minutes, stirring frequently. Reduce the heat to low, mix in the onion and nut paste and simmer until the chicken is thoroughly cooked.

5 Add the green chillies, coriander and mint leaves and stir for 10 seconds. Blend in the cream and season with salt.

6 Serve hot with boiled rice or breads.

ARIKOIDUKA THOKKU OYSTERS COOKED IN TOMATO AND COCONUT

Oysters, in Western cuisine, are a French delicacy reserved for affluent clientele. However, this is a recipe from the erstwhile Chera kingdom, which was part of present day Kerala and Coimbatore in the state of Tamil Nadu. This recipe is a modified version of the traditional one, with the addition of tomatoes.

serves 5

mildly spiced and sour, aromatic

25 fresh oysters, washed and cleaned

salt

1 tbsp lemon juice

1 tsp crushed black peppercorns

1 whole coconut, grated

3 tbsp vegetable oil

1/2 tsp mustard seeds

2 sprigs of curry leaves

1/2 tbsp chopped garlic

3 medium-sized shallots, finely chopped

2 cardamom pods

2 cloves

1 cinnamon stick, 2.5cm (1in) long

1/2 tbsp chopped ginger

1/4 tsp ground turmeric

1/2 tsp red chilli powder

1 tsp ground coriander

1/2 tsp ground cumin

1/4 tsp ground *garam masala*

5 medium-sized tomatoes, finely chopped

1/2 tsp fennel seeds

25g (scant 1oz) split and husked black lentil (*urad dal*), roasted and finely powdered

4 green chillies, slit into halves

3 tbsp finely chopped coriander leaves

1 Place the oysters in a large bowl and mix them with some salt, lemon juice and half the crushed peppercorns. Set aside to marinate for 30 minutes.

2 Meanwhile, mix half of the grated coconut with a little water to make a paste. Roast the remaining grated coconut over a moderate heat until golden brown. Set aside.

3 Heat the oil in a heavy-bottomed saucepan over a moderate heat. Add the mustard seeds, half the curry leaves and garlic and sauté until the mustard seeds crackle and the garlic turns slightly brown. Add the shallots and sauté for a minute or until light brown. Stir in the cardamoms, cloves, cinnamon stick and ginger and sauté for 1 minute. Mix in the roasted coconut and sauté for another minute. The spices and grated coconut should cook well to blend together for flavour. Add the turmeric.

4 Add the oysters and sauté for 1 minute over a moderate heat. Mix in the chilli powder, ground coriander and cumin and *garam masala*. Add 150ml (5fl oz) water and cook for 2–3 minutes, stirring occasionally.

5 Add the tomatoes, fennel seeds and cook for 4–5 minutes. If necessary, add a tablespoon or two of water to prevent the *masala* from sticking to the bottom of the saucepan. Now mix in the coconut paste and cook for 3–4 minutes, stirring occasionally. The coconut paste will thicken the gravy and enhance the taste. At this point, you may add little more water if you do not want a thick gravy. Here, I have kept the gravy thick.

6 Add the roasted lentil powder and mix well. Once the oysters are cooked, add the chillies, salt, coriander leaves and the remaining crushed peppercorns and curry leaves. Mix well and serve hot.

KARUVAPILLAI YERA PRAWNS WITH SPICY CURRY LEAVES

This delicious sea food preparation is from the Chettinad region of Tamil Nadu. Being ancient sea traders, the people of this region brought back recipes from other countries. They learnt how to preserve food in dry form with spices for long voyages, which could be prepared as curries by adding water. Karuvapillai Yera is a prawn preparation with traditional curry leaves and spices native to this region.

serves 5

mildly spiced
and velvety

15–17 raw prawns, peeled
   and deveined
250ml (9fl oz) coconut oil
$^1/_2$ tsp fenugreek seeds
1 tbsp roughly crushed garlic
2 onions, finely chopped
2 sprigs of curry leaves
6 whole red chillies
1 tbsp ground coriander
5 medium-sized tomatoes, puréed
25g (scant, 1oz) tamarind, made
   into pulp
100g (3$^1/_2$oz) coconut paste

Marinade

1 tbsp ginger and garlic paste
1 tsp ground turmeric
2 tbsp lemon juice
salt

Dry mix

50g (1$^3/_4$oz) split and husked black
   lentils (*urad dal*)
50g (1$^3/_4$oz) split *gram* lentils
   (*chana dal*)
10 whole red chillies
15 sprigs of curry leaves
1 tbsp black peppercorns
1 tbsp cumin seeds

1 Mix all the ingredients for the marinade together with 2–3 tablespoons of water. Add the prawns and turn to coat them, then cover and set aside for about 60 minutes.

2 Heat a wok or *kadhai* over a moderate heat and sauté all the ingredients for the dry mix until the lentils turn golden brown. Leave to cool, then transfer to a food processor and grind to a fine powder.

3 Coat the marinated prawns with the dry lentil powder. Heat oil in a frying pan over a moderate heat and fry the prawns until golden brown. Strain and set aside.

4 Add the fenugreek seeds, garlic, onions and curry leaves to the oil and sauté for 1–2 minutes or until the onions turn golden. Add the red chillies and coriander, sprinkle 1 tablespoon of water and sauté for a another minute.

5 Fold in the tomato purée and cook for 3 minutes, stirring frequently. Mix in the tamarind pulp and add 100ml (3$^1/_2$fl oz) water and cook for 2 minutes.

6 Reduce the heat to low, add the coconut paste along with 200ml (7fl oz) water and cook for another 2 minutes, stirring continuously. Check the seasoning and add more salt if required. Add the prawns and cook for a minute.

7 Serve the crispy prawn gravy with steamed rice.

Fenugreek seeds >

Commonly used in curry
masalas, these seeds have
a midly bitter flavour
and floury texture.

MEEN MANGO CHARRU FISH IN RAW MANGO CURRY

This popular recipe from Kerala boasts of an exceptional balance of flavours combining the tanginess of raw mangoes with the tenderness of fresh fish. I picked up this delectable recipe during one of my travels through the Chavakkad region of Kerala.

serves 5

spicy and sour

100ml (3¹/₂fl oz) coconut oil

1 tsp mustard seeds

¹/₂ tsp fenugreek seeds

3 sprigs of curry leaves

50g (1³/₄oz) shallots, finely chopped

¹/₂ tsp ground turmeric

1 tsp red chilli powder

1 tsp ground coriander

3 large-sized tomatoes, cut into quarters

2 raw mangoes, cut into 5cm x 5mm (2 x ¹/₄in) thick pieces

200ml (7fl oz) tamarind pulp

salt

1kg (2¹/₄lb) fillets of sole or cat fish, cut into chunks

200g (7oz) coconut paste

1 tsp chopped coriander leaves, to garnish

Spice mix

¹/₂ tsp black peppercorns

15 garlic cloves

1 tsp cumin seeds

4 whole red chillies

1 For the spice mix, roughly grind the peppercorns, garlic, cumin and whole red chillies in a food processor and set aside.

2 Heat the oil in a heavy-bottomed pan over a moderate heat, add the mustard seeds and reduce the heat once they start crackling. Add the fenugreek seeds and curry leaves and sauté for 20 seconds.

3 Add the shallots and sauté for 1 minute or until golden brown. Increase the heat to moderately high, add the spice mix and sauté for 1–2 minutes. Add the turmeric, chilli powder, coriander and sauté for 30 seconds. Now add the tomatoes and raw mangoes and cook for 2 minutes. Mix in the tamarind pulp and salt, cover and cook for 3 minutes.

4 Uncover and carefully add the fish chunks along with 200ml (7fl oz) water. Cover with the lid and cook for 5 minutes.

5 Once the fish is almost done, mix in the coconut paste and simmer for 5 minutes. Turn over the fish chunks to mix well, be careful not to break them. Check for the consistency of the gravy and add 4–5 tablespoons of water, if necessary.

6 Transfer to a serving dish, garnish with the coriander leaves and serve hot with plain rice or *idlis*.

GOSHT DALCHA MUTTON IN LENTILS CURRY

Muslims from the southern part of India are famous for their lentil and meat preparations. This recipe from Hyderabad is a tantalizing concoction of *chana* and *toor dal*, cooked with mutton and spices to give a mildly sour, but rich curry. Gosht Dalcha is often served as an accompaniment for biryani.

serves 5

mildly sour and aromatic

4 tbsp vegetable oil
6 green cardamom pods
6 cloves
4 cinnamon sticks, 5cm (2in) each
1/2 tsp cumin seeds
1/2 tsp ground turmeric
3 medium-sized onions, sliced
30g (1oz) split *gram* lentils (*chana dal*)
30g (1oz) split yellow lentils (*toor dal*)
1 tbsp ginger and garlic paste
1/2 tbsp red chilli powder
1/2 tbsp ground coriander
500g (1lb 2oz) neck end of mutton, washed and cleaned
50g (1 3/4 oz) each of aubergines, potatoes and pumpkins, each washed and sliced into 5cm (2in) long and 1cm (1/2 in) wide strips.
1 medium-sized raw mango
1/2 tsp ground *garam masala*
100g (3 1/2 oz) mildly sour yogurt
salt

Stock

500g (1lb 2oz) mutton neck bones, washed and cleaned
1 medium-sized onion, sliced
4 garlic cloves
2 bay leaves
25g (scant 1oz) ginger, crushed
1/4 tsp crushed black peppercorns

Tadka or tempering

1 tbsp butter
1/2 tsp cumin seeds
1/2 tsp mustard seeds
4-5 curry leaves
2 dried red chillies

To garnish

1 tbsp chopped mint leaves
1 tbsp chopped coriander leaves
juice of 1/2 lemon, (optional)

1 To prepare the stock, mix all the ingredients together in a pan. Add 1.5 litres (2 3/4 pints) water and cook for 10 minutes over a moderate heat, skimming off the scum from the surface whenever necessary. Reduce the heat to low and simmer for an hour, then strain the stock through a sieve and set aside.

2 Heat half the oil in a heavy-bottomed saucepan over a moderate heat. Add half of the cardamoms, cloves, cinnamon sticks and cumin seeds along with the turmeric and sauté for a few seconds over a moderate heat. Add half the onions and sauté until golden brown. Add the lentils and 400ml (14fl oz) water. Cover the saucepan, increase the heat and boil until the lentils are soft and broken down.

3 In another saucepan, heat the rest of the oil over a moderate heat. Add the remaining whole spices and onions and sauté until the onions are golden brown. Stir in the ginger and garlic paste, red chilli powder and ground coriander and cook for a few seconds. If necessary, add a tablespoon or two of water to prevent the mixture from sticking to the bottom of the pan.

4 Add the mutton and sauté for 5 minutes or until the mutton turns brown. Add the stock, cover the pan and cook for 50-55 minutes. Once the mutton is tender, add all the vegetables and the raw mango, stir for 2 minutes and then sprinkle over *garam masala*.

5 Reduce the heat to low and fold in the yogurt. Cover again and simmer for another 5 minutes, or until the vegetables and raw mango are tender. Now add the cooked lentils and stir for 3 minutes. Add salt to taste.

6 For the *tadka*, or tempering, heat the butter in a separate frying pan over a moderate heat. Add the cumin and mustard seeds. Once they start popping, add the curry leaves and red chillies. Stir-fry for 1 minute, then pour this tempering mixture over the *dalcha* and stir.

7 Garnish with mint and coriander leaves and serve hot. This gravy should be slightly sour to taste. If you feel it is not sour enough, squeeze some lemon juice over the top.

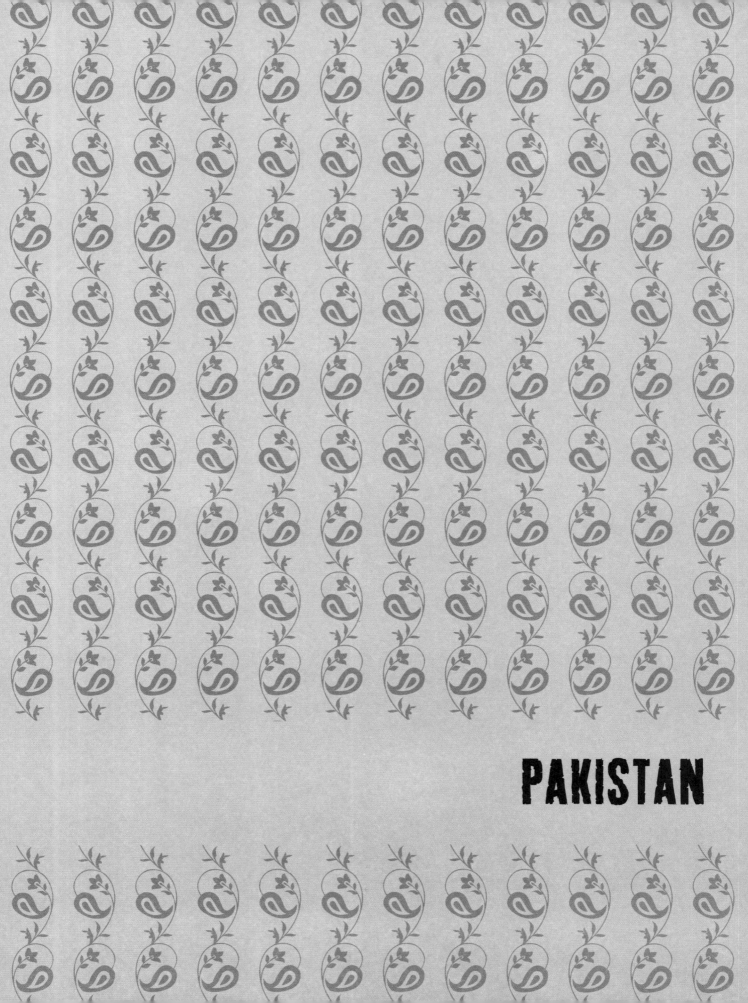

PAKISTAN

Pakistan is a country of over 160 million people and an area of almost 900,000sq km (350,000sq mi). Through various invasions and occupations and through trade, it has been greatly influenced by its neighbours – India on the east, Iran and Afghanistan to the west and China in the north, through the ancient Silk Road – and its culture, traditions and cuisine have evolved over time accordingly.

The four provinces of the country, which range in terrain from very high mountains to the coastlines of the Arabian Sea and Indian Ocean, provide a great diversity of meat, game, poultry, fruits and vegetables.

If given a choice, every Pakistani would eat meat every day. Pulses and beans are also sometimes used as the main part of a curry, but this is mainly for economic reasons, meat being more expensive. The favourite meats are lamb and mutton, although veal and beef are also eaten. Being a Muslim country, pork is never consumed. Various breeds of sheep and goats are reared in different parts of the country, most of them in a natural environment eating wild plants and herbs. Because they are free range and organic, their meat has an excellent flavour. Chicken is the most popular poultry, while game birds such as quails, pigeons and partridges are also occasionally enjoyed.

First-time visitors to Pakistan are always surprised to find so many fruits and vegetables. From the mountains to the plains there is an abundance of cherries, apples, peaches, apricots, mangoes, oranges and lychees, and from the coastal area come bananas and papayas. The array of vegetables includes potatoes, tomatoes, onions, carrots, peas, cauliflowers and many local varieties.

For everyday meals, Pakistanis add vegetables to meat – or meat to vegetables – whichever way you want to look at it. This is primarily to help the household budget, as it enables the same amount of meat to be eaten by more people. Meat is also added to beans and lentils but to a lesser extent. One very popular dish is 'chickpeas with chicken'.

In Pakistan the word 'curry' is alien. *Salan* is probably the closest word for what is called a curry in India and the rest of the world. What makes a Pakistani curry different from an Indian curry is the regular use of meat and a limited use of spices. And unlike Thai curries, in Pakistan there is no added sourness or sweetness in the seasoning.

A very important rule to follow in making a good Pakistani curry is 'less is better'. Nothing ruins a curry more than by adding too many ingredients. Each ingredient is used for a particular purpose and is not duplicated with a similar ingredient. For example, if lemon is added, then vinegar is not required. Similarly, if fresh coriander is used for flavouring, fresh mint is not needed too. Each flavour can then be appreciated for its individual characteristics.

Another vital aspect of a good Pakistani curry is the freshness of the ingredients. Food is purchased each morning and eaten by the evening. At home, cooking is mostly done by women, and the recipes are passed verbally from mother to daughter. This makes Pakistani curries all the more interesting, as the same dish will taste quite different from house to house and region to region.

Traditionally the curry cooking pot was made of earthenware, but today this has been replaced by a saucepan (without a handle). The first step in making a curry is almost always preparing the *massalla* – cooking onions, ginger, garlic and tomatoes with spices until the oil separates out. This is the basic foundation for most Pakistani curries.

Food colourings are not generally used in Pakistani curries, nor in *tikkas* and barbecued meats. Red colour from red chillies and yellow from turmeric is all that is needed. Only rice dishes such as *biryanis* and some desserts are tinted with food colourings.

The predicament of a Western curry-lover is often heartburn – when you eat a curry for dinner in a restaurant anywhere else in the world, it will still be with you for breakfast too. However, this is not the case with a Pakistani curry. It is unique: fresh in flavour, based on seasonal ingredients for the very best taste, carefully spiced, nutritious, and economical to make. A Pakistani curry can be enjoyed every day and for every occasion.

Mahmood Akbar

Making the massalla >
Fry onions, garlic, ginger and tomatoes in hot oil.

TASTE OF PAKISTAN

1. rock salt
2. cloves
3. black peppercorns
4. fresh root ginger
5. onion
6. garlic
7. tomato
8. star anise
9. mint leaves
10. fresh green chillies
11. cinnamon sticks
12. coriander leaves
13. basmati rice
14. fenugreek leaves
15. four seeds
16. ground red chilli
17. ground cumin
18. ground turmeric
19. ground coriander

THE RAW MATERIALS

The key flavouring ingredients for a Pakistani curry can be divided into four groups. The first consists of the components of the massalla base: onions, garlic, fresh ginger and tomatoes. Second is spices, followed by fresh herbs and aromatics, and then salt, which is an essential seasoning for any curry. Careful balancing of these flavourings creates a foundation for the meat, pulses and vegetables to be added.

BASMATI RICE

Probably the best rice in the world, Basmati is the one to use for all Pakistani rice dishes, in particular *biryanis*.

CHILLIES

The Dundicut is the most popular chilli in Pakistan. Bright red to deep ruby red in colour, it has a strong aroma and – Pakistanis think - a hot, pungent flavour (although in comparison with Thai and Scotch bonnet chillies, Dundicuts are quite mild). The heat level varies, ranging from 30,000 up to 150,000 Scoville units (the higher the number, the hotter the chilli).

Dundicuts are cultivated in Sindh Province. The total consumption of red chillies in Pakistan is about 180,000kg (400,000lb) per year, and over three-quarters of this is the Dundicut variety.

Red Dundicut chillies are rarely used fresh, but are usually dried and then ground into a powder. Red chilli powder is considered indispensable for many dishes. As with other spices, chillies should be freshly ground, if possible. If you are buying red chilli powder, choose small packets and do not keep for more than 2–3 months.

Hot and pungent green chillies are available fresh throughout the year. Their size varies according to the season and where they are grown, but they are generally 7–12cm (3–5in) long.

FOUR SEEDS

This combination of dried, peeled seeds from various melons, pumpkin and summer squash is used in chutney recipes (see p176) as well as in *halwas*, sweetmeats and desserts.

GARLIC

Because Pakistan has such hot weather, our garlic is more pungent than that grown in Europe. For all curries, garlic is pounded to a paste – usually in a mortar and pestle - to extract its full flavour and aroma. Garlic paste (and ginger paste, see below) can be made in larger quantity in a food processor, and kept in an airtight jar in the refrigerator for 2 weeks. The pastes can also be frozen for up to 3 months; pack into an ice cube tray lined with cling film and cover with more cling film.

SPICES

The base (*massalla*) of most Pakistani curries consists of fresh aromatics and tomatoes cooked with black pepper, red chilli powder, turmeric, coriander, cumin and salt. These spices are always added in small quantities, and each fulfils a unique requirement in the blend: black pepper provides the aroma and the bite, red chilli the heat, turmeric the colour, cumin the flavour, coriander the earthiness and salt, of course, the savour. They don't duplicate each other, nor do they overwhelm each other. Other spices are added for particular dishes. For example, star anise adds an aromatic anise-liquorice flavour to *biryanis* and other rice dishes.

While fennel, cumin, mustard and fenugreek seeds are grown locally, most of the other spices associated with curries, like cloves, cardamom, cinnamon, nutmeg, mace and so on, are imported from neighbouring countries. In everyday home cooking these spices are used only occasionally, and mainly whole rather than ground.

GINGER

Where onions and garlic are the basic ingredients in curries everywhere – and in much European cooking – almost no Pakistani curry can be made without adding ginger to this foundation, too. Ginger not only infuses curries with a warmth and earthy aroma, it also contributes positive medicinal properties. Only fresh, raw ginger is used, including for garnishing. It should be young, with a thin skin - older ginger has fibrous flesh. The skin is best scraped, not peeled. For many curries, ginger is pounded to a paste in a mortar and pestle; if very young ginger is used, the skin can be left on.

HERBS

In Pakistani cuisine mostly fresh ingredients are used, and so it is with herbs, which have been used here for centuries. Coriander, mint and fenugreek leaves are among the

most popular fresh herbs, to add extra flavouring to curries and to garnish them.

ROCK SALT

For seasoning curries, rock salt is preferred for its unique flavour, which is not overly salty or pungent. Rock salt is mined in abundance in Pakistan.

ONiONS

The purplish-red variety of onion commonly cultivated in Pakistan is more pungent and lower in water content than European onions and is also less sweet, so onions do not impart a sweet flavour in Pakistani curries.

TOMATOES

The Portuguese introduced the tomato to the Indian subcontinent via Goa, and it took more than a hundred years for the tomato to spread from there and be accepted in the rest of the region. The Italian-type plum tomato is the variety most commonly grown in Pakistan, and it is in season from mid spring until late autumn. Although a staple in curries and every salad, tomatoes are not much used otherwise, except as a garnish. If tomatoes are not in season, you can substitute canned Italian plum tomatoes in the recipes.

YOGURT

Thick plain yogurt is added to curries to give a slightly sour flavour and to make them milder. Coconut milk and cream are not used in Pakistani curries.

< Fresh fenugreek leaves

NIHARI SPICE POTLI

Whole spices add depth to any recipe with their woody, wholesome flavours. This bouquet garni is a mixture of aromatic Asian spices and is used in slow-cooked mutton recipes and mutton stock in the India and Pakistan region.

2 onions, roughly chopped

20g (³/₄oz) ginger

25g (scant 1oz) coriander leaves

25g (scant 1oz) mint leaves

10g (¹/₄oz) vetiver roots

5 garlic cloves

6 black cardamom pods

6 cloves

2 cinnamon sticks

2 bay leaves

1 tsp black peppercorns

1 tsp cumin seeds

pinch of grated nutmeg

2 blades mace

2 star anise

10g (¹/₄oz) dried rose petals

1 tsp caraway seeds

1 Roughly chop the onions, ginger, coriander and mint leaves and the vetiver roots. Roughly crush the garlic cloves. Place all the ingredients on a plate and mix together.

2 Take a 46cm (18in) square muslin cloth, put all the ingredients in the centre of the cloth. Gather together the cloth and tie a knot around it.

3 Add this bouquet garni to the stock for mutton curries. Remove and discard the spices once the stock is prepared.

MUSTARD RAITA

The sharp and tangy taste of crushed mustard seeds blends perfectly with the creaminess of the thick yogurt. This combination acts as a wonderful appetizer that scintillates the taste buds. it is also a perfect accompaniment to rich dishes, such as *biryani* and pilau.

serves 4–5

1 tsp mustard seeds

250g (9oz) yogurt

salt

1 tsp black salt

1 tsp black peppercorns, coarsely crushed

1 tsp chopped coriander leaves, plus extra for garnishing

pinch of red chilli powder, for garnishing

1 Soak the mustard seeds in lukewarm water for an hour.

2 Meanwhile, whisk the yogurt in a bowl until thick and smooth.

3 Drain the water from the mustard seeds and grind them to a coarse paste with a mortar and pestle. Alternatively you could use a food processor.

4 Add the mustard seed paste, both the salts, peppercorns and coriander leaves to the yogurt and mix well. Garnish with red chilli powder and the remaining coriander leaves.

PALAK GOSHT SPINACH AND LAMB CURRY

No wedding meal or special dinner is considered complete without this curry. It is almost always made with mutton or lamb, although some people prefer to use chicken. The vast popularity of this dish is due to the fact that it is pretty indestructible – whichever way you cook it, it still somehow comes out tasting good. You can make it ahead and reheat it, serve it for lunch or dinner and eat it with any kind of rice – plain boiled to chickpea pilau (p180) – or with *nan* or *roti*, plus some onion *raita* (p179). It is loved by people of all ages, in all seasons, and is the ultimate comfort food.

serves 4–5

spicy and fragrant

4 tbsp sunflower oil

2 large onions, finely sliced

1 tsp garlic paste

2 medium tomatoes, skinned and chopped

1 tsp red chilli powder

1 tsp ground turmeric

1 tsp cumin seeds

salt

500g (1lb 2oz) boned leg of lamb, cut in small pieces

500g (1lb 2oz) fresh spinach leaves or well-drained frozen spinach

To garnish

chopped green chillies

slivers of fresh root ginger

1 Heat the oil in a saucepan, add the onions and cook until slightly browned. Add the garlic paste and tomatoes and stir for a minute. Add the chilli powder, turmeric, cumin seeds and salt to taste and stir. If necessary, add a tablespoon or two of water to prevent the mixture from catching on the bottom of the pan and burning. Stir until the oil separates out.

2 Now add the lamb pieces together with 350–500ml (12–16fl oz) water. Put the lid on and leave to cook on a moderately low heat for 30–40 minutes or until the lamb is 80 per cent cooked. Add the spinach and continue cooking, covered, for 12–15 minutes or until the lamb is tender.

3 Remove the lid and simmer for a further 10–15 minutes or until excess liquid has evaporated and the oil separates out. Garnish with chopped green chillies and slivers of ginger, and serve.

NOTE The curry can be made in advance (it's great for freezing) and reheated in the pan on a low heat or in a microwave.

TAMATAR GOSHT LAMB AND TOMATO CURRY

Make this curry when tomatoes are in peak season and full of flavour – Tamatar Gosht is simply pieces of lamb and lots of tomatoes cooked into a curry. Lamb (or mutton) works well with the slightly sharp taste of tomatoes; however, beef or veal shoulder or rump can be substituted for the lamb, as can chicken, quail, fish or even squid. Serve with plum chutney (p175) and leavened *roti* (p172) or *nan*.

serves 2–3

tangy and slightly sweet

4 tbsp sunflower oil

1 large onion, finely chopped

1 tsp ginger paste

1/2 tsp garlic paste

500g (1lb 2oz) tomatoes, skinned and chopped

salt

1 tsp red chilli powder

1 tsp cumin seeds

3 black cardamom pods

5 cloves

1 bay leaf

500g (1lb 2oz) boned lamb leg or shoulder, cut into small pieces

4 tbsp chopped coriander leaves

To garnish

slivers of fresh root ginger

chopped green chillies

1 Heat the oil in a saucepan, add the onion and fry until slightly browned. Add the ginger and garlic pastes and stir, then add the tomatoes. Add some salt, the chilli powder, cumin seeds, cardamoms, cloves and bay leaf. Stir until the oil separates out.

2 Add the lamb and fry, stirring, for 5 minutes. Pour in 250ml (9fl oz) water and stir well, then put the lid on the saucepan and reduce the heat to moderately low. Cook for 45–60 minutes or until the lamb is cooked and tender.

3 Remove the lid and keep cooking gently, stirring, until the oil separates out. Stir in the chopped coriander leaves. Garnish with the ginger and green chillies, and serve.

NOTE The curry can be made in advance (it's good for freezing) and reheated in the pan on a low heat or in a microwave.

Cloves >
Use cloves in small quantities, as their assertive, warm aroma can easily overpower other spices.

GURDA KEEMA MINCED LAMB AND KIDNEY CURRY

Keema, or mince, is the staple food in every household, every roadside restaurant and every cafeteria in Pakistan, and *keema* is probably the first curry to be mastered and consumed over and over again by every Pakistani student in the UK or US. The meat traditionally used to be beef, then mutton or lamb became popular. Nowadays among the urban population chicken mince is picking up. Vegetables, such as potatoes, peas and onions, pulses and beans are often added for flavour and to extend the dish. But kidneys lift ordinary mince to a higher status, making this curry worthy to be served to a special guest. Instead of including kidneys, you can, of course, add potatoes or peas. Serve this with plain yogurt and Pratha (p172).

serves 4–5

meaty and spicy

6 lamb's kidneys, sliced

1¹/₂ tsp garlic paste

1 tsp ground turmeric

4 tbsp sunflower oil

2 large onions, finely sliced

1 tsp ginger paste

4 medium tomatoes, skinned and chopped

1 tsp red chilli powder

1 tsp cumin seeds

1 tsp ground coriander

salt

500g (1lb 2oz) coarsely minced lamb

4 tbsp chopped coriander leaves

To garnish

green chillies cut into julienne

fresh root ginger cut into julienne

1 Pour 250ml (9fl oz) water into a small saucepan. Layer the sliced kidneys in the pan, cut side down. Add ¹/₂ tsp of the garlic paste and ¹/₂ tsp turmeric. Bring to the boil, then drain the kidneys. This helps to remove their strong smell.

2 Heat the oil in a saucepan, add the onions and cook until golden brown. Add the remaining garlic paste, the ginger paste and tomatoes and stir well, then add the chilli powder, remaining turmeric, the cumin seeds, ground coriander and salt. Cook, stirring, until the oil separates out.

3 Add the minced lamb and stir to mix with the *massalla*. Add the kidneys and mix them in. Put the lid on the saucepan and cook for 30–35 minutes on a low heat.

4 Remove the lid and cook for a further 8–10 minutes or until excess liquid has evaporated and the oil separates out.

5 Stir in the chopped coriander. Garnish with green chillies and ginger, and serve.

NOTE The curry can be made in advance (it's good for freezing) and then reheated in the pan or in a microwave.

PASSANDA CURRY SLICED BEEF CURRY

The word *passanda* means a thin slice of meat, usually beef or veal, although lamb is also sometimes used. Prepared like this, a simple piece of meat is transformed into a lavish dish. The curry is ideal for any occasion, and is best served with mint *raita* (p179) and *roti* or *nan*. A less expensive cut of beef or veal can be used, as long as it is very lean and tender.

serves 4-5

thick and warmly spiced

500g (1lb 2oz) fillet of beef

3 tbsp sunflower oil

2 large onions, finely chopped

1 tsp garlic paste

1 tsp ginger paste

1 large tomato, skinned and finely chopped

5-6 tbsp chopped coriander leaves

Marinade

200g (7oz) plain Greek-style yogurt

1 tsp red chilli powder

$\frac{1}{2}$ tsp ground turmeric

1 tsp ground black pepper

1 tsp cumin seeds

1 tsp ground coriander

salt

1 Cut the beef into 5mm ($\frac{1}{4}$in) slices. With a meat mallet beat the slices until they are even thinner. Mix together the yogurt, spices and salt to taste. Add the slices of beef and turn to coat with the spiced yogurt. Leave to marinate for 2-3 hours.

2 Heat the oil in a saucepan, add the onions and cook until lightly browned. Stir in the garlic and ginger pastes, then immediately add the tomato. Stir for a few minutes. Add the marinated beef with all the spiced yogurt. Stir around for 1 minute, then put the lid on the saucepan and turn the heat to low. Cook for 15-20 minutes or until the beef is very tender.

3 Remove the lid and stir for a few more minutes or until the oil separates out. Stir in 4 tbsp of the chopped coriander. Garnish with the remaining chopped coriander and serve.

NOTE The curry can be made in advance (it's good for freezing) and reheated in the pan on a low heat or in a microwave.

Turmeric powder >
In the Indian subcontinent, turmeric powder mixed with other spices form the basis of most curries. It imparts a yellow-orange colour and a warm flavour to dishes.

DESI MURGH CURRY SPECIAL CHICKEN CURRY

In the fifties and sixties, if you were invited to dinner and served this curry, it would show that your hosts had spared no expense or effort in your honour, and you would have been duly thankful. Thus was the status of a 'Desi Murgh' curry, when chickens were hard to obtain, quite expensive and difficult to cook. Farmed chicken changed all this and turned a glorious curry into an ordinary one. To get the real taste of the original, you have to use a *desi murgh* – a young, male, organic free-range chicken. It should be slowly cooked until tender to allow all the herbs and spices to penetrate and release the full flavour of the chicken. If necessary, a regular chicken can be used instead of a free-range organic bird; however, you will probably need to reduce the amount of water for cooking. Serve with mango pickle (p176) and *nans* or boiled or pilau rice.

serves 4

flavourful and wet

4 tbsp sunflower oil

2 large onions, finely sliced

2 tsp garlic paste

2 tsp ginger paste

4 tomatoes, skinned and finely chopped

50g (1³/₄oz) plain Greek-style yogurt

1¹/₂ tsp red chilli powder

1 tsp ground turmeric

1 tsp cumin seeds

2 tsp ground coriander

3 large black cardamom pods

6 cloves

1 bay leaf

salt to taste

1 free-range organic chicken, about 1.2kg (2³/₄lb), cut into 8 pieces and skinned if preferred

5-6 tbsp chopped coriander leaves

1 Heat the oil in a large saucepan, add the onions and cook until dark golden brown. Remove the onions with a slotted spoon. Allow to cool, then grind them finely in a food processor. Set aside.

2 Add the garlic and ginger pastes to the hot oil in the saucepan and stir for a few minutes. Add the tomatoes and stir in well, then stir in the yogurt. Cook for 5-6 minutes. Add the browned onion paste and stir to mix, then add all the spices, the bay leaf and salt to taste. Cook, stirring, until the oil separates out.

3 Put the chicken pieces in the pan and spoon the spice mixture over them. Add 500ml (16fl oz) water. Put the lid on the pan and cook on a low heat, stirring occasionally, for 40-50 minutes or until the chicken is cooked through and tender. Add more water if needed.

4 Remove the lid and continue cooking for 10 minutes or until the oil in the sauce separates out. Stir in 4 tbsp of the chopped coriander. Garnish with the remaining chopped coriander and serve.

NOTE The curry can be made in advance and reheated in the pan on a low heat or in a microwave.

BATAIR DAHI WALA QUAILS IN YOGURT CURRY

Until a few years ago, quails (*batair*) were only available as wild game and were considered a great delicacy, deemed fit only for *nawabs* and *maharajas*. Now, however, quails are farmed and easily available to everyone. This combination of quails and yogurt is ideal as the yogurt tenderizes the birds and the tartness highlights their flavour. Other game birds like partridges can be cooked in the same way – use 6 partridges and increase the cooking time slightly. Serve with fresh coriander chutney (p176) and chickpea pilau (p180) or *nans*.

serves 4

light and gamy

4 tbsp sunflower oil
1 large onion, finely sliced
salt
12 red chillies
1/2 tsp red chilli powder
2 cinnamon sticks
4 black cardamom pods
8 cloves
20 black peppercorns
2 bay leaves
1 tsp cumin seeds
12 quails, about 75g (2½oz) each, skinned if preferred
300g (10oz) plain Greek-style yogurt
coriander leaves to garnish

1 Heat the oil in a large saucepan, add the sliced onion and cook until lightly golden brown. Add some salt, the whole chillies and all the spices and stir for a few minutes. Add the quails and stir for a few more minutes to be sure they are well coated with the spice mixture.

2 Add the yogurt and stir to mix, then reduce the heat to moderately low and cook, uncovered, for 20–25 minutes, stirring occasionally.

3 With the tip of a sharp knife check that the quails are fully cooked and tender. Then continue stirring gently until all excess liquid has evaporated and the oil separates out. Garnish with coriander leaves and serve.

NOTE The curry can be made in advance and reheated in a microwave.

< Red chillies
Be careful when using red chillies, because changing the specified quantity can significantly alter the balance of flavour in a dish.

JHINGA CURRY PRAWN CURRY

Prawns (*jhinga*) are found abundantly in the warm waters of the Arabian Sea, which lies to the south of Pakistan. White shelled prawns, which are delicate in flavour, are the most common variety, followed by tiger prawns. If available, use white shelled prawns for this curry as they blend beautifully with the aromatic, spicy *massalla*. The *massalla* can be cooked in advance; however, the prawns must be added and cooked just before serving. Cumin *raita* (p179) and vegetable *biryani* (p166) are good accompaniments.

serves 4–5

fragrant and spicy

500g (1lb 2oz) raw king or tiger prawns

3 tbsp sunflower oil

1 onion, chopped

1 tsp garlic paste

1 tsp ginger paste

1 medium tomato, skinned and finely chopped

225g (8oz) plain Greek-style yogurt

1 tsp red chilli powder

1/2 tsp ground black pepper

1/2 tsp ground turmeric

1/2 tsp cumin seeds

1/2 tsp ground coriander

salt

2 tbsp coarsely chopped green chillies

4 tbsp chopped coriander leaves

coriander leaves to garnish

1 Peel the prawns, leaving the last tail section on. Devein the prawns, then set aside.

2 To make the *massalla*, heat the oil in a saucepan, add the onion and fry until light golden brown. Add the garlic and ginger pastes and stir for 1–2 minutes. Add the tomato and yogurt and cook, stirring, for another few minutes. Add the chilli powder, black pepper, turmeric, cumin seeds, ground coriander and salt to taste, and cook, stirring, until the oil separates out.

3 Add the prawns and cook on a moderately high heat, stirring frequently, for 4–5 minutes or until the prawns turn pink. Make sure you don't overcook them. Stir in the green chillies and chopped coriander, and garnish with coriander leaves. Serve hot.

< Coriander leaves
These are generally added at the end of cooking, as prolonged heat reduces their fresh, delicate flavour.

SUBZI BIRYANI VEGETABLE BIRYANI

If you want a rice dish that is more than a rice dish, if you want one that is versatile and colourful, if you want it to be a centrepiece on your table and a dish to show your masterly skills, then this is the one to make. It is appropriate with any curry or condiment, great for picnics and barbecues, can be eaten hot or cold and is loved by children. You can use any vegetables that are in season.

serves 4-5

colourful and aromatic

500g (1lb 2oz) Basmati rice

125ml (4fl oz) sunflower oil

2 large onions, sliced

1 tsp ginger paste

1 tsp garlic paste

225g (8oz) skinned and finely chopped tomatoes

1 tsp red chilli powder

1 tsp ground turmeric

1 tsp ground coriander

2 cinnamon sticks

4 black cardamom pods

1 tsp cumin seeds

1 tsp black peppercorns

1 tsp cloves

4 star anise

2 bay leaves

salt

250g (9oz) plain Greek-style yogurt

250g (9oz) potatoes, peeled and diced

150g (5½oz) shelled fresh or frozen peas

150g (5½oz) carrots, peeled and diced

4 tbsp finely chopped coriander leaves

fried brown onions to garnish (p180)

1 Thoroughly wash the rice in running cold water, then leave to soak, covered in water, for at least 1 hour. Drain the rice and cook in plenty of boiling salted water until it is 90 per cent cooked. Drain the rice and set aside.

2 Heat the oil in a saucepan, add the onions and fry until golden brown. Add the ginger and garlic pastes and cook for 1 minute, then stir in the tomatoes, all the spices, the bay leaves, some salt and the yogurt. Cook for about 10 minutes or until the oil separates out.

3 Add the potatoes, fresh peas and carrots with 125ml (4fl oz) water and cook for 5-8 minutes or until the vegetables are tender. (Add frozen peas when the potatoes and carrots are almost done.) Remove from the heat.

4 Spread half the cooked rice over the bottom of a large saucepan. Put the cooked vegetables on this layer of rice and sprinkle with the chopped coriander. Cover with the remaining rice.

5 Dampen a clean, thick kitchen cloth with water and cover the saucepan. Put the lid tightly on the cloth and set the saucepan on a very low heat. (You can place the saucepan in a thick frying pan to further reduce the heat.) Cook like this for about 30 minutes.

6 Mix the rice gently with the vegetables, then spoon into a large, flat dish. Garnish with fried brown onions and serve.

LOBIA CURRY BLACK-EYE BEAN CURRY

A typical family meal consists of a meat dish, a vegetable dish and a dish of pulses or beans. This curry would be quite a common choice, as it is economical and ideal for winter or summer. It's also great for those who don't eat meat, because if served with garlic *nan* and a rice dish, plus cucumber *raita* (p179), it makes a whole meal. The closest equivalent to what we call *lobia* are black-eye beans, although you can also use other pulses such as red kidney beans (cooking time may vary, according to the bean you use).

serves 4–5

warmly spiced and earthy

3 tbsp sunflower oil

2 onions, chopped

1 tsp ginger paste

1 tsp garlic paste

3 medium tomatoes, skinned and chopped

1 tsp red chilli powder

½ tsp ground turmeric

1 tsp cumin seeds

2 tsp ground coriander

½ tsp ground black pepper

salt

300g (10oz) dried black-eye beans, soaked for 8–10 hours, then drained

4 tbsp chopped coriander leaves

To garnish

chopped green chillies

coriander leaves

1 Heat the oil in a saucepan, add the onions and fry until light golden brown. Add the ginger and garlic pastes and the tomatoes, and stir for a few minutes, then add the dry spices and salt to taste. Cook, stirring, until the oil separates out.

2 Add the black-eye beans and stir to blend with the spice mixture. Pour in 750ml (1¼ pints) fresh water and bring it to the boil. Put the lid on the saucepan, reduce the heat to low and cook for 45–50 minutes or until the beans are tender.

3 Remove the lid and simmer over a gentle heat until excess liquid has evaporated and the oil separates out. Stir in the chopped coriander and remove from the heat. Garnish with chopped green chillies and coriander leaves, and serve.

NOTE The curry can be made in advance (it freezes well) and then reheated in the pan on a low heat or in a microwave.

< Black-eye beans
Quick to cook, these robust beans impart a creamy texture and can make a delicious meal all by themselves.

SUBZI CURRY MiXED VEGETABLE CURRY

Although Pakistan is a meat-eating nation, various *subzi* (vegetable) curries feature very frequently in everyday meals. This curry is eaten on its own by the poor or as part of a meal by the more affluent. For a lot of people, it is the curry of choice, preferred over meat for its healthiness and taste, excellent served with fresh coriander chutney (p176) and *roti*. Almost any vegetable can be made into a curry, following the right technique and method. The key factors are to use very fresh vegetables and subtle spicing, and to eat the curry as soon as it is cooked.

serves 3–4

fresh and fragrant

3 tbsp sunflower oil

1 large onion, finely chopped

1 tsp garlic paste

1 tbsp fresh root ginger cut in slivers

2 large plum tomatoes, skinned and chopped

½ tsp ground turmeric

1 tsp red chilli powder

1 tsp cumin seeds

salt

500g (1lb 2oz) potatoes, peeled and diced

500g (1lb 2oz) cauliflower, cut into medium florets

5–6 tbsp chopped coriander leaves

1 Heat the oil in a saucepan, add the onion and cook until slightly browned. Add the garlic paste and ginger slivers, then add the tomatoes, spices and salt to taste and stir well. Add the potatoes and cauliflower together with 125ml (4fl oz) water. Stir well, then put the lid on the pan. Cook for 15–20 minutes or until the vegetables are tender.

2 Remove the lid and continue cooking until the oil separates out. Stir in most of the chopped coriander leaves. Garnish with the rest of the coriander and serve.

NOTE The curry can be made in advance and reheated in the pan on a low heat or in a microwave.

Plum tomatoes >
Thanks to their rich flavour and meaty interior, plum tomatoes are used when preparing the *masala* base of most of the curries in this region.

ALLOO CURRY POTATO CURRY

When you are not sure what to cook, or you have to prepare a meal in a hurry, potato curry is always the answer. It will never let you down. You can eat it for breakfast (serve it on toasted country bread, topped with a couple of fried eggs), lunch or dinner, alone or as part of a meal, with any kind of bread or rice. It's great as a left-over too. All varieties of potatoes can be used, even young new potatoes. This is a true comfort food, delicious with apple chutney (p176) and plain *nan*.

serves 3-4

savoury and comforting

2 tbsp sunflower oil

1 large onion, finely chopped

2 large plum tomatoes, skinned and chopped

8 red chillies

$1/2$ tsp red chilli powder

1 tsp cumin seeds

salt

500g (1lb 2oz) potatoes, peeled and diced, or whole new potatoes

chopped coriander leaves to garnish

1 Heat the oil in a saucepan, add the onion and cook until slightly browned. Add the chopped tomatoes, then stir in the chillies, chilli powder, cumin seeds and salt to taste. Add 125ml (4fl oz) water and cook, stirring, until excess liquid has evaporated.

2 Add the potatoes together with another 125ml (4fl oz) water. Stir well to coat the potatoes with the spice mixture, then put the lid on the pan. Cook for 15–20 minutes or until the potatoes are tender but not breaking up.

3 Remove the lid and continue cooking until the oil separates out. Garnish with chopped coriander and serve hot.

NOTE The curry can be made in advance and reheated in the pan on a low heat or in a microwave.

KHAMIRI ROTI LEAVENED ROTI

A *roti* spread with *ghee* or butter is a combination made in heaven. Serve these slightly puffy breads hot, straight from the oven.

Makes 5–6

1 tsp dried yeast
¼ tsp sugar
500g (1lb 2oz) white or
   wholemeal bread flour
1 tsp salt

1 Dissolve the yeast and sugar in 2 tbsp warm water, then leave for 15 minutes to become frothy.

2 Sift the flour and salt into a large mixing bowl. Add the yeast mixture and more water (about 275ml/9fl oz) to make a dough. Knead for 8–10 minutes or until pliable.

3 Divide the dough into equal portions and shape each into a ball. Leave in a warm place to prove for 30 minutes. The dough will rise slightly.

4 Preheat the oven to 180°C (350°F/Gas 4).

5 With a rolling pin roll out each ball of dough to a 23cm (9in) disc. Place on a non-stick baking sheet and bake for 3–5 minutes or until lightly browned and a bit puffy. Serve immediately.

PRATHA FRIED ROTI

The crisp, crackling texture and taste of a fried *roti* goes well with just about every curry ever created. They are best freshly fried, but can be frozen or refrigerated, then reheated in the oven (wrapped in foil), in the microwave or in a frying pan.

Makes 4–5

250g (9oz) white bread flour
250g (9oz) wholemeal flour
1¼ tsp salt
2½ tsp sunflower oil
250ml (9fl oz) sunflower
   oil for frying

1 Sift the flours and salt into a large mixing bowl. Add 350ml (12fl oz) water and the 2½ tsp oil, and knead to make a pliable dough. Leave to rest for 30 minutes.

2 Divide the dough into equal portions and shape into balls. Roll out into 20cm (8in) diameter discs. Heat the oil for frying in a large frying pan. Fry the breads on a moderate heat for about 2 minutes on each side or until golden brown. Drain on kitchen paper and serve hot.

Leavened roti >

ALLOO BUKHARA CHATNEY PLUM CHUTNEY

For this chutney we use dried round purple or black plums, which are a different variety from the plums that are dried to make prunes. Due to its high sugar content, the chutney can be kept in the refrigerator for 2–3 months.

Makes 1.1kg (2½lb)

750g (1lb 10oz) sugar

500g (1lb 2oz) dried plums, soaked for 30 minutes and drained

small pinch of salt

small pinch of red chilli powder

¼ tsp black peppercorns, crushed

good pinch of white cumin seeds

5g (scant ¼oz) four seeds (p154)

1 Put the sugar and 300ml (10fl oz) water in a large saucepan and bring to the boil, stirring to dissolve the sugar. Add the dried plums and cook for 20 minutes on a moderate heat.

2 Stir in the salt, red chilli powder, crushed pepper and cumin seeds. Mix in the four seeds. Allow to cool before serving or storage.

LASSAN ACHAR PICKLED GARLIC

This *achar* (pickle) can be stored in a cool cupboard for 2–3 months or in the refrigerator for up to 6 months.

Makes 1kg (2¼lb)

125ml (4fl oz) white vinegar

40g (1¼oz) salt

15g (½oz) red chilli powder

10g (⅓oz) ground turmeric

½ tsp black onion seeds

25g (scant 1oz) fennel seeds

15g (½oz) fenugreek seeds

500g (1lb 2oz) garlic cloves, peeled

500ml (16fl oz) mustard oil

1 Combine the vinegar with the salt and all the spices in a large glass or ceramic jar. Add the garlic cloves. Leave in a cool place to marinate for 15 days.

2 Add the mustard oil and leave to marinate for a further 5-10 days or until the garlic cloves are slightly soft and have lost their pungent smell.

< Lassan achar

DHANIA CHATNEY CORIANDER CHUTNEY

Serve this chutney as soon as it is made, to preserve its fresh green colour.

makes 350g (12oz)

140g (5oz) coriander leaves
2 tbsp chopped green chillies
1 tsp red chilli powder
salt

1 In a food processor or blender, grind the coriander leaves with the green chillies to make a fine paste. Add a little water, if necessary.

2 Stir in the chilli powder and salt to taste, and serve immediately.

SAIB CHATNEY APPLE CHUTNEY

This can be kept in the refrigerator in an airtight container for up to 2 months.

makes 600g (1lb 5oz)

500g (1lb 2oz) green apples
lemon juice
300g (10oz) sugar
¼ tsp salt
small pinch of red chilli powder
¼ tsp black peppercorns, crushed
5g (scant ¼oz) four seeds (p154)

1 Peel and core the apples and cut into slices. Dip into a bowl of water acidulated with lemon juice to prevent discoloration.

2 Put the sugar and 150ml (5fl oz) water in a large saucepan and bring to the boil, stirring to dissolve the sugar. Add the drained apple slices and cook on a moderate heat for 15 minutes or until the apples have softened.

3 Stir in the salt, red chilli powder, crushed pepper and four seeds. Allow to cool before serving.

AAM KA ACAR MANGO PICKLE

Use very unripe, green mangoes for this pickle. In a cooler climate, the marinating time may need to be extended – it can easily be doubled. All home-made pickles improve with age. Keep this in a cool place or the refrigerator.

makes 1kg (2¼lb)

500g (1lb 2oz) small unripe mangoes
125ml (4fl oz) white vinegar
40g (1¼oz) salt
15g (½oz) red chilli powder
10g (⅓oz) ground turmeric
½ tsp black onion seeds
25g (scant 1oz) fennel seeds
15g (½oz) fenugreek seeds
500ml (16fl oz) mustard oil

1 Cut the unpeeled mangoes lengthways into quarters, keeping the stones in.

2 Combine the vinegar, salt and all the spices in a large glass or ceramic jar. Add the mangoes and stir. Leave to marinate in a cool place for 10–15 days or until the mangoes are slightly softened.

3 Add the mustard oil. Leave to marinate for a further 5–10 days before using.

Coriander chutney (top), Apple chutney (centre) and Mango pickle (bottom) >

ZEERA RAITA CUMIN RAITA

Popular during the winter months, when fresh herbs and other vegetables are scarce, cumin *raita* has an aromatic, mildly spicy flavour. It is great with meat, fish and seafood curries and goes well with all rice dishes too.

serves 4–5

225g (8oz) plain Greek-style yogurt
½ tsp salt
½ tsp white cumin seeds

Whisk the yogurt in a bowl to be sure it is well combined and thick, then add the salt and cumin seeds, mixing well. Chill for at least 30 minutes before serving.

PODINA RAITA MINT RAITA

Mint has a wonderful aromatic fragrance and flavour and it gives yogurt a beautiful green colour, which is why this is the most popular of all the *raitas*. It enhances the flavour of the food it is eaten with and also acts as a mouth-cleanser between each bite.

serves 4–5

225g (8oz) plain Greek-style yogurt
salt to taste
4 tbsp finely chopped mint leaves
1 tsp finely chopped green chilli

Whisk the yogurt in a bowl to be sure it is well combined and thick, then add the salt, chopped mint and green chilli, mixing well. Chill for at least 30 minutes before serving.

PIYAZ RAITA ONION RAITA

With its sharp onion flavour, this *raita* is a good partner for curries made from vegetables, pulses and beans. It also goes well with rice dishes.

serves 4–5

225g (8oz) plain Greek-style yogurt
4 tbsp finely chopped onion, squeezed dry
½ tsp crushed dried chillies
salt

Whisk the yogurt in a bowl to be sure it is well combined and thick, then add the onion, crushed chillies and salt to taste. Chill for at least 30 minutes before serving.

KHEERA RAITA CUCUMBER RAITA

Cucumber *raita* is very popular during the summer months as it is known for its cooling properties. Serve it with vegetable and bean curries. It is also delicious eaten on its own with a fresh salad.

serves 4–5

225g (8oz) plain Greek-style yogurt
4 tbsp grated cucumber, squeezed dry
½ tsp red chilli powder
salt

Whisk the yogurt in a bowl to be sure it is well combined and thick, then add the cucumber, chilli powder and salt to taste, mixing well. Chill for at least 30 minutes before serving.

< (Clockwise from top) Zeera raita, Podina raita, Piyaz raita and Kheera raita.

CHANA PULAO CHICKPEA PILAU

This is a great combination of protein and carbohydrates, and makes a complete meal if served with a salad and yogurt. It can be made spicy or mild, according to your taste. A rice dish like this is a good way to introduce people – including children – to the wonderful world of curries. It can be packed into lunchboxes to take to school or work and is perfect eaten outdoors on a warm summer evening.

serves 5

aromatic and hearty

500g (1lb 2oz) Basmati rice
125ml (4fl oz) sunflower oil
115g (4oz) thinly sliced onion
1 tsp fresh root ginger, cut into slivers
3 cinnamon sticks
1 tsp black peppercorns
1 tsp cumin seeds
3 black cardamom pods
salt
115g (4oz) dried chickpeas, soaked overnight and cooked until tender, or 400g canned chickpeas, drained

Fried brown onions

2 tbsp sunflower oil
1 large onion, thinly sliced

1 Thoroughly wash the rice in running cold water, then leave to soak in a bowl of water to cover for at least 1 hour. Drain and set aside.

2 Heat the oil in a saucepan, add the onion and fry until golden brown. Add the ginger, all the spices and salt to taste and stir for about 1 minute. Add 750ml (1¼ pints) water and bring to the boil. Add the soaked rice and cooked or canned chickpeas. Cover the saucepan, reduce the heat and simmer for about 15 minutes or until the rice is about 90 per cent cooked.

3 Dampen a clean, thick kitchen cloth with water. Remove the lid from the saucepan. Cover with the cloth, then put the lid back on tightly and set the pan on a very low heat. (You can place the saucepan in a thick frying pan to further reduce the heat.) Cook like this for 25–30 minutes.

4 Meanwhile, heat the oil in a large saucepan, add the onion and cook until dark golden brown and crisp. Remove the onion with a slotted spoon and drain on kitchen paper.

5 Garnish the pilau with the fried brown onions and serve.

< Chickpeas
With a nutty flavour and buttery texture, chickpeas are ideal for curries as they hold their shape well when cooked.

BALTI FISH CURRY

Balti is a cooking container, similar to a wok, in which the food is cooked. Balti curries are mostly semi-thin to thin gravies. Mutton or chicken are mostly cooked using this process, however, I have made this recipe with fish.

serves 5

aromatic and slightly spicy

1kg (2¼lb) sole or any other white fish fillet, cut into 4cm (1½in) cubes

300ml (10fl oz) vegetable oil

1 tbsp grated ginger

1 tbsp roughly crushed garlic

3 medium-sized onions, finely chopped

1 tsp crushed coriander seeds

1 tsp red chilli powder

½ tsp ground cumin

½ tsp ground turmeric

400g (14oz) tomatoes, finely chopped

80g (3oz) red pepper, diced

salt

150ml (5fl oz) coconut cream

Marinade

25g (scant 1oz) garlic cloves

1 tbsp lemon juice

salt

To garnish

1 tbsp chopped coriander leaves

1 tsp chopped mint leaves

1 To prepare the marinade, peel the garlic and grind to a fine paste. Add a tablespoon or two of water and mix well. Pour the mixture into a piece of muslin. Gather the muslin and squeeze to extract the garlic juice. Mix the garlic juice with rest of the ingredients for the marinade. Add the cubes of fish and turn to coat them, then cover and set aside for 30 minutes.

2 Heat the oil in a *karahi* or wok over a moderate heat. Add the ginger and garlic and sauté for a minute or until light brown. Add the onions and sauté for 2–3 minutes or until translucent. Stir in the crushed coriander seeds, chilli powder, ground cumin and turmeric, mix well and cook for another minute. Now add the tomatoes and cook for 6–7 minutes, stirring frequently.

3 Lower the heat, add 200ml (7fl oz) water and cook the spice mix for 15 minutes. Add the red pepper, the marinated fish and salt and simmer for 10 minutes.

4 Now mix in the coconut cream and simmer for another 3–4 minutes or until the fish is cooked through.

5 Garnish with the coriander and mint leaves and serve hot with rice, *rogini naan* or *roti*.

Red peppers >
Fleshy peppers add a mild sweet taste and a peppery flavour to curries.

NIHARI GOSHT SLOW-COOKED MUTTON STEW

This rich and aromatic mutton stew is a traditional Muslim dish cooked during festivals and other special occasions. It is a simple dish but requires a considerable amount of time to prepare. There are various methods of cooking Nihari and here I have used the traditional Pakistani method to prepare this flavoursome dish.

serves 5

rich and aromatic

4 tbsp *ghee*

4 medium-sized onions, sliced

1kg (2¼lb) mutton with bones, washed, chopped into cubes

1 tsp ginger paste

½ tsp ground turmeric

1 tbsp red chilli powder

4 cardamom pods

4 cloves

2 cinnamon sticks

1 tsp black peppercorns

1 tsp cumin seeds

3 tbsp yogurt, whisked until smooth

2 tbsp brown onion paste (p30)

¼ tsp ground *garam masala*

¼ tsp ground fennel seeds

¼ tsp dried ground ginger

2 pinches of ground mace

2 pinches of round nutmeg

salt

2 tbsp refined white flour

Garnish

1 tbsp finely chopped coriander leaves

½ tsp finely chopped ginger

1 tsp chopped green chillies

10g (¼oz) fried onion

Stock

1kg (2¼lb) mutton bones

5 mutton leg pieces, each 5cm (2in) long, cleaned and roasted

3 cinnamon sticks

10 cardamom pods

7 cloves

1 tsp cumin seeds

1 tbsp fennel seeds

1 tsp crushed dried ginger

salt

1 To prepare the stock, take a large pot and add the mutton bones and roasted leg pieces along with 1 litre (1¾ pints) water. Boil over a high heat for 5 minutes. Drain the water to remove the scum. Add another 2 litres (3½ pints) water along with the rest of the ingredients for the stock and boil. Reduce the heat to low and simmer for 60–90 minutes. You could add the Nihari spice potli (p156) to enhance the flavour of the stock. Pour the stock through a sieve into a bowl and set aside.

2 Meanwhile, in a heavy-bottomed saucepan, heat the *ghee* over a moderate heat. Add the onions and sauté for 3–4 minutes or until brown. Add the mutton and cook for 3–4 minutes, stirring continuously, until light brown.

3 Stir in the ginger paste and cook for a minute. Add the turmeric, chilli powder, cardamoms, cloves, cinnamon sticks, peppercorns and cumin seeds and sauté for 2 minutes. Add 2 tablespoons of water and cook for a minute, stirring constantly. Reduce the heat to low, slowly fold in the yogurt and mix well.

4 Pour the stock into the saucepan, cover and simmer for about an hour. Once the mutton is three-fourth done, add the brown onion paste, mix well, cover and simmer for another 40 minutes. (Check if the meat is cooked by piercing a fork in a mutton piece. If the piece starts to break but does not fall apart, it is three-fourth done.)

5 Uncover the saucepan, add the rest of the spices, cover and simmer for 10 seconds. Season to taste.

6 Mix the refined white flour with a little water to make a paste. Add the paste to the gravy and mix well to acquire a slightly thick consistency.

7 Garnish with the coriander leaves, ginger, green chillies and fried onion and serve with rogini *naan*.

KEEMA ALOO MINCED MEAT AND POTATO CURRY

This is an extremely popular Pakistani curry. It is simple, quick and yet a tasty, wholesome dish that can be served as part of a regular meal and also when entertaining. This recipe was given to me by the wife of a senior diplomat from Pakistan, who put her own unique twist on it.

serves 5

aromatic and spiced

200g (7oz) *ghee*

7 green cardamom pods

7 cloves

3 cinnamon sticks, each 5cm (2in) long

3 bay leaves

1 tsp cumin seeds

3 onions, finely chopped

1 tbsp garlic paste

1kg (2¼lb) minced goat or lamb, leg piece

300g (10oz) tomatoes, finely chopped

6 green chillies, slit lengthways

250g (9oz) plain yogurt

300g (10oz) large potatoes, peeled and cut into 2.5cm (1in) cubes

1 tbsp Kashmiri chilli powder

1 tbsp ground coriander

¹/₂ tsp ground turmeric

1 tbsp ground *garam masala*

1 tsp black peppercorns

salt

1 tbsp, finely chopped coriander leaves, to garnish

1 To make the *masala*, heat the *ghee* in a heavy-bottomed saucepan over a moderate heat. Add the cardamoms, cloves, cinnamon sticks and bay leaves and sauté for 2–3 minutes. Then add the cumin seeds and fry until brown.

2 Stir in the onions and sauté for 5 minutes or until golden brown. Mix in the garlic paste and fry until brown.

3 Now add the meat and cook for 10 minutes, stirring frequently. Mix in the tomatoes, half of the green chillies and the yogurt and sauté for another 8–10 minutes.

4 Add the potatoes along with the chilli powder, ground coriander, turmeric, *garam masala* and peppercorns. Season and cook for 7–8 minutes, stirring frequently. Cover the pan, reduce the heat to low and simmer until the potatoes and meat are tender and cooked.

5 Remove the whole spices and transfer to a serving dish. Garnish with the coriander leaves and the remaining green chillies and serve hot with *rogini naan* or *roti*.

MYANMAR & MARITIME SE ASIA

Almost everyone in Southeast Asia eats rice, and most people eat it two or even three times a day. With rice is eaten the best meat, fish and vegetables that can be afforded, which not only provides a balanced diet, but also gives the pleasure of contrasting textures and tastes, among them the strong, aromatic flavours of herbs and spices. Sauces are also sometimes included in a dish, partly to blend and distribute the flavours of the ingredients, and partly to moisten the food. People in Southeast Asia have been cooking and eating in this way for centuries, but at some fairly recent date – perhaps around 200 years ago – these dishes became known as 'curries'.

How much sauce must there be to make a dish a curry? It's hard to say. The sauce may be runny, or it may be reduced to make it thick; there may be more sauce than solids in the dish; or there may be very little liquid at all. At one extreme, it would be correct to speak of a curry soup, such as the Burmese chicken noodle soup called Ohno Kwautskwe (p204) or the lamb stew of central Java called Gulé Kambing (p221). *Gulé*, which in Indonesia and Malaysia is usually spelled *gulai*, is a general term for stews with plenty of sauce, and a *gulai* is simply a curry: the Malaysian Gulai Kepala Ikan (p216) translates into English as Fish Head Curry. In Singapore this is considered a typical local dish, and most people call it by its English name.

In the four countries in this chapter – Myanmar (Burma), Malaysia, Singapore and Indonesia – the flavouring ingredients that add zest to a curry are generally incorporated into a paste, which traditionally is made at home, fresh each day. This is hard work, and many modern cooks will not refuse commercial curry powders (Filipino curries are usually spiced with curry powder). There are many locally produced brands and varieties: powders for beef, lamb or goat, for fish, for vegetables or for well-known recipes like Vindaloo, all available in the local market. For meat, the mix usually contains more of the stronger spices and extra garlic, to counteract the smell and flavour of the meat. The names of the curry powders usually suggest an Indian connection, as of course does the word 'curry' itself, even in its original Tamil form, *kari* or *karé*. For the Tamils, that meant either pepper, or a mix of water with hot spices.

In addition to the aromatics and spices, curries also need colour: yellow from turmeric root, red from red chillies. Mixed, they tint the sauce an appetizing reddish-orange colour.

A creamy texture is achieved with coconut milk, which is used in this part of the world just as Western cooks use dairy products. Coconut cream can be compared to double cream, coconut milk to single cream or milk.

In the Philippines, curries are particularly popular in Mindanao and other southern parts of the country. The people here broadly agree with their Malaysian and Indonesian neighbours on curry's Indian connections, on the fact that it should have sauce, and on how the sauce should be made. The shopping list is quite short and there are only minor differences between regional cuisines. Aromatics, such as lemongrass, galangal and curry leaves or kaffir lime leaves are needed, as well as the three universal essentials: shallots or onions, ginger and garlic. In addition, a curry must be seasoned with strong-tasting spices like ground coriander, nutmeg, cumin, cardamom, pepper and, of course, chillies.

Filipinos have a unique cookery tradition in *adobo*, a stew of pork, beef or chicken, whose dominant flavour is sourness. This comes from vinegar, following a long tradition of vinegar-making in the Philippines. Different vinegars produce different tastes: palm sugar and sugar cane vinegars make an *adobo* sweeter than other vinegars would. The late Doreen Fernandez, in writing on the food of the Philippines, showed that *adobo*-type dishes were popular long before the Spanish arrived, and one of these, called Adobo sa Gata, was (and still is) made with coconut milk. So it is fair to say that *adobo* recipes could represent curries from the Philippines.

Adobo is, in fact, the Filipino form of the word *adobado*, the name given by the Spanish conquistadores to a Mexican stew that they particularly liked. So there may be an ironic parallel in this naming of dishes: the Spaniards brought *adobado* to Manila and the islands just as the British – perhaps – brought 'curry' to their colonies in Southeast Asia.

Sri Owen

Toasting peanuts >
Fry in hot oil to enhance their nutty flavour

THE TASTE OF MYANMAR & MARITIME SE ASIA

1. candlenuts
2. kaffir limes
3. apple aubergines
4. green mango
5. green chillies
6. red chillies
7. galangal
8. turmeric root
9. shrimp paste
10. dried shrimps
11. lemongrass
12. dried shelled peanuts
13. blanched dried peanuts
14. peanuts in shell
15. *asam gelugur*
16. tamarind pods

THE RAW MATERIALS

The key ingredients used in the curry pastes or spice mixtures for Burmese, Malaysian, Singaporean, Filipino and Indonesian curries provide the characteristic tastes and flavours of the cooking of this region. These ingredients are now generally available in the West, as are different types of shrimp paste and fish sauce, and the fruits, vegetables and nuts described here.

KAFFIR LIME

Kaffir lime leaves are easily recognised by their figure-of-eight shape and their delicious fragrance. Though they are edible and have a refreshing taste, they are rather tough, even after being cooked for a long time. So it is best to discard them before serving. The zest of the kaffir lime is also used in cooking to add an appetizing perfume. If a recipe calls for lime juice (usually as a substitute for the souring agent, tamarind water), it will be the juice of ordinary lime, not kaffir lime, which isn't a very juicy fruit.

TAMARIND

Tamarind, which has a sourness different from that of any citrus fruit, is important for giving depth to and balancing the sweetness of much Southeast and South Asian cooking. If available, fresh tamarind pods can be used in a curry sauce – simply crack the shell and take out the pod. More common is tamarind pulp, which is sold in a small compact block. This is used in the form of tamarind water, made by simmering or soaking tamarind pulp in water, then squeezing it and passing it through a sieve to extract the flavourful liquid (p355).

ASAM GELUGUR

This souring agent is often sold with a misleading label that says 'tamarind slices', 'tamarind skins' or (the latest version) 'assem skins'. The shrivelled, blackened contents of the bag are, in fact, slices of *asam gelugur* (*Garcinia atroviridis*). They are easy to use: rinse 2 slices under the cold tap, then drop them into the boiling curry sauce. The asam slices will expand, at the same time exuding their sour juice. Discard the slices before serving. *Asam gelugur* can also be used in any recipe to replace tamarind water (and save the work of making it): a slice equals 2 tbsp tamarind water.

CHILLIES

Although chillies are very important in Asian cooking today, they were only introduced to this area in the 16th century, when seeds and plants were brought from Central America. There are many different varieties of chilli, ranging widely in their heat, but generally speaking, the larger the chilli, the milder the taste. In Southeast Asian curries, all kinds of chillies are used, from large, long red chillies, which are not too hot, to tiny bird's eye or bird chillies (in Malaysian, *chilli padi*; *cabe rawit* in Indonesian), which are the hottest.

GALANGAL

This pinkish rhizome, known as *laos* or *lengkuas* in Indonesia and Malaysia, resembles ginger, but is not as hot, and it has a bitter taste. It is very tough and hard – a large piece can damage the blades of a food processor. So peel and dice galangal before blending it in a curry paste. Alternatively, you can put a 2cm (³/₄in) piece of galangal into a curry while it's cooking. Just remember to take it out before serving – if you bite on it, it can break a tooth.

LEMONGRASS

This aromatic ingredient is one of the first to come to mind when thinking about Southeast Asian cooking. Pieces of lemongrass may be added to a curry sauce whole (sometimes slightly bruised by pressing with the flat of a knife) and removed before serving. Alternatively, the outer, tougher leaves are stripped off (they can be added to a sauce as a flavouring) and the inner tender part is then chopped into rounds like spring onion and blended into a curry paste.

COCONUT

Coconut oil is the traditional frying medium in Indonesia and Malaysia, and coconut milk and cream (p241) are used in curries all over the region. Another coconut preparation is *kerisik*, which is freshly grated coconut that is dry roasted and then blended to make a brown, oily paste. It is used in the rich Malaysian beef rendang (p212).

MANGO

This tropical fruit has been cultivated in India for several thousand years and is now grown over almost all of South and East Asia. There are more than 40 varieties, but it is the green or unripe mango that is used as a

Fresh red chilli >

souring agent in Southeast Asian curries. The Thai variety, which is used in this chapter's recipes, is normally larger than the Indian, and its sourness is checked by a pleasant slight sweetness.

RICE

Throughout Southeast Asia, rice is not just a staple food, it is a symbol of good living, and the foundation of every meal. To accompany any curry, plain boiled or steamed rice is always the best choice. Malaysians and Indonesians love compressed rice (p200). With no added flavouring, not even salt, rice absorbs the tastes and aromas of the curry, moderates and blends them. Cooking rice in an electric steamer will ensure perfect results without any effort.

To cook white, long-grain rice, such as Basmati or Thai fragrant (jasmine) rice conventionally, use a thick-bottomed pan, preferably non-stick. Measure the rice in a cup, and use the same cup to measure the water (equal quantities of rice and water). Wash the rice in two or three changes of water, then put into the pan with the measured water and bring to the boil. Stir once with a wooden spoon, then leave the rice to simmer, without a lid, until it has absorbed all the water. Stir once more, then turn the heat to low and cover the pan tightly. Leave on this low heat, undisturbed, for about 10 minutes, then serve.

TURMERIC

Both red and white varieties of turmeric have been in popular use for a very long time all over Southeast Asia. As with galangal and fresh ginger, turmeric root needs to be peeled and chopped before use. If you can't get fresh red turmeric root, you can use ground turmeric instead – just

< Crushing dried shrimps

½–1 tsp is all you need in a curry paste if you are cooking for 4. Aromatic turmeric leaves are also used in Southeast Asian curries, but are rarely found in Europe.

AUBERGINE

Many kinds of aubergines, in all sizes, colours and shapes, are used in Southeast Asian cooking. One popular variety is the apple aubergine, which is slightly bigger than a golf ball. Apple aubergines come in different shapes, but are typically globular or egg-shaped. They also come in different colours – purple, bright yellow, white, or shades of green ranging from light to intense – as well as multi-coloured, with whites and greens often delicately fading into each other.

OKRA

Although more commonly found in Indian cooking, this vegetable is also much enjoyed in Southeast Asia. One popular use for okra is in the Singaporean dish known as Fish Head Curry (p216).

DRIED SHRIMPS

The one ingredient the Burmese simply cannot do without is dried shrimps. They are the main ingredient in the Burmese relish called Balachaung (p201), which is normally eaten with curries in Myanmar, and can be served as a relish or accompaniment to other curries eaten with rice. The tiny dried shrimps are usually roasted before being packaged for sale. Before use, soak them in hot water for 10 minutes, then drain and chop, crush with a pestle and mortar, or blend in a blender.

FISH SAUCE

Another salty and strong-smelling condiment, fish sauce is used all over Southeast Asia. Various fish sauces are

made in Myanmar, the Philippines and Vietnam, but Thai fish sauce (nam pla) is the most widely available.

SHRIMP PASTE

Another essential ingredient in the cooking of this region is shrimp paste, called terasi or trassie in Indonesia and balachan or blachen in Malaysia. In Myanmar they have their own fish paste (ngapi), but they also use terasi and balachan. Shrimp paste is sold in hard blocks or individually wrapped slices, and is extremely strong smelling and salty. Use it very sparingly.

CANDLENUTS

Resembling macadamia nuts in appearance, candlenuts, which are called kemiri in Indonesia and buah keras in Malaya, are used in many Indonesian and Malaysian dishes, as well as in Nonya cooking in Singapore. Candlenuts are always crushed or ground before being mixed with other ingredients and then blended to make a curry paste. Never eat candlenuts raw, because they are mildly toxic until they are cooked. Raw macadamia nuts make a satisfactory substitute. Another alternative is blanched almonds.

PEANUTS

These are used all over Southeast Asia because they are cheap, filling and nutritious. You can buy them in their shells, or already shelled in the form of dried nuts. Their thin outer skins range in colour from pink to almost red or, if they have been blanched and dried, to an off-white colour. Peanut sauce (p202) tastes and looks much better if you use pink or reddish peanuts. To bring out their nutty flavour and aroma, roast the peanuts first in a dry wok for 6–8 minutes, stirring constantly, or deep-fry them in hot oil for 4 minutes. Drain on kitchen paper and leave to cool before grinding finely.

SPICED TAMARIND RELISH

This relish can be used as a dipping sauce for crudités or plain cooked vegetables, or be served in place of the chutney that would conventionally accompany a curry. Additionally, you can stir 1–2 tbsp of this relish into any curry while it is cooking, and it can take the place of plain tamarind water.

Makes about 250ml (8fl oz)

2 tbsp groundnut oil

4 shallots, finely chopped

2 tsp very finely chopped or grated fresh root ginger

1/2 tsp chilli powder, or 1 large red chilli, deseeded and finely chopped

2 garlic cloves, crushed

1 tsp brown sugar

1 tsp ground coriander

1 tsp coarse sea salt

250ml (9fl oz) thick tamarind water (p355)

1 Heat the oil in a wok or saucepan, add the shallots and stir-fry for 2 minutes to soften.

2 Add the ginger, chilli powder and garlic, and stir-fry for 2 minutes.

3 Add the brown sugar, ground coriander and salt and stir.

4 Continue stirring on a low heat until the mixture becomes quite sticky.

5 Add the tamarind water and simmer for 5 minutes, stirring often.

6 Taste and adjust the seasoning, adding more salt if necessary. Simmer, stirring continuously, until the relish has become quite thick. Leave the relish to cool, then transfer it to a jar with a tight-fitting lid, and refrigerate until needed.

Tamarind ˄

Tamarind is used for adding a sweet-sour flavour and a brown-black colour to many Asian curries.

PREPARING CHICKEN STOCK

This flavoured liquid is prepared by simmering chicken bones along with various vegetables and spices in water. It is used as a base for many recipes, particularly soups. Either cool and use the stock immediately, or pour it into ice cube trays and freeze.

makes 1 litre (1³/₄ pints)

50g (1³/₄oz) onions
50g (1³/₄oz) ginger
30g (1oz) garlic cloves
45g (1¹/₂oz) celery sticks
100g (3¹/₂oz) spring onions
100g (3¹/₂oz) carrots
500g (1lb 2oz) chicken bones, cleaned and washed

1 Wash and clean all the ingredients except the chicken bones. Roughly chop all the vegetables.

2 Wash and clean the chicken bones and put them, along with the rest of the ingredients, into a large pan. Pour over enough cold water to cover the ingredients completely. You will probably need about 2 litres (3¹/₂ pints) of water.

3 Bring to the boil, reduce the heat and simmer for 30 minutes, stirring frequently.

4 Skim the white scum from the surface of the boiling stock as it gathers.

5 After 30 minutes, strain the contents of the pan through a sieve into a bowl and leave to cool.

< Celery

With a crunchy texture and a mild, salty taste, this vegetable is one of the essential ingredients in stocks and soups.

LONTONG COMPRESSED RICE

Lontong is always eaten cold. In Indonesia, Singapore and Malaysia, it is cooked inside a rolled-up banana leaf, or in a container woven from a coconut frond. It is then called *ketupat*, but the taste and texture are the same. By being cooked in this confined space, the rice grains, as they absorb moisture, are pressed into a soft but solid mass. In most parts of the world you can now buy boil-in-the-bag rice, and this saves you the trouble of rolling or weaving any containers. Make sure, though, that it is not 'easy cook' or 'pre-cooked', because these won't work for this method. Buy a plain long-grain rice, preferably Basmati. Check, too, that the bags (made of a special plastic with tiny holes) are the right size – the rice should fill them one-third full, not much more or less. If the bags are too big, machine or hand-stitch a seam across the bag to reduce the size.

---

2 bags of boil-in-the-bag long-grain rice

serves 4–8

1 Fill a large saucepan two-thirds full of cold water and bring it to a rolling boil. Put in the bags of rice and let them boil for 1¹⁄₄ hours, topping up the pan with very hot water when necessary to make sure the rice is always covered.

2 Pour out the water and take out the bags, which will now be plumped like small white cushions. Let them cool, then store them overnight (or for up to 3 days) in the fridge.

3 To serve, cut open and strip off the plastic bags, then cut the lontong into chunks and put these in a bowl to go to the table.

BALACHAUNG DRIED SHRIMP RELISH

This is a Burmese hot relish, made of dried shrimps with plenty of garlic and chillies. Once made, it can be kept in an airtight jar in the fridge for up to a month. It is worth making a good quantity. Among the recipes, it appears in the Burmese chicken curry with limes and tomatoes (p203).

makes about 250ml (8fl oz)

225g (8oz) dried shrimps, soaked in hot water for 10 minutes, then drained

3 tbsp groundnut oil

4 shallots, finely chopped

4 garlic cloves, finely sliced

2 tsp toasted sesame oil

2-4 red chillies, deseeded and finely chopped, or 1/2-1 tsp chilli powder

2 tsp finely chopped fresh root ginger

1/2 tsp ground turmeric

1/2 tsp salt, or more to taste

juice of 1 lime or lemon

1 Finely chop the shrimps with a sharp knife, pound them in a mortar and pestle, or put them in a small blender and blend until fine. Set aside.

2 Heat the groundnut oil in a wok or saucepan and fry the shallots and garlic for 2-3 minutes or until they are slightly coloured. Remove with a slotted spoon and reserve.

3 Add the sesame oil to the wok or pan, heat and then add the chillies, ginger, turmeric and salt. Fry for 2 minutes, stirring all the time.

4 Put in the ground shrimps and continue stir-frying for 1 minute. Now add 2 tbsp hot water and the lime or lemon juice. Stir until the liquid is absorbed by the shrimps. Mix in the reserved fried shallots and garlic.

5 The relish should be moist, not dry. Taste and add salt if you think it is needed. When cold, store in an airtight jar. Serve cold as a relish.

Lemon >
This citrussy fruit is used to give a tang and tartness to various recipes and is even used for preserving.

SAMBAL KACANG PEANUT SAUCE

This sauce is used in the Philippines Karé-karé (p228), and it is a very popular sauce with all kinds of satay, in Malaysia, Singapore and Indonesia. It makes an excellent dipping sauce for crudités (called *lalab* in Indonesia), and it is the sauce for various cooked vegetable salads called *gado-gado*, which are claimed by Indonesians and Malaysians as among their national dishes.

Makes about 500ml (16fl oz)

120ml (4fl oz) vegetable oil

225g (8oz) raw peanuts

2 garlic cloves, chopped

4 shallots, chopped

thin slice of shrimp paste (optional)

salt to taste

1/2 tsp chilli powder

1/2 tsp brown sugar

1 tbsp dark soy sauce

2 tbsp tamarind water (p355) or lemon juice, or to taste

1 Heat the oil in a wok or large, shallow saucepan and fry the peanuts over a moderate heat for about 4 minutes, stirring them frequently. With a slotted spoon, transfer them to a colander lined with kitchen paper and leave them to cool. Then grind them in a blender or coffee grinder to a fine powder. Remove and set aside. Pour off all but 1 tbsp oil from the wok.

2 Put the garlic, shallots, shrimp paste (if using) and a little salt into the blender and blend to make a smooth paste.

3 Heat the oil in the wok, then add the garlic and shallot paste and fry for 1 minute. Add the chilli powder, sugar, soy sauce and 600ml (1 pint) water and bring to the boil. Add the ground peanuts and stir to mix. Simmer, stirring occasionally, until the sauce has reduced to the thickness you want. This should take 8–10 minutes. Taste, and add the tamarind water and more salt, as needed.

4 This sauce can be stored for up to 1 week in an airtight jar in the fridge. It can also be frozen for up to 2 months. Thaw it out completely before reheating it in a saucepan. If it has become too thick, add water and continue heating until it reaches the right consistency.

< Peanuts
Though peanuts are consumed in different forms, only whole, freshly roasted peanuts are used when preparing the spicy sauce in Southeast Asian cuisine.

KYE THAR HIN CHICKEN CURRY WITH LIME AND TOMATOES

This curry is very popular all over the region, perhaps because, although it is an authentic Burmese curry, it is not made with coconut milk or yogurt, but with tomatoes. If you have an abundance of tomatoes during the summer in your garden, use them. They must be very ripe. Alternatively, your curry will be just as good made with the best canned chopped plum tomatoes you can get.

Serves 4–6

pungent, citrussy and spicy

2 tbsp groundnut oil

2 onions, finely chopped

2 garlic cloves, finely chopped

1 tsp ground turmeric

1 tbsp ground coriander

2 cinnamon sticks

4 cloves

1 stalk lemongrass, cut into 2 pieces

4 kaffir lime leaves

2 boneless chicken breasts, each cut in half

8 chicken thighs, boned

450g (1lb) ripe tomatoes, skinned and chopped, or 400g canned chopped plum tomatoes, drained

juice of 2–3 limes

3 tbsp Balachaung (p201)

1/2 tsp cayenne pepper (optional)

1 tbsp fish sauce

1 tbsp toasted sesame oil

salt, if needed

1 Preheat the oven to 160°C (325°F/Gas 3).

2 Pour the groundnut oil into a large saucepan. Place over a high heat and, when hot, stir-fry the onions and garlic for 2–3 minutes, stirring often. Add the turmeric, ground coriander, cinnamon, cloves, lemongrass, kaffir lime leaves and the chicken pieces. Stir-fry for 6–8 minutes or until the chicken pieces are slightly browned.

3 Add the tomatoes, lime juice, *balachaung*, cayenne pepper (if using) and fish sauce, stirring well. Cover the pan and simmer for 3 minutes. Uncover and stir in 4 tbsp hot water and the sesame oil. Go on cooking, covered, on a moderate heat for 20 minutes.

4 Using a slotted spoon, transfer the chicken pieces to an ovenproof dish and place in the oven. Cook for 20–25 minutes.

5 Meanwhile, continue cooking the sauce for 4–6 minutes or until it has become thick and oily. Spoon out some of the oil and discard it, at the same time removing the solid seasonings (lime leaves, cinnamon sticks and lemongrass). Taste and adjust the seasoning, adding salt if needed.

6 Take the chicken from the oven and pour the curry sauce over it. Serve hot, with plain boiled rice.

< Lemongrass
A tropical grass, this herb imparts a refreshing lemon fragrance and flavour to most Southeast Asian curries.

OHNO KWAUTSKWE BURMESE CHiCKEN NOODLE SOUP

In Myanmar, this is a popular breakfast dish. Thick coconut milk and chickpea flour give the soup extra richness, and the flavours are delicious. My Burmese friend, who gave me the recipe, said that instead of round rice noodles, you can use the flat rice noodles called rice sticks. As a starter for 6–8, use only 60g (2oz) noodles.

serves 4

creamy and rich

175g (6oz) round rice noodles

2 skinless, boneless chicken breasts, cut into bite-size pieces

1 tbsp fish sauce

1 small onion, chopped

2 garlic cloves, chopped

1 tsp chopped fresh root ginger

1 tsp chopped turmeric root or ½ tsp ground turmeric

1 large red chilli, deseeded and chopped

300ml (10fl oz) thick coconut milk (p241)

2 tbsp groundnut oil

1.2 litres (2 pints) chicken stock

3–4 tbsp chickpea flour, dissolved in 120ml (4fl oz) cold water

To garnish

hard-boiled eggs, quartered or sliced

1 red onion, thinly sliced, soaked in cold water for a few minutes, then drained

slices of lemon

deep-fried shallots (p239)

crushed dried chillies

chopped coriander leaves

1 Cook the noodles in boiling water for 2–3 minutes; drain and refresh under the cold tap. Set aside in a colander. Just before serving, reheat the noodles by pouring boiling water over them while they are still in the colander and give this a shake to drain as much water from them as possible.

2 Rub the chicken with the fish sauce, then set aside.

3 Blend together the onion, garlic, ginger, turmeric and chilli in a food processor or blender. When smooth, add 3 tbsp of the coconut milk or stock to make a paste.

4 Fry the paste in the groundnut oil in a saucepan over a moderate heat for 2–3 minutes, stirring constantly. Add the chicken and stir-fry for another 2–3 minutes. Add half of the stock and bring to the boil. Continue cooking the chicken for 8–10 minutes.

5 Heat the other half of the stock in another pan until it starts to boil. Add the dissolved chickpea flour, stirring to prevent lumps. When thickened, pour the stock through a sieve into the pan containing the chicken mixture. Stir well. When the soup starts to boil add the remaining coconut milk. Taste and adjust the seasoning by adding salt or more fish sauce, if necessary. Bring the soup back to a rolling boil.

6 At the same time ask your guests to help themselves to the hot noodles, ready for the chicken soup to be ladled into their bowls. When everyone has soup, they should then help themselves to the garnishes, and eat while the soup is hot.

WETHER HIN LAY PORK CURRY WITH MANGO

I think this is a really delicious curry. My Burmese friend, Kyu Kyu, suggested that I should make a Golden Pork Curry (Wet Thani) with bamboo shoots, not mango. For a pork curry with mango, she said that dried or pickled mangoes should be used. So it was a challenge for me to devise a new version. I decided to use a fresh green mango to give sourness to the sauce, as well as bamboo shoot, because it goes so well with pork. Instead of a fresh green mango, you can use a few slices of pickled mango. Another Burmese friend calls this a 'sour stew of pork'.

serves 4

savoury and sour

675g (1½ lb) pork fillet/tenderloin or boned pork chops, cut into 2.5cm (1in) medallions

2 tbsp fish sauce

2 tsp lime juice

5 tbsp groundnut oil

6 shallots, finely sliced

1 small, unripe Thai or Indian green mango, about 115–175g (4–6oz), peeled and cut into fine julienne strips

1 tbsp thick tamarind water (p355)

salt and pepper

200g (7oz) canned sliced bamboo shoots, drained and rinsed

Paste

4 garlic cloves, finely chopped

5mm (¼in) piece shrimp paste (the size of a small postage stamp)

2 tsp grated fresh root ginger

2 large red chillies, deseeded and finely chopped

1 Marinate the pork medallions in a mixture of the fish sauce and lime juice for 20 minutes.

2 Meanwhile, make the paste by crushing the ingredients in a mortar and pestle until smooth.

3 Heat the oil in a wok or frying pan and fry half of the pork medallions over a moderate heat for 3 minutes, stirring often. Using a slotted spoon, transfer these to kitchen paper to drain. Repeat this process for the rest of the pork, and set aside.

4 There should still be enough oil in the pan for the next step (if not, add another tbsp). Heat the oil again over a moderate heat, then stir-fry the shallots for 2 minutes. Reduce the heat to low, add the paste from the mortar and stir for 2–3 minutes. Add 300ml (10fl oz) hot water, stir and bring to the boil. Put in the mango and tamarind water. Simmer for 10 minutes or until the sauce is reduced by half. Adjust the seasoning, adding salt if needed and a few turns of the pepper mill.

5 Return the pork to the wok and add the sliced bamboo shoots. Stir to mix, then continue cooking for 3–5 minutes or until everything is very hot. Serve straight away, with rice or noodles.

DAGING MASAK MERAH RED CURRY OF BEEF

You will find this curry on the menu of many Malaysian restaurants, a slightly different version each time. Mine is from Pontianak, a town in West Kalimantan (Indonesian Borneo) near the Malaysian border. This recipe differs from the original only in the quantity of red chillies: instead of 40, I use only four.

serves 2–4

spicy and savoury

2 tsp chopped fresh root ginger

2 tsp chopped turmeric root, or 1 tsp ground turmeric

½ tsp coarse sea salt

500–600g (1lb 2oz–1lb 5oz) rump or sirloin steak, cut into pieces (2 per person)

3 tbsp groundnut oil

3 tbsp thick tamarind water (p355)

6 ripe red tomatoes, skinned and chopped, or 400g canned chopped tomatoes, drained

300ml (10fl oz) coconut cream (p241), single cream or (my own choice) plain yogurt

handful each of mint leaves and coriander leaves, roughly chopped

Red paste

3 shallots, chopped

6–8 garlic cloves, chopped

4 large red chillies, deseeded and chopped

1 red pepper, deseeded and chopped (optional)

4 tbsp tomato purée

4 candlenuts, roughly chopped, then roasted until slightly coloured (optional)

2 tbsp groundnut oil

To garnish

4 tbsp deep-fried shallots (p239)

60g (2oz) unsalted cashew nuts, fried in a little oil until browned

60g (2oz) sultanas, fried briefly in a little oil until plump

1 Grind the ginger, turmeric and sea salt in a mortar to make a paste. Rub the pieces of beef all over with this paste, and set aside for at least 30 minutes before cooking.

2 To make the red paste, blend all the ingredients together with 3 tbsp water until smooth. Transfer the paste to a large saucepan and simmer over a moderate heat for 6–8 minutes, stirring often. Remove from the heat and set aside.

3 Heat the oil in a frying pan and fry the pieces of beef, a few at a time, for 2 minutes on each side, turning them over once only. Set aside.

4 Reheat the paste in the saucepan for 2 minutes, stirring well, then add 120ml (4fl oz) hot water and the tamarind water. Bring to the boil. Put in the beef, stir and cover the pan. Continue cooking on a moderate heat for 6–8 minutes.

5 Add the tomatoes and stir to mix with the beef. Cook for 3 more minutes. Now add the coconut milk, or cream or yogurt, and continue cooking, turning the beef over several times, until the sauce is well reduced. This will take only a few minutes. For the final minute of cooking, put in the mint and coriander leaves.

6 Serve hot, with the garnish of fried shallots, cashews and sultanas scattered over all.

LAKSA LEMAK LAKSA WITH PRAWNS AND TOFU

The original meaning of the word *laksa* is fine rice noodles or rice vermicelli, but nowadays a *laksa* is a spicy soup made with coconut milk and whatever noodles you fancy, plus chicken, fish, prawns, scallops and so on. *Lemak* literally means 'fat', but it should be understood here as rich, lavish and delicious. This will make a substantial one-bowl meal; a smaller bowl could provide a starter for 8.

serves 4

rich and spicy

1 block Chinese tofu, about 400–450g (14–16oz)

2–3 tbsp groundnut oil

16 raw king prawns, heads removed, peeled and deveined

1 tsp salt

1.2 litres (2 pints) chicken or vegetable stock

300ml (10fl oz) thick coconut milk (p241)

225–350g (8–12oz) rice vermicelli, soaked in hot water in a covered bowl for 5 minutes, then drained

115–175g (4–6oz) beansprouts

2 hard-boiled eggs, quartered

Paste

1–2 large red chillies, chopped

2 shallots, chopped

1 garlic clove, chopped

2 candlenuts, chopped, or 1 tbsp ground almonds

1 tsp chopped fresh root ginger

1 tsp chopped galangal

1 tsp ground coriander

1 tsp sea salt

2 tbsp tamarind water (p355)

2 tbsp groundnut oil

To garnish

2 tbsp chopped spring onions

handful of flat-leaf parsley

2 tbsp deep-fried shallots (p239)

1 First make the paste by blending the ingredients together until smooth. Transfer to a small pan and cook on a moderate heat for 4 minutes, stirring. Remove from the heat and set aside.

2 Cut the tofu into quarters, then cut each quarter into quarters again (handle these carefully, as they break easily). Heat the oil in a non-stick frying pan and fry the tofu pieces, turning them over several times, until they are just slightly coloured. Drain on kitchen paper and set aside.

3 Rub the prawns with the salt and set aside. Bring the stock to the boil in a large saucepan. Stir in the paste and boil for 2 minutes. Add the prawns and cook for 2 minutes, then remove them with a slotted spoon and keep them aside in a bowl.

4 Pour the coconut milk into the stock and bring back to the boil. Simmer for 4–5 minutes while you distribute the noodles, prawns and tofu pieces equally among the bowls. Then distribute the beansprouts and quartered hard-boiled eggs, putting these on top of the prawns and tofu.

5 Adjust the seasoning of the soup, and bring it to a rolling boil, then ladle the boiling soup into the bowls. Garnish with the spring onions, parsley and crisp-fried shallots. Serve immediately.

RENDANG DAGING BEEF RENDANG

This is a long-cooked stew, with the beef simmered for 2–3 hours in coconut milk. Most of the liquid boils away, and you are left with a thick, rich-tasting, spice-laden sauce, in which the meat is no longer boiling but frying. Eventually all the sauce is absorbed into the meat, which becomes moist, almost black and very tender. In Malaysia, the meat is usually either beef or chicken, but the other ingredients differ from one state to the next. In some areas, tamarind water is added, in others spices like cinnamon, cumin and cardamom are used. My own favourite recipe is that of my grandmother, in whose home in West Sumatra I grew up. The recipe here is from Trengganu. It is almost the same as my grandmother's but with an additional ingredient that we don't normally use in rendang, called *kerisik*.

serves 8-10

meaty, rich and spicy

1.35kg (3lb 3oz) boneless beef, preferably brisket or good stewing steak, cut into 2cm (³/₄in) cubes

2 litres (3¹/₂ pints) thick coconut milk, made from 2 coconuts (p241)

8 shallots or 2 onions, finely chopped

1cm (¹/₂in) piece galangal

3 kaffir lime leaves

1 tsp salt

1 stalk lemongrass, cut across in half

1 turmeric leaf (optional)

4 tbsp *kerisik* (p192)

Paste

6 garlic cloves, chopped

6 large red chillies, deseeded and chopped

1 tbsp chopped fresh root ginger

2 tsp chopped turmeric root or 1 tsp ground turmeric

1 To make the paste, blend together the garlic, chillies, ginger and turmeric in a blender or food processor until smooth.

2 Put the beef into a large saucepan and add the coconut milk, shallots, galangal, lime leaves, salt, lemongrass and the paste. Bring to the boil on a moderate heat. Stir once, then leave to bubble gently for 1¹/₂–2 hours, stirring occasionally. Taste and add more salt, if necessary.

3 When the mixture is thick, continue cooking slowly, stirring constantly. Add the turmeric leaf (if using) and the *kerisik*. By now the meat will be getting brown and very tender. Continue stirring for perhaps 20 more minutes.

4 Take out the piece of galangal and the leaves, and serve the rendang hot, with rice. In many parts of Malaysia, it is the custom to eat rendang with compressed rice (p200).

Turmeric leaf >
Native to Asia, turmeric leaves impart a distinctive flavour to curries. These aromatic leaves are also used to wrap food.

IKAN MASAK KUAH BELIMBING SOUR FISH CURRY

Belimbing is the usual Malay word for carambola, also called star fruit, which is widely available in the West. However, the traditional souring agent in this fish curry is what in Indonesian is called *belimbing wuluh*, or *belimbing asam* in Malay. If you can get this, use 10–12 of the tiny fruits, thinly sliced. I've used *asam gelugur* (p192). Another alternative is 115g (4oz) thinly sliced unripe mango. My choice for this curry is a fresh halibut. Other suitable fish are pomfret, red snapper fillets, turbot fillets or whole small trout.

serves 4

sweet and sour

½ tsp sea salt

¼ tsp ground turmeric

1 tsp lime juice

black pepper

4 good-sized halibut steaks, 175–250g (6–9oz) each

600ml (1 pint) coconut cream (p241)

2 slices *asam gelugur*

1 stalk lemongrass, cut across in half

Paste

6 shallots, chopped

4–6 large red chillies, deseeded and chopped

2 tsp chopped turmeric root, or ½ tsp ground turmeric

1 tsp coarse sea salt

2 tbsp groundnut oil

1 Mix together the sea salt, turmeric, lime juice and a few turns of the pepper mill. Rub the fish with this mixture. Leave in a glass bowl in a cool place for 10 minutes or so.

2 Blend all the ingredients for the paste together with 2 tbsp water in a food processor or blender until smooth.

3 Put 3 tbsp of the coconut cream into a saucepan big enough to accommodate the fish. Heat on a moderate heat until the oil comes to the top. Add the paste and cook, stirring, for 2–3 minutes. Put in the *asam gelugur* and stir, then add the lemongrass. Put in half of the remaining coconut cream, bring to the boil and cook for 8 minutes or until the liquid has reduced by half.

4 Add the rest of the coconut cream and bring back to the boil, then add the fish steaks. Cook for 4–6 minutes, depending on the thickness of the fish.

5 Remove from the heat. Adjust the seasoning, and take out the *asam gelugur*, if used, and the lemongrass. Cover the pan and leave the fish in the sauce for just another minute or two, then serve straight away with rice or noodles and a mixed green salad.

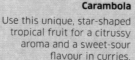

Carambola >
Use this unique, star-shaped tropical fruit for a citrussy aroma and a sweet-sour flavour in curries.

KARI KEPITING PEDAS CHILLI CRAB

This is my variation on a well-known Singaporean dish. I ate an excellent version a few years ago in the Courtyard Restaurant of the then newly renovated Raffles Hotel, made with crabs brought in alive from Sri Lanka. Live crabs are recommended for this recipe, although you can use frozen uncooked crab claws (not frozen cooked claws). If you intend using live crabs, my advice is not to buy one weighing less than 2kg (4½lb). Under that a crab probably has very little meat in it.

serves 4

chilli-hot and rich

3–4kg (6½–9lb) frozen uncooked crab claws, thawed in the fridge (this may take up to 36 hours)

600ml (1 pint) chicken stock or hot water

120ml (4fl oz) groundnut oil

Curry paste

6 shallots, chopped

4 garlic cloves, chopped

1 tbsp chopped turmeric root or 1 tsp turmeric powder

2–4 red bird chillies, chopped

6 large, dried red chillies, soaked in hot water for 5 minutes, drained and chopped

2 tbsp yellow bean paste

1 tsp salt

1 tsp sugar

1 tbsp groundnut oil

Ginger and tomato sauce

6 large red chillies, deseeded and thinly sliced diagonally

5 tsp grated fresh root ginger

450g (1lb) ripe red tomatoes, skinned and chopped, or 400g canned chopped plum tomatoes, drained

1 tsp salt

1 tsp paprika (optional)

2 tbsp white malt vinegar, wine vinegar or cider vinegar

To finish

2 egg yolks, beaten

1 tbsp light soy sauce

4 spring onions, cut into thin rounds

1 To make the curry paste, blend all of the ingredients together in a blender or food processor until smooth. Transfer the paste to a saucepan and simmer for 5–8 minutes, stirring frequently with a wooden spoon. Remove from the heat and leave to cool.

2 Mix all the ingredients for the ginger and tomato sauce in a glass bowl and keep aside.

3 Wash the crab claws thoroughly under cold running water, then dry on kitchen paper. Crack each claw with a mallet.

4 Put the cooked curry paste into a large saucepan and add the chicken stock. Bring to the boil.

5 Meanwhile, heat 2 tbsp of the oil in a wok and stir-fry the crab claws, in several batches, for 3 minutes each batch. Add more oil if necessary. As they are fried, drain the fried claws on kitchen paper.

6 When all the claws are fried, stir the curry sauce in the saucepan, increase the heat and put in the crab claws, stirring so that every claw is well coated. With a slotted spoon, transfer the claws to a large heated platter, leaving some sauce in the pan.

7 Pour the egg yolks and soy sauce into the bowl containing the ginger and tomato sauce and mix well. Then pour this into the curry sauce in the saucepan. Cook on a low heat, stirring constantly, until the sauce is hot and slightly thickened. Take care not to scramble the egg.

8 Pour the curry sauce over the claws on the platter. Scatter the chopped spring onion over all and serve immediately. You should, of course, eat this with your fingers, so provide finger bowls for everyone plus French bread to soak up the sauce. I like to eat this curry with plain boiled white rice or with compressed rice (p200).

GULAI KEPALA IKAN FISH HEAD CURRY

On my first visit to Kuala Lumpur and Singapore, many years ago, I was instructed that whenever a curried fish is served whole the most honoured guest must receive the head. In his or her turn, this person must show great pleasure and acknowledge the privilege gracefully. There is not a great deal of meat on the fish head, but the cheeks and eyes are considered delicacies. If I were hosting such a party, I would make sure that the head is cut off with the neck and the shoulders, if fish can be said to have these. Joachin, my Singaporean friend who gave me this recipe, tells me that what is really good in this dish is the sauce, which penetrates both the fish and the vegetables – usually okra and aubergines. In West Sumatra, my grandmother used to put *pakis* (edible fern shoots) into her fish curry. If you cannot find fish curry powder, use a mixture of 1 tbsp ground coriander, 2 tsp ground cumin, 1 tsp ground turmeric, 1 tsp paprika, 1 tsp ground fennel seed, $^1/_2$ tsp freshly ground black pepper and $^1/_4$ tsp chilli powder.

serves 4

sweet and sour

juice of $^1/_2$ lime (2–3 tsp)

$^1/_4$ tsp ground turmeric

$^1/_4$ tsp chilli powder

1 tsp coarse sea salt

4 whole trout, with heads, 1–1.25kg ($2^1/_4$–$2^3/_4$lb) in total

2 tbsp groundnut oil

1 tsp cumin seeds

1 tsp fennel seeds

1 tsp black mustard seeds

4–6 curry leaves or kaffir lime leaves

2 large red chillies, deseeded and sliced diagonally

8 small okra

8 apple aubergines or baby purple aubergines, cut into halves

6 ripe tomatoes, skinned and chopped

Curry sauce

6 garlic cloves, chopped

1 tbsp chopped fresh root ginger

3 tbsp groundnut oil

6 shallots, finely sliced

3 tbsp fish curry powder

3–4 tbsp thick tamarind water (p355)

250ml (9fl oz) coconut milk (p241)

250ml (9fl oz) coconut cream (p241)

salt and pepper

1 Mix together the lime juice, turmeric, chilli powder and coarse salt. Rub the fish inside and out with this, then put them back in the fridge in a large bowl, covered with cling film, until you are ready to cook.

2 Preheat the oven to 180°C (350°F/Gas 4). Arrange the fish in a casserole or braising pan that will accommodate them tightly side by side.

3 To make the sauce, crush the garlic and ginger in a mortar until they are puréed and well mixed. Heat the oil in a wok or a large, shallow saucepan and fry the shallots, stirring often, until they are soft. Add the garlic and ginger and continue stirring, then add the fish curry powder. Stir in the tamarind water and coconut milk. Bring to the boil and let the sauce bubble gently for 15 minutes. Add the coconut cream and simmer for a further 10 minutes. Season with salt and pepper. (The sauce can be made ahead of time and refrigerated. If you do this, take it out of the fridge when you turn on your oven, and heat it for 5 minutes in a saucepan before pouring it over the fish.)

4 Pour half of the sauce over the fish in the casserole. Put it into the oven to cook for 25 minutes.

5 When the fish has been in the oven for about 15 minutes, start the vegetables. Heat the oil in another saucepan and, when it is hot, put in the cumin, fennel and black mustard seeds. Stir until the seeds are popping, then add the curry leaves and the chillies. Keep on stirring for a minute or so, then add 120ml (4fl oz) hot water and $^1/_2$ tsp of salt. Bring to the boil. Add the okra and aubergines, cover and cook for 4 minutes. Uncover the pan and put in the tomatoes. Continue cooking, uncovered, for 2 minutes, then adjust the seasoning, adding more salt if necessary.

6 Pour the rest of the curry sauce into the vegetable mixture. Stir gently to mix, then cook on a high heat for 2–3 minutes.

7 Check to see if the fish are cooked. If they are, take the casserole out of the oven. Place the curried vegetables on top of the fish and serve, with plain boiled rice or cold compressed rice (p200).

BEBEK BUMBU BALI DUCK BREASTS IN BALINESE SPICES

This recipe is an adaptation of a renowned traditional duck dish called Bebek Betutu. There are three reasons why I feel I can include it in a curry book. The first is that this was traditionally a long-cooked duck with a sauce, though the sauce was very much reduced because the duck was wrapped in a banana leaf and the meat absorbed much of it. Secondly, the spice paste, or *bumbu*, contained a long list of ingredients that would not be at all out of place in an Indian curry. And finally, this is an endangered recipe, like those of many traditional dishes. I hope that my modern version may help it to survive. Note that the duck breasts should be left to marinate in the fridge for at least 4 hours, and preferably overnight. The paste and marinade should be prepared a day in advance.

serves 6-8

aromatic and savoury

450ml (15fl oz) thick coconut milk (p241), chicken stock or water

6-8 duck breasts, with skin

450g (1lb) spinach leaves, finely shredded

Paste

6 shallots or 2 medium onions, chopped

4 garlic cloves, chopped

4-6 large red chillies, deseeded and chopped, or 1 tsp chilli powder

3 candlenuts or macadamia nuts, chopped, or 2 tbsp slivered almonds

1 tbsp coriander seeds

1 tsp cumin seeds

2 tsp chopped turmeric root, or 1 tsp ground turmeric

1 small piece of shrimp paste (optional)

3 tbsp lime juice

1 tsp coarse sea salt

Spice mixture

3 cloves

2 green cardamoms

2.5cm (1in) cinnamon stick

$1/4$ tsp grated nutmeg

$1/4$ tsp black pepper

1cm ($1/2$in) piece galangal

1 stalk lemongrass, cut across in half

1 Blend all the ingredients for the paste together with 4 tbsp water in a food processor or blender until smooth. Transfer the paste to a saucepan. Combine all the ingredients for the spice mixture and add to the paste, stirring well to mix. Bring to the boil on a moderate heat and stir for 2 minutes.

2 Add about 4 tbsp of the coconut milk, then continue cooking for 5-8 minutes, stirring often. Transfer to a large glass bowl and set aside to cool completely.

3 Score two deep incisions through the skin and fat of each duck breast (not cutting into the meat). Put the breasts into the cold spice mixture and turn each one once or twice to make sure it is well coated on all sides. Leave to marinate in the fridge for at least 4 hours, or overnight if possible.

4 There are two ways to cook the duck. To long-cook, preheat the oven to 160°C (325°F/Gas 3). Loosely wrap the duck breasts with half of the marinade in two layers of banana leaves or aluminium foil, making sure that the edges are tightly sealed. Cook in the oven for 30 minutes, then turn the heat down to 75°C (170°F/Gas 1/4) and cook for a further $1^1/_2$-2 hours.

5 Alternatively, to short-cook the duck, preheat the oven to 200°C (400°F/Gas 6). Take the breasts out of the marinade and, with a knife or the side of a fork, scrape off all the marinade from the skin. Put the breasts, skin side up, on a rack in a roasting tin and roast for 25-30 minutes.

6 While the duck is cooking, take the lemongrass, cardamoms, cinnamon and galangal out of the remaining marinade, then put 2-4 tbsp of the marinade, or the remaining half (depending on how strong you want the sauce to be), into a saucepan. Add the rest of the coconut milk. Bring to the boil and simmer for 10 minutes.

7 Add the spinach and continue cooking for 4-5 minutes. Adjust the seasoning and set aside until ready for use. Reheat for serving. If you have long-cooked the duck breasts, skim off and discard the oil from the cooking juices, then mix the cooking juices into the spinach sauce. Cut each duck breast diagonally into several slices, and serve hot with the sauce and rice, potatoes or pasta.

GULAI BAGAR WEST SUMATRAN MUTTON CURRY

In West Sumatra, this curry is made with a leg or shoulder of goat cooked on the bone, then cut up in big chunks, bones and all, for serving. I prefer to use a boned, rolled and tied shoulder of mutton, served in thick slices.

serves 4-6

rich and spicy

1 boned shoulder of mutton, 1.35kg (3lb)

salt and pepper

6 tbsp freshly grated or desiccated coconut

1 tbsp coriander seeds

4-6 candlenuts, finely chopped, or 85g (3oz) slivered almonds

3 tbsp groundnut oil

8 shallots or 3 medium onions, finely sliced

2 tsp finely chopped fresh root ginger

4 large red chillies, deseeded and finely chopped, or 1 tsp chilli powder

4 garlic cloves, crushed

1 tsp ground turmeric

1 cinnamon stick

3 cardamoms

2 cloves

1/2 tsp ground cumin

pinch of grated nutmeg

300ml (10fl oz) coconut milk (p241)

300ml (10fl oz) coconut cream (p241)

2 tbsp tamarind water (p355)

1 stalk lemongrass, cut into 3

2 kaffir lime leaves

2 large purple aubergines, cut into large chunks

1 Preheat the oven to 220°C (425°F/Gas 7). Rub the mutton joint with salt and pepper. Lay it on a rack in a roasting tin and roast for 20 minutes. Turn off the oven, but leave the meat inside it.

2 In a frying pan, roast the coconut for 6 minutes, stirring constantly, until it turns brown. Add the coriander seeds and candlenuts and stir for a further 2 minutes. Transfer to a plate and cool, then process in a blender or food processor to a powder. Put this back on the plate and set aside.

3 Heat the oil in a large saucepan and fry the shallots, ginger, chillies and garlic for 3-4 minutes, stirring. Add the turmeric, cinnamon, cardamoms, cloves, cumin, nutmeg and the powdered coconut mixture. Cook, stirring, for 2 more minutes. Pour in the coconut milk and bring to the boil. Simmer for 30 minutes. Put the mutton into the sauce, cover and simmer for another 30 minutes.

4 Uncover the pan. Add the coconut cream, tamarind water, lemongrass and kaffir lime leaves. Continue cooking, uncovered, over a moderate heat (the sauce should bubble gently) for 10-15 minutes longer, turning the mutton every 5 minutes or so. Taste and add more salt, if necessary.

5 By now the sauce will be quite thick. Take out the meat and leave it to rest on a plate or a wooden board for 10-15 minutes. Remove the cinnamon stick, cardamoms, lemongrass and leaves from the sauce. Put the aubergines into the sauce and cook them, over a high heat, for 8 minutes. Add a little hot water if you think the sauce is becoming too thick and is sticking to the bottom of the pan.

6 To serve, cut the meat into thick slices. Arrange these, with the aubergines, on hot serving plates and pour the sauce over. Serve with plenty of rice.

GULÉ KAMBING JAVANESE LAMB CURRY

This is a liquid stew, or a curry soup. When I was at school in central Java, this *gulé*, made with goat meat, was a treat that we bought at least twice a week from a street vendor whose stall was a block away from our house. For us, *gulé* was a one-bowl meal, with a small helping of boiled rice or compressed rice added to the piping-hot curry. You could also have rice noodles in your *gulé*.

serves 4

aromatic and spicy

900ml (1½ pints) thick coconut milk (p241)

1 tbsp ground coriander

1 small stick of cinnamon, about 3cm (1¼in)

3 cloves

2 kaffir lime leaves

1cm (½in) piece galangal

1 stalk lemongrass, cut across in half

3 tbsp tamarind water (p355)

salt and pepper

1kg (2¼lb) boneless lamb shoulder or leg, cut into 2.5cm (1in) cubes

Paste

6-8 shallots or 2 onions, chopped

4-6 large red chillies, deseeded and chopped, or 1 tsp chilli powder

1 bird chilli, or ½ tsp cayenne pepper (optional)

4 garlic cloves, chopped

4 candlenuts, chopped, or 2 tbsp ground almonds

1 tbsp finely chopped fresh root ginger

1 tbsp chopped turmeric root, or 1 tsp ground turmeric

2 tbsp groundnut oil

1 tsp coarse sea salt

To garnish

2 tbsp deep-fried shallots (p239)

handful of chopped flat-leaf parsley

1 First make the paste, put all the ingredients in a blender or food processor with 2 tbsp of water and blend until smooth. Transfer the paste to a saucepan, bring to the boil on a moderate heat and simmer, stirring often, for 4-5 minutes. Add 4 tbsp of the coconut milk and continue simmering and stirring for 4 minutes or until the oil from the coconut milk comes to the top.

2 Add the coriander, cinnamon, cloves, kaffir lime leaves, galangal, lemongrass, tamarind water, and salt and pepper to taste. Cook, stirring, for 2 minutes. Then add the lamb cubes and turn up the heat a little. Keep stirring with a wooden spoon until all the meat is coated with the spice paste. Stir in 170ml (6fl oz) hot water. Cover the pan and continue cooking for 5-8 minutes. (The curry can be prepared to this point ahead of time; reheat before continuing.)

3 Pour in half of the remaining coconut milk and stir to mix. Bring to the boil, then leave to bubble gently for 10 minutes. Add the rest of the coconut milk, stir well and bring back to the boil. Stir again, then cook for 2 more minutes so that the *gulé* is piping hot. Scatter the shallots and parsley over and serve straight away with rice or noodles.

UDANG ASAM PEDAS HOT AND SOUR PRAWN CURRY

This is one of the wide variety of prawn curries that are popular all over Indonesia. There are hot and sour prawns, prawn *sambal goreng*, prawn curry with potatoes, and many more cooked in coconut milk and tamarind. The hotness, of course, comes from chillies, so reduce the quantity of these if you prefer your food less hot. The sourness in this case comes from a combination of tamarind and tomatoes. There is no need to add any sugar, because the dish contains so much onion, and the tamarind itself is sweet as well as sour. For convenience, you can fry the prawns and make the sauce ahead of time. Then, before serving, reheat the sauce and, when hot, add the prawns to finish the cooking.

serves 4

chilli-hot and sour

12-16 raw king prawns or tiger prawns, peeled, but last tail section left on, and deveined

1 tsp coarse sea salt

$1/2$ tsp ground turmeric

$1/2$ tsp chilli powder

3 tbsp groundnut oil

Sauce

3 tbsp groundnut oil

3 large red onions, chopped

4 garlic cloves, finely sliced

1 tbsp finely chopped fresh root ginger

2-6 large green chillies, deseeded and thinly sliced diagonally

1 tsp ground coriander

6-8 large, red and ripe tomatoes, skinned and chopped

3-4 tbsp tamarind water (p355)

salt

To garnish

chopped spring onions

deep-fried shallots (p239)

1 Rub the prawns with the sea salt, turmeric and chilli powder, then set aside for 10-12 minutes. Heat the oil and, when hot, fry the prawns, in two batches, for not more than 2 minutes each batch. They will not be fully cooked at this point. Drain on kitchen paper.

2 To make the sauce, heat the oil in a wok or large frying pan. Add the onions and fry, stirring often, for 8-10 minutes or until they are soft and just starting to colour. Add the garlic, ginger and chillies and stir-fry for a minute or so, then add the ground coriander and stir for another minute. Put in the chopped tomatoes and the tamarind water, stir them around and cook on a low heat for 3-4 more minutes. Adjust the seasoning.

3 Add the prawns to the sauce and stir them around for 2 minutes or until hot and cooked through. Serve immediately, with the spring onions and shallots scattered on top. As a main course dish, the accompaniment can be rice, noodles or bread, with salad or plain cooked vegetables.

KELIA ITIK RICH CURRY OF DUCK

This is a West Sumatran dish. In Java, 'duck' is *bebek*, but I use the Sumatran word *itik* here because this is the word for duck in Malaysia, where a variation of this dish is called Gulai Itik. Most Southeast Asians consider duck to be rather strong-smelling, so they cook it with plenty of garlic, or they use chicken instead – the chicken is simply chopped into ten pieces, and bones and all go into the pot. I prefer my duck with as few bones as possible, in fact no bones at all, so I use boneless breasts. This dish will freeze well. Make sure that the sauce covers the duck when it is packed. To serve, thaw at room temperature for 2–3 hours, then put it into a pan or a wok and heat until the sauce is thick and hot.

serves 4

garlicky, rich and spicy

1.2 litres (2 pints) thick coconut milk, made from 2 fresh coconuts (p241), or 3 cans (400g each) coconut milk

8-10 garlic cloves, chopped

4-6 large red chillies, deseeded and chopped

1 tbsp chopped fresh root ginger

1 tbsp chopped turmeric root

2 tsp chopped galangal

6 shallots or 2 onions, finely chopped

3 kaffir lime leaves

1 stalk lemongrass, cut in half

4 duck breasts, skin and fat removed and each breast cut into 2 or 3 portions

1 tsp coarse sea salt

1 If using canned coconut milk, heat it slowly in a large saucepan for 5 minutes or until the thick and thin parts of the 'milk' are well mixed. Remove from the heat.

2 Put 4 tbsp of the coconut milk into a blender and add the garlic, chillies, ginger, turmeric root and galangal. Blend until smooth. Put this paste and the chopped shallots into the saucepan containing the rest of the coconut milk. Add the kaffir lime leaves, lemongrass, duck pieces and salt.

3 Bring to the boil. Stir once, then leave to bubble gently on a moderate heat, without stirring, for at least 45 minutes. By this time the coconut milk will have become quite thick and oily. From this point on, you need to stir often, cooking until the sauce becomes really thick and very little oil is left on top of it. Taste and add more salt if needed. Serve hot, with rice.

< Galangal
A member of the ginger family, galangal adds a sharp, peppery taste to curries.

ADOBONG MANOK CHICKEN ADOBO

Although people in the Philippines prefer not to call *adobo* 'curry', the sauce, when cooked, does closely resemble a curry sauce. (Note that this *adobo* is cooked with coconut milk.) My version of it adapts the traditional method and starts by cooking the chicken, whole, in vinegar; this gives the finished dish an attractive appearance.

serves 4-6

mild and creamy

1 chicken, 1.1-1.35kg (2½-3lb)

6-8 garlic cloves, finely chopped

250ml (8fl oz) sugar cane vinegar, white vinegar or rice vinegar

1-2 kaffir lime leaves or bay leaves

½-1 tsp coarsely ground black pepper or chopped fresh red chillies

1 tsp salt

2 tbsp groundnut oil

½-1 tsp ground turmeric

½-1 tsp paprika

150ml (5fl oz) coconut cream (p241)

2 tbsp light soy sauce

1 Put the chicken into a large saucepan and add the garlic, vinegar, 1.2 litres (2 pints) water, the kaffir lime leaves, black pepper and salt. Bring to the boil, then cover the pan, reduce the heat and simmer for 30 minutes.

2 Transfer the chicken to a colander. Turn the heat up under the saucepan and boil the stock until it has reduced to half its original volume. This will take 20-25 minutes.

3 Heat the oil in another large saucepan, add the turmeric and paprika and stir, then add about half the coconut cream. Put in the chicken, cover the pan and simmer for 10 minutes. Uncover and pour in the reduced stock and the rest of the coconut cream. Bring back to the boil and leave to bubble gently for 15 minutes. Add the soy sauce and adjust the seasoning.

4 Take the chicken out of the pan and put it on a chopping board. Let it cool a little, while you continue to simmer the sauce. Then either cut the chicken into 4 equal portions, or carve it as you would carve a roast chicken, discarding the bones.

5 Arrange the chicken portions or slices on a heated serving plate and pour the sauce over them. Serve hot, with rice.

Kaffir lime leaves >
The highly aromatic kaffir lime leaves are responsible for the tangy, citrussy flavour in South Asian curries.

ADOBONG PUSIT SQUID ADOBO

This is my adaptation of a recipe sent to me by my friend Pia Lim-Castillo in Manila. I like to serve this as a first course before a main course of, perhaps, a chicken curry or the Javanese lamb curry on p221. If you want to serve this *adobo* as a main course, offer a vegetable curry with it, and rice, bread or a noodle salad.

serves 4

sweet, sour and savoury

600g (1lb 5oz) small squid, each 12–16cm (5–6¹/₂in) long, or 12–16 baby squid, cleaned and the tentacles and wings reserved for the stuffing

7 tbsp groundnut oil

coarse sea salt

6 shallots, finely chopped

2 green chillies, deseeded and thinly sliced diagonally

3 garlic cloves, chopped

2 kaffir lime leaves or bay leaves

6 ripe vine or plum tomatoes, skinned, partly deseeded and finely chopped

100g (3¹/₂oz) day-old bread, crust removed, soaked in water or milk and squeezed dry, or 100g (3¹/₂oz) cooked rice

2 egg yolks, beaten

6 tbsp chopped flat-leaf parsley

90ml (3fl oz) rice vinegar or white wine vinegar

1 tsp sugar, if needed

1 Chop the squid tentacles and wings into small dice. Heat 2 tbsp of the oil in a wok or saucepan and stir-fry the tentacles and wings for 2 minutes. Add a pinch of salt and remove from the heat.

2 Heat 2 tbsp oil in another wok or saucepan and stir-fry the shallots, green chillies and garlic for 2–3 minutes. Add the kaffir lime leaves and the chopped tomatoes. Simmer for 2 minutes. Season with a little salt, then remove from the heat.

3 Using a slotted spoon, transfer half of this mixture to a bowl, leaving the cooking juices and leaves in the wok. Add the squid tentacles and wings to the bowl, taking care not to include the oil from the pan. Then add the bread or rice, egg yolks and half the parsley. Mix well. Using a small spoon, fill the squid with this stuffing. Close the openings with wooden cocktail sticks.

4 Put the chilli and tomato sauce back on a low heat and add the vinegar. Simmer, without stirring, for 5 minutes. Add the rest of the parsley and a little water if the sauce looks too dry. Remove from the heat. Taste the sauce and add the sugar, if necessary.

5 Heat the remaining 3 tbsp oil in a large flameproof casserole and carefully put in the stuffed squid. Cook until they are opaque all over, turning them after every minute. Pour in the vinegared sauce and turn the squid in this. Cover the casserole and cook on a moderate heat for 10–12 minutes. Alternatively, you can cook in a preheated 150°C (300°F/Gas 2) oven for 30–60 minutes, depending on the size of the squid.

6 When cooked, remove the cocktail sticks from the squid. Serve whole or cut into thick slices, with the sauce spooned over.

KARÉ-KARÉ BRAISED OXTAIL WITH PEANUT SAUCE

We in Southeast Asia love offal, and oxtail is a favourite meat for soup. Sop Buntut (Indonesian oxtail soup) is a well-known and popular one-bowl meal served with rice or rice noodles. Karé-karé is a Philippines variation on the theme, using oxtail as the basis of a substantial main course. It is customary to serve it with two or three kinds of cooked vegetables, mixed with the peanut sauce. Filipinos also like to serve a chilli-hot shrimp paste, which they call *guisadong bagoong alamang*, with this dish. My suggestion is to serve Karé-karé with the dried shrimp relish on p201.

Serves 4-6

nutty, garlicky and rich

4 tbsp white vinegar

1.5-2kg (3lb 3oz-4½lb) oxtail, trimmed of excess fat and cut into segments 6-8cm (2½-3in) long

3 tbsp groundnut oil

4 shallots, chopped

1 head of garlic, chopped (use less if preferred)

1 tsp shrimp paste

1 tsp coarse sea salt

1 tsp ground turmeric

1 tbsp black pepper

175-225g (6-8oz) yard-long beans, cut into 10cm (4in) pieces, or fine French beans

175-225g (6-8oz) white cabbage or Chinese cabbage, roughly sliced

175-225g (6-8oz) carrots, cut into thin rounds

300ml (10fl oz) Sambal Kacang (p202)

1 Add the vinegar to a bowl of water. Wash the oxtail pieces in this, then drain them in a colander and dry them with kitchen paper. Put the oxtail into a large saucepan and add enough cold water to cover. Bring to the boil and boil for 5 minutes. Drain the oxtail pieces.

2 In another saucepan, heat the oil over a moderate heat and fry the shallots, stirring often, until they start to colour. Add the oxtail and stir the pieces around in the oil for a few minutes.

3 Crush the garlic, shrimp paste and coarse salt together in a mortar, then add to the pan with the turmeric and pepper. Stir well, then add enough cold water just to cover the meat. Bring to the boil, then reduce the heat a little and cover the pan. Simmer for 2-2½ hours or until the meat is tender and the sauce quite thick. Skim every half hour or so during the simmering, and add a little hot water when the cooking liquid gets too low.

4 Remove the oxtail from the pan and transfer to an ovenproof serving dish; keep warm in a low oven. Turn the heat under the saucepan to high and bring the cooking juices to the boil. Cook uncovered for 5-10 minutes or until reduced by half.

5 At the same time, cook the vegetables in boiling water for 3-4 minutes or until tender; drain. Arrange the cooked vegetables on top of the oxtail. Keep hot.

6 Stir the Sambal Kacang into the reduced cooking juices. Add 125ml (4fl oz) hot water if the sauce is too thick. Heat until very hot, then pour all over the vegetables. Serve immediately, with rice.

THAILAND

Thai food is one of the world's great cuisines. It has fine traditions and intricate culinary practices, great regional diversity and a vast array of ingredients. Together these combine to produce the most wonderful cooking. Thailand has a venerable past that stretches back to the arrival of the Thais on to the plains of ancient Siam. During the ensuing thousand years, a remarkable cuisine evolved with a complex repertoire that reflects the ornate and sophisticated culture of the people.

Although Thailand is quite a small country, it has many distinct styles of cooking: royal and peasant food, street cooking and the diverse cuisines of the four major regions. The food of the court of Thailand is the most elegant, sadly now almost extinct. It delights in unusual combinations with surprising textures and enticing perfumes, such as a red curry of shredded beef with orange blossoms accompanied by a dish of sweet and salty clams. Peasant food, on the other hand, is robustly flavoured, firmly rooted in the land and prepared with rudimentary techniques. A pungent curry of shrimp paste with shallots and chillies, with fish and local seasonal vegetables added, is perhaps the most common of peasant-style curries. But whatever the curry, rice is always served with it.

Rice is of fundamental importance to the Thais and their cooking. Its cultivation has transformed the countryside from impenetrable and uninhabited forests to verdant expanses of rice paddies feeding an increasing population. Its crucial role is reflected at table. Rice is most often cooked with elemental simplicity, boiled or steamed, plain and unseasoned, although some cooks enhance its natural perfume by adding pandanus leaf. Normally a selection of dishes arrives with the rice. While each and every dish shares the same importance as any other in the meal, they are merely accompaniments to rice.

Curries are perhaps the most familiar of Thai dishes and many people will have eaten such standards as a red or green curry from the central plains. But the rich traditions make for a huge range of styles. From village to village, house to house and, of course, region to region, all have their own preferred type of curry. It can be made with coconut cream, a light stock or even just with water, and the paste can be fried, grilled, steamed or simply dissolved in simmering liquid. Almost all are seasoned with fish sauce, but some have the addition of palm sugar, tamarind and, of course, chilli to help lift it from the ordinary to the memorable. This is what makes Thai food so good: the interplay of textures and seasonings to create a deft balance of sweet, sour, salty and hot tastes in each dish and every meal.

In every market place there is always a section where prepared food is sold, and among these stalls are those that specialize in curries. Some offer the curry paste already prepared – a boon that a Westerner can only dream of. Others, called *raan kao geng* in Thai, sell curries complete and ready to go. Up to 20 different varieties may be available. The national favourites are there, of course – sour orange, green and red curries – as well as mussaman and aromatic curries and the more unusual local specialities.

There are four main regional styles of cooking with a great many more variations in each area. The north of the country is mountainous and misty, and has a gentler style of cooking that seems to reflect the comparatively milder climate. Freshwater fish and pork are heavily used as are uncultivated vegetables and wild mushrooms collected from nearby forests. Pork curry with shredded ginger, pickled garlic and cardamom is a firm favourite.

The northeast is the poorest and most remote of the regions. The food here is extremely spicy and uses many fermented or preserved products, in particular fermented fish in all its forms. A pork and mustard green curry is a typical dish. In both of the northern regions the preference is for glutinous or sticky rice. Coconut cream is not much used, because at certain times of the year it becomes too cold for the coconut tree to grow well here.

The central plains are the heartland, dominating the country both politically and economically. Bangkok is at its centre. The style of cooking here is the most familiar to non-Thais: a green curry of chicken, for instance, or red curries of many kinds. The south of the country winds sinuously around the Gulf of Thailand, so naturally this region's food is based on seafood. Prawns, crabs and fish are grilled or fried, and curries here are redolent of turmeric, coconut and chillies.

Recipes have been honed down, over generations, to ensure a harmonious balance. The recipes that follow are only a small selection from the huge repertoire of Thai curries, but they reflected the diversity, complexity and elegance of this wonderful cuisine.

David Thompson

Frying the curry paste >
Simmer in cracked
coconut cream until fragrant

THE TASTE OF THAILAND

1. Thai basil leaves
2. holy basil leaves
3. dried bay leaves
4. turmeric root
5. galangal
6. kaffir lime
7. kaffir lime leaves
8. wild ginger
9. coriander stalks and root
10. lemongrass
11. garlic
12. fresh green bird chillies
13. dried red Thai chillies
14. dried large red chillies
15. cassia
16. white cardamom
17. star anise
18. palm sugar
19. coriander seeds
20. cumin seeds
21. shrimp paste
22. tamarind
23. apple aubergine
24. heart of coconut
25. long green aubergine
26. pea aubergines
27. fresh green peppercorns

THE RAW MATERIALS

In the markets of Thailand, row after row of stalls sell tempting produce along with inviting prepared curries of all kinds. Here is a brief description of the ingredients used in most curry pastes, in the order of addition if using a pestle and mortar, followed by the seasoning ingredients added to balance the hot, sweet, salty and sour flavours, and vegetables, herbs and other aromatics used as garnishes.

CURRY PASTE
RED SHALLOTS

Small red shallots are one of the most common ingredients used in Thai cooking, and they give a curry paste substance and sharp pungency. Although onions can be substituted, they are much stronger than shallots, so if using, reduce the amount slightly.

CHILLIES

Dried large, red chillies, which are fruity and hot, are most common in red curries; when fresh, large chillies (red or green) are only occasionally used in curry pastes. If large chillies are called for, it is best to remove the seeds and the surrounding membrane, which contains much of the heat. Then soak dried chillies in lightly salted water to remove yet more of the heat and to soften them. This means more chillies can be used without increasing the heat to lethal levels and gives a deeper, more substantial chilli flavour to the paste. When small chillies are specified, either fresh or dried, the seeds and membranes are normally not removed. Those most often used are the very hot, fresh, green bird's eye or bird chillies (what I like to call 'scuds').

CORIANDER ROOT

The lingering herbaceous taste of coriander root gives length to a curry's flavour. Before use, clean the root well, trim off the fuzzy strands at the bottom and cut off most of the green stalk. Scrape or peel off the skin, then soak the root in water to dislodge any dirt that might still be lurking. Chop the root finely before pounding with the other ingredients.

GALANGAL

Slightly older galangal is the best to use, because it has a stronger, more peppery taste than young galangal. It brings a sharp, almost medicinal quality to the paste, but use too much and the paste will be bitter. Peel the rhizome well and cut into a fine dice before pounding.

GARLIC

Thai garlic has smaller cloves, and is sweeter and less pungent than Western garlic, although, of course, these larger cloves can be used instead. Garlic is an essential component in a curry paste, giving a rich sweetness to the flavour. It is good practice to remove the green germ, if any, which can give the curry a slightly bitter aftertaste.

KAFFIR LIME

Only the outer, green zest should be used – the white, fleshy pith is unrelentingly bitter – and it should be freshly grated, because the aroma – kaffir lime's essential role in a curry paste – dissipates quickly. A fresh kaffir lime is best, of course, but the frozen fruit can be used quite satisfactorily. Grate off the zest while the fruit is still frozen, because once thawed it becomes too soft. Too much lime zest in a curry paste will make it soapy and slightly bitter.Although dried kaffir lime zest is available, the aromatic oils are so desiccated as to make it a worthless addition. If only dry is available, omit completely.

LEMONGRASS

This imparts a citrussy, floral perfume. The outer leaves, the top third and the hard root need to be discarded before slicing the remainder finely. Prepare just before use as its perfume dissipates quickly. Too much lemongrass makes a paste taste oily and bitter; too little and the paste has a metallic aftertaste.

RED TURMERIC

Fresh red turmeric is used mainly in curries from the south of Thailand, although it also makes an appearance in a green curry paste to enliven the colour. Although ground dried turmeric can be substituted, it must be used with caution – one-third of the quantity of fresh peeled root. Red turmeric has an agreeable mustiness that becomes bitter if too much is used.

SALT

This acts as an abrasive to help break down the other ingredients. It also seasons the curry paste and acts

Wild ginger

All dried spices should be roasted individually before being ground and then sieved (p354).

WILD GINGER

Also called Chinese keys, wild ginger (*grachai*) is a pencil-like rhizome. Its earthy heat is used to counteract the muddiness of freshwater fish and bloodiness of game. It is most used in jungle curries. Peel and trim before use.

SEASONINGS

FISH SAUCE

This salty seasoning is made by fermenting fish with salt in water. From such an unpromising start comes one of the staples of Southeast Asia. Fish sauce (*nam pla*) should always be added last as it is the most pervasive seasoning and the most difficult to adjust if too much is used.

SUGAR

Whether palm sugar or white sugar, this has always been a component of the Thai seasoning spectrum. White sugar imparts a simple, clear sweetness. It is most often used in boiled curries and in curries fried in oil. Palm sugar is richer and rounder in taste and gives body to a curry. It is most often used in curries where the paste is cooked in cracked coconut cream.

TAMARIND

Tamarind water is the most common souring agent in Thai curries. It is best made fresh, using 1 part tamarind pulp to 2 parts water (p355). Take care after adding tamarind water to a curry as it can scorch quite easily.

as a preservative to delay any fermentation that might develop during storage.

SHRIMP PASTE

Thai shrimp paste (*gapi*) is the soul of Thai food. It is made by fermenting small shrimps with salt – an unpromising start for a delicious result. The best quality varieties are rich and earthy. Sadly, the more common commercial versions are salty and can be acrid. Shrimp paste should be used carefully, as too much

will smother the curry, making it murky and heavy, while too little will mean a curry without depth.

SPICES

Most Thai curry pastes use very few dried spices – just enough to imbue the paste with aroma. The spices most employed are white peppercorns, Thai coriander seeds and cumin seeds, with cassia bark, white cardamom and star anise added occasionally. A large amount of spice usually indicates a Muslim origin for the dish.

GARNISHES

HOLY BASIL

The somewhat pointed, purple-tinged leaves of holy basil have a surprisingly clove-like intensity when very fresh. This volatile aroma dissipates quickly as the herb loses its freshness or is subjected to heat, so add just before serving. Once holy basil was used in many curries from the central plains, but now it is mainly reserved for jungle curries.

THAI BASIL

While Thai basil appears to be quite similar to European basil, it is very different: it has a pronounced anise taste. The leaves are usually added just before the curry is served so their aroma is at its best. Thai basil is used in many curries from the central plains, especially red and green curries.

THAI BAY LEAVES

These dried leaves are only used in a mussaman curry, where their musty, spicy taste enhances the cardamom and peanuts. Bay leaves will make an almost unnoticeable alternative.

PEPPERCORNS

The peppercorn is indigenous to this region and was the main spicing component before the arrival of the chilli in the 16th century. Thais use three types of peppercorns: green, white and black. Green peppercorns are the fresh berries, simply washed and perhaps de-stemmed before use. White peppercorns are soaked in a brine, then rubbed to remove the skin so that only the spicy kernel is dried.

< Kaffir lime

Black peppercorns retain the skin, which blackens as the berry dries.

Green peppercorns are mainly used as a finishing garnish in jungle curries but are rarely if ever used in a curry paste itself, whereas dried and processed pepper is an important spice in almost every curry paste. White pepper is used mostly in curries from the central plains, black pepper in curries from the south and those of Muslim origin.

KAFFIR LIME LEAVES

The verdant and aromatic leaves of the kaffir lime are normally added as a final garnish to a curry after it is cooked. Their perfume helps to cover any bitter or muddy flavours. When adding, crush the leaves slightly to help to release their fragrance. Frozen kaffir lime leaves have little of the characteristic smell, while dried leaves have none.

AUBERGINES

There are many kinds of aubergines used in Thai cooking, but perhaps the three most common are the pea, apple and long green varieties. The little pea aubergine grows in clusters and should be picked from the stalk before being washed and added to a curry. It imparts a pleasing bitterness. Apple aubergine has a less pronounced flavour and is mainly used for its texture. Top and slice just before adding to a curry, otherwise it will oxidise and the once white flesh will develop an unsightly black-mottled tone. Some Thai cooks steep the sliced aubergine in salted water to delay this, but it can then take on too much salt. The long green aubergine needs to be cooked and tender to eat it at its best. Once sliced and simmered, it is rich and silken in both taste and texture.

HEART OF COCONUT

This is the crunchy, nutty shoot of the coconut. It is ideal to use in curries where its texture poses a pleasing contrast. If cooked, this is done quite briefly. Before use, wash and peel away any yellowing areas. The meat from a young green coconut is a possible alternative to heart of coconut.

DEEP-FRIED SHALLOTS

These are an important garnish in Thai cooking. Although they can be bought, it is much better to fry your own. Cut peeled shallots lengthways into very thin, even slices, then deep-fry in hot oil, stirring constantly with tongs. As the shallots begin to colour, they will lose their onion-like aroma and begin to smell enticingly nutty. When they become quite golden, remove from the oil and spread out on kitchen paper to drain. They will crisp as they cool. Deep-fried shallots will keep for 2 days in an airtight container.

PREPARING LEMONGRASS

This aromatic grass with fibrous leaves is one of the most common ingredients in Southeast Asian cuisine and is used commonly in curries from Thailand. It is either sliced or chopped to flavour curries and soups, often mixed with other spices and herbs for curry pastes.

1 Peel away and discard the tough outer leaves from the stalks until you get to the softer inner layer, which is light yellow in colour and easy to peel.

2 With a sharp knife, slice off the lower bulb. Cut off about 2.5cm (1in) from the lower end to remove the bulb and a little more.

3 Take out the inner layer and rinse under cold running water to remove any dirt and soil that may have collected on the inside of the stalk.

4 Lay the stem on the chopping board and either slice, dice or chop them. You could also dry the leaves and make a fine powder to garnish dishes.

COCONUT MILK AND CREAM

The taste of fresh coconut cream is incomparably luscious, with a complexity and depth of flavour that justifies the labour required to produce it. Both coconut milk and cream are best used within a few hours. They can be refrigerated for 1–2 days, but will harden and become difficult to use. One Thai trick worth trying is to add a bruised chilli to retard the hardening.

1 Use the back (blunt) side of a cleaver or a light hammer to split open the coconut, hitting it all the way around. Score the flesh or cut it into segments, to make it easier to prise from the shell. Peel away and discard the brown inner skin, then chop the flesh and blend in a food processor with an equal amount of hot water.

2 Pour the coconut mixture into a piece of muslin – or a very clean tea towel – draped over a glass, china or plastic bowl (metal taints the cream). Gather up the muslin and squeeze the flesh to extract the liquid. If a recipe calls for thick coconut milk, use immediately, before separation occurs (see bottom, left).

3 For coconut cream, leave for at least 20 minutes. The cream is the thicker, opaque liquid that separates and floats on top of the thinner liquid, which is called coconut milk in the book. Normally one good coconut yields about 250ml (9fl oz) of coconut cream. Often the squeezing process is repeated, but this second pressing will yield more coconut milk than cream.

'Cracked' coconut cream
Curries that are fried in coconut cream often call for the cream to be 'cracked', or separated. For this, simmer the cream until most of the water evaporates. The cream then separates into thin oil and milk solids. Once cracked, coconut cream lasts for several weeks. The separated oil can also be used for deep-frying and the solids can be used in desserts when a weighty sumptuousness is required.

KREAUNG GENG GENG GWIO WARN GREEN CURRY PASTE

Some of the paste recipes in the curries in this chapter make more paste than is needed for the individual dish. This is because when making a paste, either using a pestle and mortar or a blender, a certain volume is required before the ingredients will purée successfully. Leftover paste can be stored for up to 2 weeks in the fridge: put it in an airtight container, pressing cling film against the surface of the paste before closing the top.

1 heaped tbsp bird's eye chillies

1–2 long green chillies, deseeded

a few blades of mace, roasted (optional)

1 tsp roasted coriander seeds

1 tsp white peppercorns

1 tsp Thai shrimp paste

2¹/₂ tbsp chopped garlic

2¹/₂ tbsp chopped red shallots

1 rounded tbsp chopped wild ginger

2 tsp chopped red turmeric

2 tsp chopped coriander root

1 tsp chopped kaffir lime zest

2¹/₂ tbsp chopped lemongrass

1 rounded tbsp chopped galangal

pinch of salt

1 Pound the fresh ingredients in a mortar with a pestle, adding them one at a time and starting with the hardest, driest and most difficult (which is always the chillies), and working through to the softest and wettest. (In recipes where dried chillies are used, they are often soaked first; this means they are no longer the driest or hardest, but they are still pounded first.) Follow the order of ingredients as listed. Reduce each ingredient to a pulp before adding the next.

2 Grind the peppercorns, coriander seeds and mace, if using, then sieve to be sure the powder is fine. Combine the spices with the rest of the ingredients in the pestle and mortar.

Using a blender
Put the ingredients into the blender at once and blend to a paste, adding a water to facilitate the blending. Stop the machine and scrape down the sides of the goblet from time to time. Take care not to overwork the paste – 3–4 minutes of blending should be sufficient.

PREPARING GALANGAL

This rhizome is used extensively in Thai, Malaysian and Indonesian recipes. From the ginger family, with an orangy-brown rind and pale yellow or white flesh, it has a pungent flavour and a sharp, gingery taste. Peel off the hard scale on the surface before using it in recipes.

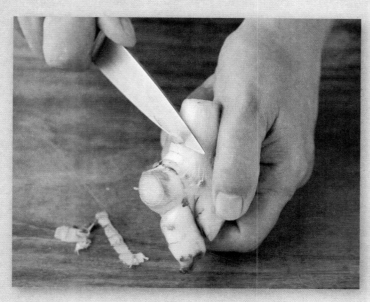

1 Cut off the amount of galangal you require from the main piece. Then remove the nodes on the surface and peel off the skin. Wash the piece thoroughly under cold running water to remove any dirt.

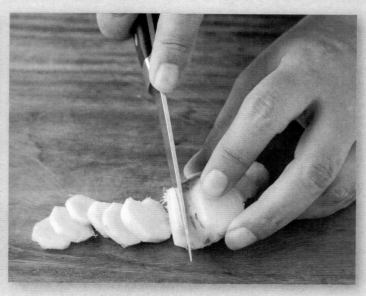

2 There are a variety of ways in which galangal can be prepared, depending how it is used in the recipe. To cut into discs, use a sharp knife and slice the piece thinly across the grain into small discs.

3 To shred, hold each disc firmly with your fingers and slice into fine slivers. Shredded galangal is mainly used for garnishing.

4 To use finely chopped, gather the slivers and cut across. Chop them further for finer cuts. Chopped galangal is mixed with other spices for curry pastes. It is also used for garnishing.

RED CHILLI PASTE

Use thick dried red chillies to prepare this paste. Garlic topped with hot oil gives a pungent, garlicky flavour to this paste. This pungent red chilli paste can be used in a number of Thai curries to enhance their flavour.

makes 1 kg (2¼lb)

250g (9oz) dried
 red chillies

1 tbsp salt

100ml (3½fl oz) vinegar

30g (1oz) garlic, peeled
 and finely chopped

3 tbsp vegetable oil

1 Half-fill a saucepan with water. Add the red chillies and boil for 10 minutes over a moderate heat.

2 Once boiled, drain the water, then transfer the chillies to a food processor and blend to a paste.

3 Transfer the paste to a bowl. Add the salt and vinegar and mix well.

4 Top the paste with the chopped garlic but do not mix the garlic with the paste yet.

5 Heat the oil in a saucepan over a high heat, then pour the hot oil over the garlic. This will burn the garlic and release its flavour.

6 Mix the oil and garlic with the paste and set aside to cool completely. You can use the paste immediately in a curry or transfer it to an airtight container and store in the fridge for up to 20 days.

COOKING THAI CURRIES

The Thai word for curry, *geng*, has a much looser meaning than its English equivalent. In its widest sense it means a liquid seasoned with a paste and can include soups and braised dishes, but when the paste is spicy it comes closer to our understanding of the word. At its most basic, then, a curry can be a simple paste of chillies, red shallots and shrimp paste dissolved in simmering seasoned stock or water, quite similar to the sour orange curry on p252. This is the most common and probably most popular type of curry in the Kingdom. From this, curries become increasingly complex, reaching the harmonious intricacy of a mussaman curry where up to 20 ingredients go into the paste, not to mention the subsequent seasoning, the meat and garnishes. There are three main parts to making a Thai curry: preparing the paste, cooking and seasoning the paste, and adding garnishes, such as herbs, aromatics, and meat, fish and so on.

Preparing the curry paste

While making a curry paste in a blender or food processor is undoubtedly more convenient, purists believe that the best paste is made by hand, using a pestle and mortar (p242). The larger the mortar, the more practical, as it allows for easier, quicker achieving of a fine paste.

By whatever the means a good-quality paste is one where the original, often rough initial state is reduced to a fine purée. To ensure this, each ingredient should be pulverized completely before the next is added. The normal order is the hardest, most fibrous ingredients first, the softer ones last.

All the ingredients must be prepared in advance. This means that most ingredients need to be washed, peeled and chopped prior to adding to the mortar. The more finely chopped, the less time required to reduce the ingredient to a pulp. Perhaps this is rather obvious but it is certainly a welcome relief when actually pounding.

Cooking the paste

There are two methods for cooking the paste. The simplest and oldest is to dissolve it in simmering seasoned liquid, be it water, stock or, in the south of Thailand, coconut milk. After this the 'boiled curry' is seasoned, usually with fish sauce and with tamarind water. Sometimes a pinch of white sugar is added to balance the tartness.

The alternative method is to fry the paste. Depending on the style of curry and the region, frying is done either in oil (some older recipes use rendered pork fat) or in cracked coconut cream (p241). With oil, the paste is fried over a searingly high heat for just a minute or two, until it smells piercingly aromatic. Pastes cooked in oil are mostly seasoned with fish sauce, rarely with sugar, and are then moistened with stock. This forms the basis of 'jungle' curries and many other curries from the north and northeast of the country, where coconuts are less common.

More familiar are curries based on coconut, where the paste is fried in coconut cream that has been simmered until the oil begins to separate out ('cracked'). The frying takes quite a long time – up to 5 minutes over a moderate heat, stirring regularly. The aroma develops and deepens, conveying the changes in the paste as it cooks. The longer the cooking, the more mellow the flavour becomes as the disparate elements become unified.

Seasoning

Seasoning transforms the curry paste – it is this process that so distinguishes Thai food. Thai cooking is a deft balance of hot, sweet, salty and sour. Most curries are salty, some are also sweet, many can be sour as well, and a few have all these elements. Wise cooks refrain from complete seasoning at this stage, since it removes the possibility of a final adjustment just before serving. After the seasoning process the curry is moistened with either stock or coconut milk and then simmered gently for a few minutes to incorporate all the components.

Adding the garnishes

The third stage is where the garnishes are added. To the Western sensibility this defines a curry, but to a Thai it is but one element in a complex dish. Garnishing is quite straightforward with a boiled curry, since it is usually only made with

Thai red curry paste

fish or seafood cut up into bite-sized pieces that cook quickly. Any vegetables, fresh herbs and other aromatic garnishes are added in order of the time it takes to cook them.

With a fried curry the meat is cut into very small pieces to allow for an easy and equal share for all, as well as to ensure that tough meat will become tender. Then the aromatic garnishes are added, usually including kaffir lime leaves, fresh chillies and picked herbs such as holy, Thai or lemon basil. Once garnishing is completed, the curry is left to rest for a minute or so, to allow the flavours to mingle and mellow. Then the seasoning is checked one more time so any final adjustments can be made before serving.

Making a Thai curry is an complex process where the layers of taste are finely poised and the seasonings finely balanced: it is as sophisticated as Thai culture is itself.

KAO SUAY STEAMED JASMINE RICE

Most Asian cooks now use electric rice cookers, which make perfectly cooked rice simple and almost failsafe. However, you need to take care not to overfill the cooker: one-third full is enough. Any more and the rice might cook unevenly. Below is the method for cooking rice in the traditional way.

jasmine rice
water
pandanus leaf (optional)

1 Wash the rice in cold water, carefully combing your hands through the rice grains in the water to remove any husks and excess starch and dust that aided in polishing the grains. With cupped hands, gently rub the grains together. Drain and repeat two or three times until the water is clear. This washing prevents gluggy rice.

2 Put the rice in a heavy pot – tall rather than wide for small amounts, yet the converse for larger amounts – and cover with cold water. Traditionally the water level should be about an index-finger joint above the rice. Surprisingly, this joint is almost always the same length! For the less traditional, the proportions of approximately $2^1/_2$ cups of rice to $3^1/_2$ cups of water will give you plenty of rice for 4 people. Significantly, the rice is not seasoned with salt – the accompanying dishes are sufficiently seasoned.

3 Cover the pot with a tightly fitting lid and bring quickly to the boil, then turn the heat to very low and cook for 10-15 minutes. Do not stir rice during cooking, because this breaks down the grains, releasing starch and making it gluggy.

4 Remove from the heat and allow the rice to rest for 10 minutes or so – it will remain quite warm for 30 minutes, covered in the pot. A pandanus leaf is sometimes added after the rice is cooked, while it rests, to enhance its perfume.

5 If the rice on top is dry at the end of cooking, sprinkle with a little warm water and cover with a piece of banana leaf or greaseproof paper. Return to a low heat for a few minutes, and the top rice should be cooked and moist.

GENG GUWA PLA DTAENG COCONUT AND TURMERIC CURRY OF RED SNAPPER

Most southern curries are rich with coconut cream and this curry should be hot, salty and a little tart. It is important that the cream does not separate but forms a suave emulsion with the paste. Naturally, almost any seafood can be used in place of the snapper. I find crab is an especially good alternative. Serve with slices of cucumber, sprigs of mint and coriander, grilled prawns and rice.

serves 4

salty and sour

500ml (16fl oz) coconut milk (p241)

250ml (9fl oz) light chicken stock or water

2 stalks lemongrass, bruised

white sugar

4 tbsp tamarind water (p355)

4 tbsp fish sauce, or to taste

200g (7oz) red snapper fillet or 400g (14oz) whole red snapper, gutted and scaled

handful of torn 'betel' leaves (optional)

120ml (4fl oz) coconut cream (p241)

5 kaffir lime leaves, finely shredded

Curry paste

6 dried long red chillies, soaked and chopped

3–4 dried small red chillies

pinch of salt

a few bird's eye chillies

50g (1³/₄oz) chopped lemongrass

4 tbsp chopped red shallots

2¹/₂ tbsp chopped garlic

1 rounded tbsp chopped red turmeric

1 rounded tbsp Thai shrimp paste

1 First make the curry paste (p242).

2 Combine the coconut milk with the stock in a saucepan, add the lemongrass and bring to the boil. Season with a little sugar, the tamarind water and fish sauce and add 4 tbsp curry paste. Simmer for a minute before adding the fish and 'betel' leaves. Continue to simmer until the fish is cooked.

3 Check the seasoning, then finish by stirring in the coconut cream. Serve sprinkled with the shredded kaffir lime leaves.

GENG SOM PLAA LING MAA SOUR ORANGE CURRY OF BRILL AND ASIAN GREENS

This is perhaps the most common of all Thai curries – certainly in the central plains. In every marketplace you will see pots of prepared boiled curries made with all manner of ingredients. It is extremely versatile: almost any seafood or freshwater fish can be used and many alternative vegetables can be added, such as Siamese watercress, *cha-om* or spring onions. Traditionally it is served with pickled ginger, salted beef, steamed eggs and, of course, rice.

serves 4

thin, salty, sour and hot

500ml (16fl oz) light chicken stock or water

pinch of salt

250g (9oz) brill, turbot, sea bass, barramundi or whiting fillets, cut into elegant lozenges (keep the trimmings)

1 bunch of *choy sum* or other Asian greens, trimmed into 3cm (1¼in) lengths

2½–4 tbsp tamarind water (p355), as needed and to taste

pinch of white sugar (optional)

2½ tbsp fish sauce, or more to taste

pinch of chilli powder (optional)

a few deep-fried or roasted, dried small or long red chillies (optional)

Sour orange curry paste

3–4 dried long red chillies, soaked and chopped

2–3 dried small red chillies (optional)

1–2 bird's eye chillies (optional)

pinch of salt

4 tbsp chopped red shallots

2 tsp chopped coriander root

1 rounded tbsp Thai shrimp paste

1 First make the curry paste (p242).

2 Bring the chicken stock and salt to the boil over a moderate heat. Reduce the heat to low, add some of the fish trimmings and poach for 5 minutes. Remove with a slotted spoon, draining well, and allow to cool, then pound to a fine paste in a mortar and pestle. Keep the poaching liquid.

3 Combine 1 heaped tbsp of the pounded fish paste with 2½ tbsp of the curry paste.

4 Strain the stock and return to the saucepan. Bring back to the boil, then add the *choy sum*. Reduce the heat to low and simmer for a few minutes or until quite tender. Season with tamarind water, sugar and fish sauce.

5 Stir in the curry paste mixture, increase the heat to high and boil for a minute or so. Then add the fish to the boiling curry, turn down the heat and poach for 5–6 minutes or until cooked.

6 Add the chilli powder and deep-fried chillies. Check the seasoning and adjust as required, then serve.

< Choy sum
A member of the cabbage family, these flowering greens add a mild mustard-like flavour to curries.

GENG TAEPO RED CURRY OF OYSTER MUSHROOMS AND BEAN CURD

This is a tart, rustic curry from the central plains. Quite often a piece of freshwater fish or cut of pork is simmered in this curry, but it can be equally enjoyed as a vegetarian curry, as here. Siamese watercress is a vegetable common throughout all of Asia. Sometimes it is referred to invitingly as morning glory, less happily as swamp cress or in Chinese as *ong choi*. But whatever its appellation, this soft green vegetable with its long crunchy stalks and spear-like leaves is a perennial favourite.

serves 4

sour, salty, hot and sweet

120ml (4fl oz) cracked coconut cream (p241)

1 rounded tbsp palm sugar

pinch of salt

2 tsp light soy sauce

about 2$\frac{1}{2}$ tbsp tamarind water (p355)

500ml (16fl oz) coconut milk (p241)

200g (7oz) oyster mushrooms

1 small cake soft bean curd (tofu), about 220g (7$\frac{1}{2}$oz)

100g (3$\frac{1}{2}$oz) Siamese watercress, cut into 3cm (1$\frac{1}{4}$in) lengths

7 kaffir lime leaves

2 small kaffir limes, cut in half and deseeded)

Red curry paste

5-10 large dried chillies, deseeded, soaked and chopped

pinch of salt

4 tbsp chopped lemongrass

6 slices galangal

2$\frac{1}{2}$ tbsp chopped wild ginger

1 rounded tbsp chopped coriander root

2$\frac{1}{2}$ tbsp chopped red shallots

2$\frac{1}{2}$ tbsp chopped garlic

1 tsp toasted coriander seeds

1 First make the curry paste (p242).

2 Simmer 2$\frac{1}{2}$ tbsp of the curry paste in the cracked coconut cream until fragrant. Season with the palm sugar, salt, soy sauce and tamarind water. Add the coconut milk and, when it has come to the boil, add the mushrooms, bean curd, watercress and kaffir lime leaves.

3 Squeeze the kaffir limes and add them and their juice. Simmer until the mushrooms and watercress are cooked. Check the seasoning and adjust accordingly, then serve.

Oyster mushrooms >

These mushrooms have a mild flavour with a hint of anise and add a rich texture to curries. Use them young, because they become tough and pungent with age.

BPUU PAT PONG GAREE CRAB STIR-FRIED WITH CURRY POWDER

Although not technically a curry, this easy street dish is eaten throughout the country and I thought its inclusion was justified by the use of curry powder. Most Thai cooks would use a prepared curry powder and, I must confess, it is one of the few instances where store-bought is better than home-made. While crab is the most common version of this dish, on the streets and along the beaches, prawns, squid and sea bass are also used. Serve with rice and, perhaps, a grilled fish or some stir-fried Chinese broccoli with oyster sauce.

serves 4

aromatic, rich and salty

1 crab, about 1kg (2¼lb)

1 egg, lightly beaten

2 garlic cloves, peeled

equivalent amount peeled fresh root ginger

pinch of salt

400ml (14fl oz) cracked coconut cream (p241)

4 tbsp curry powder

4 tsp fish sauce

smallest pinch of white sugar

4 tsp rice vinegar

125ml (4fl oz) coconut cream (p241)

125ml (4fl oz) coconut milk (p241)

1 small bunch of Asian celery, cleaned and cut into 2cm (¾in) lengths, about 30g (1oz)

½ small white onion, sliced

handful of chopped coriander leaves

1 Kill the crab humanely (drowning in fresh water is probably the best, least stressful way for the beast). Clean by lifting off its carapace, scraping out but retaining any mustard and roe, and removing its tail and the 'dead man's fingers'. Rinse, then segment the crab into about 8 pieces, cracking the claws. Mix the mustard and roe with the beaten egg.

2 Using a pestle and mortar, pound the garlic, ginger and salt into a rather coarse paste. Heat a wok, add the cracked coconut cream and, when sizzling, add the paste.

3 As the paste mixture is just beginning to colour, add the crab and fry for a few moments over a moderate heat. Sprinkle in the curry powder. Continue to fry for a few more moments, stirring constantly. When fragrant, season with the fish sauce, sugar and vinegar.

4 Enrich with the fresh, uncracked coconut cream and moisten with the coconut milk, stirring well to mix. Cover the wok and simmer until the crab is cooked, tossing and stirring the pieces of crab regularly to ensure that they cook evenly.

5 Remove the lid and turn up the heat, then stir in the egg and roe mixture. Stir until the egg has thickened and begun to separate.

6 Check the seasoning. Mix in the celery and sliced onion, then sprinkle with coriander and serve.

GENG LAO UBON RACHTANI
NORTHEASTERN CURRY OF PORK RIBS AND MUSTARD GREENS

This curry comes from the northeast of the country. The dominant tastes are of *pla raa* (fermented fish), peppery mustard greens, the sweetness of the pork and dill. Dill is quite a common culinary herb in this region, where it is called *pak chii lao* (Laotian parsley). The curry can be either very hot or mild, according to the cook's preference. Normally, however, it is searingly hot. The northeast is a poor area, and most food is pungently seasoned, because a meal consists mainly of rice with just a little curry mixed into it. There are many alternatives to pork. Since this is such a pungent curry, the choices should also be pungent. A rich freshwater fish like carp is ideal, or an eel. Duck or chicken chopped on the bone with their offal is another option. Rather than making fermented fish sauce (below) ordinary fish sauce can be used. However, much of the character of this curry would be lost and it would become indistinguishable from its central plains' equivalents.

serves 4

hot, salty and aromatic

2½ tbsp pork fat or oil, less if using pork belly

150g (5½oz) boned pork belly or ribs, sliced

500ml (16fl oz) light chicken or pork stock or water

5 tbsp Nahm Pla Raa (below)

100g (3½oz) picked pea aubergines

200g (7oz) mustard greens, shredded

20g (¾oz) dill, coarsely chopped

Northeastern curry paste

10–15 dried red chillies, soaked and chopped

a few small dried red chillies

½ tsp salt

1 rounded tbsp chopped galangal

1 rounded tbsp chopped lemongrass

1 rounded tbsp chopped red shallots

1 rounded tbsp chopped garlic

1 First make the curry paste (p242).

2 Heat the fat or oil in a heavy pan or wok. Add 2½ tbsp of the curry paste and cook until fragrant. Add the pork and continue to fry over a moderate heat for several minutes as the pork begins to cook and the paste deepens in colour. Moisten, if necessary, with a little stock to prevent the paste from catching and burning.

3 Season with the *nahm pla raa* and cover with the remaining stock. Simmer gently until the pork is tender. Replenish with more stock should the curry become too dry during the cooking.

4 When the meat has cooked sufficiently, add the aubergines and mustard greens and simmer for a further 10 minutes or so, or until the vegetables are cooked. Finish with the dill.

5 Check the seasoning and adjust as preferred, then serve.

NAHM PLA RAA FERMENTED FISH SAUCE

makes about 500ml (16fl oz)

3 stalks lemongrass

5 red shallots

3 coriander roots, or a handful of coriander stalks

200g (7oz) fermented fish (*pla raa*)

1 whole kaffir lime, or several kaffir lime leaves

10 slices galangal

1 Bruise the lemongrass, shallots and coriander. Combine all the ingredients in a pot and cover with 500ml (16fl oz) water. Bring to the boil, then simmer for at least 10 minutes or until the fish has completely dissolved.

2 Strain and set aside to cool. Refrigerated, the sauce keeps indefinitely. Store in an airtight container.

GENG BPAA GAI JUNGLE CURRY OF CHICKEN WITH VEGETABLES AND PEPPERCORNS

A jungle curry is a country curry that is simple and robust in flavour and technique. Coconut cream is never used but either a green or a red curry paste can be its base. This version is perhaps the most common; however, there are many variations, using frog, game, freshwater fish and prawns as well as a myriad of vegetables reflecting the bounty of the local market. It can be served with pickled red shallots and dried fish or prawns.

serves 4

hot and salty

200g (7oz) boneless chicken thigh or breast, skinned if preferred

2 apple aubergines

1½ tbsp vegetable oil

2½ tbsp fish sauce

250-300ml (9-10fl oz) light chicken stock

2 heaped tbsp picked pea aubergines

2 heaped tbsp snake beans cut into 2cm (¾in) lengths

3 baby corn, cut into small pieces

a little sliced boiled bamboo (optional)

3 stalks wild ginger, julienned

1 long green chilli, thinly sliced at an angle

2 kaffir lime leaves, torn

handful of holy basil leaves

3 sprigs of fresh green peppercorns

Red jungle curry paste

10 dried red chillies, deseeded, soaked and chopped

3-4 dried small red chillies, soaked and chopped

a few bird's eye chillies (optional)

good pinch of salt

2 tsp chopped galangal

2½ tbsp chopped lemongrass

1 rounded tbsp chopped wild ginger

1 tsp chopped coriander root

1 tsp chopped kaffir lime zest

2½ tbsp chopped red shallots

2½ tbsp chopped garlic cloves

1 tsp Thai shrimp paste

Garlic and chilli paste

2 garlic cloves, peeled

pinch of salt

3 stalks wild ginger

3-5 bird's eye chillies

1 Slice the chicken into pieces about 2cm (¾in) long and 5mm (¼in) thick. Remove the stalks from the apple aubergines, then cut each one into sixths; keep in salted water to prevent discolouration.

2 Next make the curry paste (p242). To make the garlic and chilli paste, grind all the ingredients with a mortar and pestle. Heat the oil in a wok or heavy saucepan and, when very hot, add the garlic and chilli paste. Fry over a high heat until golden and almost starting to burn. Quickly add 2½ tbsp of the curry paste and continue to fry, stirring to prevent scorching, until explosively fragrant.

3 Season with the fish sauce, then add the stock and bring to the boil. Add the chicken and all the aubergines. Simmer for a minute or so or until cooked.

4 Add the remaining ingredients. Simmer for a few more moments. Check the seasoning, then serve.

KRUA GLING NEUA SOUTHERN CURRY OF CHOPPED BEEF

This is quite possibly the hottest curry of them all – certainly in Thailand. It comes from the southern area around the ancient city of Nakorn Siri Thammarat. Although pork or chicken could be used, the most popular version is made with beef. Having a little of the fat attached prevents the meat from becoming too dry when cooking. However, this curry is not oily – it is in fact very dry, and it looks deceptively mild. As with most pungent curries from the south, a plate of raw vegetables and herbs makes a welcome and cooling accompaniment. In Thailand local herbs such as mango shoots and cashew nut sprouts are eaten with it, but cucumber, snake beans and apple aubergines are perhaps more likely candidates to soothe the palate of Western cooks.

serves 4

dry, very hot and salty

300g (10oz) boned beef brisket and blade with some fat attached

500ml (16fl oz) light chicken stock or water

pinch of salt

4 tbsp vegetable oil

1½–2½ tbsp fish sauce

palm sugar, to taste

5 kaffir lime leaves, shredded

Curry paste

35g (1¼oz) dried small red chillies

20 bird's eye chillies

pinch of salt

60g (2oz) sliced lemongrass

2½ tbsp chopped galangal

2 tsp chopped kaffir lime zest

90g (3oz) peeled red shallots

90g (3oz) peeled garlic cloves

1 tsp chopped red turmeric

1 rounded tbsp mixed white and black peppercorns, ground

1 rounded tbsp Thai shrimp paste

1 First make the curry paste (p242).

2 Trim the beef and cut into roughly 5mm (¼in) pieces. Add to the stock with the salt and bring to the boil, then simmer until cooked. Drain the beef, reserving the braising stock.

3 Heat the oil and fry the curry paste for 5 minutes or until fragrant. Add the beef and continue frying for 10–15 minutes or until it is quite dry. The curry can be moistened with a little of the braising stock during frying, but it must be simmered until dry again.

4 Season with fish sauce and a little palm sugar. Serve sprinkled with the kaffir lime leaves.

GENG PANAENG NEUA RED CURRY OF BEEF WiTH PEANUTS

A *panaeng* curry is rich and thick, redolent of peanuts, cumin and nutmeg. A firm favourite in the Thai repertoire, its origins are in the Muslim community, probably from the south. Beef is the most common meat used in this style of curry and with beef, nutmeg and plenty of it must also be used. However, chicken or prawns are common alternatives and long, green aubergines can be used for a vegetarian option. The curry paste must be cooked for at least 10 minutes to ensure that it is mellow and well balanced before seasoning it. Some regions prefer a decidedly sweeter version of this curry, which can be shocking to the Western palate. While this version uses some sugar and is sweet, it is not unsettlingly so. Add only half the amount of sugar called for and taste, then add as much of the remaining sugar as preferred. Serve with steamed rice, naturally. Some pickled ginger or shallots would be nice too, and as an accompanying dish perhaps steamed fish or scallops.

serves 4

rich, salty, spicy and a little sweet

300g (10oz) boned beef shank, shin or flank, trimmed

about 1 litre (1¾ pints) coconut milk (p241) or stock

1 pandanus leaf (optional)

2–3 Thai bay or cardamom leaves (optional)

Thai basil stalks (optional)

salt

Panaeng curry paste

6–12 dried long red chillies, deseeded, soaked and chopped

1 rounded tbsp chopped galangal

2½ tbsp chopped lemongrass

1 tsp chopped kaffir lime zest

1 tsp chopped coriander root

2½ tbsp chopped red shallots

4 tbsp chopped garlic

1 tsp Thai shrimp paste

2 tsp coriander seeds, roasted

1½ tsp cumin seeds, roasted

good pinch of freshly ground white pepper

1 tsp freshly grated nutmeg

2½ tbsp roasted peanuts

Curry

120ml (4fl oz) cracked coconut cream (p241)

good pinch of freshly grated nutmeg

2–3 tbsp palm sugar, to taste

3–4 tbsp fish sauce, to taste

150ml (5fl oz) coconut milk (p241)

chilli powder (optional)

2 kaffir lime leaves, torn

2 long red or green chillies, thinly sliced at an elegant angle and deseeded

good handful of Thai basil leaves

1 For the braised beef, put the meat in a pan of cold salted water and bring to the boil, then drain and rinse. Put the coconut milk in a large pan and bring to the boil. Add the beef with the optional pandanus leaf, cardamom leaves and basil stalks, and salt to taste. Braise over a low heat for about 1 hour or until the beef is tender. Replenish with additional coconut milk, if necessary. While the beef is simmering, make the curry paste (p242).

2 Once sufficiently cooked, remove the beef from the liquid and allow to cool. Keep the braising liquid to moisten the curry paste. Trim off excess fat and sinew, then slice the beef into elegant pieces across the grain, about 1.5cm (⅝in) in size and 5mm (¼in) thick.

3 To make the curry, heat the cracked coconut cream over a moderate heat, then add 4 tbsp of the curry paste and the grated nutmeg. Cook for at least 10 minutes, stirring often to prevent it from catching. Season with the palm sugar and then, after a minute or so, the fish sauce.

4 Moisten with the coconut milk (some of the beef braising liquid can be used too, but do not just use this, as it makes the curry very meaty). Add the coconut milk a bit at a time and allow it to evaporate while simmering for no less than 5 minutes. Within reason, the longer the better, as this not only gives depth to the curry, ensuring the paste is completely cooked and mellow, but encourages a good separation – a defining characteristic of this curry. It may be necessary to add a little chilli powder and a pinch more grated nutmeg, to ensure that the curry is sufficiently spicy.

5 Add the beef. Continue to simmer for several minutes, then finish with the remaining ingredients.

GENG SAPPARROT HOI MALAENG PUU PiNEAPPLE CURRY OF MUSSELS

This curry comes from Phetchburi, a prosperous trading province to the southwest of Bangkok. The most traditional version uses the roe of the helmet crab, a sinister-looking beast with very firm, almost chalky eggs. Prawns, clams, mussels, pork or chicken can very easily be used as more available alternatives. Some cooks like to take the mussels out of the shell and cook them directly in the curry. It is served with steamed rice, as well as, perhaps, steamed salted duck eggs, salted beef or pork. If the pineapple is either too green and tart or too sweet, wash it briefly in salted water to reduce its pungency.

serves 4

salty, smoky, sweet and sour

120ml (4fl oz) cracked coconut cream (p241)

2–2¹/₂ tbsp palm sugar, to taste

2¹/₂ tbsp fish sauce

2–2¹/₂ tbsp tamarind water (p355)

500ml (16fl oz) coconut milk (p241)

300g (10oz) finely chopped pineapple

300g (10oz) mussels, scrubbed and debearded

3 kaffir lime leaves, torn

1 long red or green chilli, deseeded if preferred and thinly sliced at an elegant angle

Curry paste

10 large dried red chillies, soaked and chopped

3 heaped tbsp red bird's eye chillies

pinch of salt

2¹/₂ tbsp chopped galangal

5 tbsp chopped lemongrass

2 tsp finely chopped kaffir lime zest

1 tsp chopped coriander root

5 tbsp chopped garlic

2¹/₂ tbsp chopped red shallots

1 rounded tbsp Thai shrimp paste

1 First make the curry paste (p242).

2 Heat the cracked coconut cream over a moderate heat, add 4 tbsp of the curry paste and fry until it is fragrant and redolent of the fish in the paste. This can take as long as 10 minutes, much longer than a normal red curry.

3 Season with the palm sugar and fish sauce (not too much as the mussels will add their own salt) and then the tamarind water. Do not fry the paste for more than a minute or so after adding the tamarind water, otherwise it will develop a somewhat scorched taste.

4 Moisten with the coconut milk, then add the pineapple and the mussels. Simmer until the shells have opened, stirring regularly. (Discard any mussels that remain closed.)

5 Finish with the lime leaves and chilli. Check the seasoning and adjust accordingly, then serve.

NGOB PLA DTAA DTIAW GRILLED HALIBUT CURRY

This is a refined, restaurant version of a homely market-style curry. Cook the curry paste in plenty of cracked coconut cream to ensure the fish does not dry out as it cooks. The addition of freshly grated coconut gives body and substance to the curry. Almost any fish can be used, as can any shellfish. To accompany, this doesn't need much more than steamed rice, although it is nice with a soup, salad and so on. Once the curry is cooked, seasoned and wrapped, grill or barbecue it gently and slowly, charring the banana leaves. They impart a pleasing bitterness to the curry and help give it an inviting crust.

serves 4

rich, nutty, hot and salty

1-2 large banana leaves

250ml (9fl oz) cracked coconut cream (p241)

70g (2¼oz) Thai basil leaves

6-10 kaffir lime leaves, finely shredded

250ml (9fl oz) coconut cream (p241)

4 skinned halibut fillets, each weighing 180g (6oz)

Red curry paste

6-10 dried red chillies, soaked and chopped

a few bird's eye chillies

pinch of salt

4 tbsp chopped garlic

5 tbsp chopped red shallots

4 tbsp chopped lemongrass

1 rounded tbsp chopped galangal

1 tsp chopped kaffir lime zest

1 tsp chopped coriander root

1 tsp Thai shrimp paste

good pinch of freshly ground white peppercorns

good pinch of freshly ground mace (optional)

Coconut mixture

120ml (4fl oz) cracked coconut cream (p241)

2½ tbsp palm sugar

4 tbsp fish sauce, or to taste

100g (3½oz) freshly grated coconut

120ml (4fl oz) coconut cream (p241)

1 First make the curry paste (p242).

2 To make the coconut mixture, simmer 5 tbsp of the curry paste in the cracked coconut cream over a moderate heat until fragrant, then season with the palm sugar and fish sauce.

3 Add the grated coconut and continue to simmer, adding some fresh coconut cream and/or water to moisten as required. The water will ensure that the grated coconut is completely cooked and that the mixture is sufficiently oily.

4 Simmer until the additional water has evaporated and the mixture is indeed oily. (The coconut mixture can be made in advance; if refrigerated, it lasts for a few days. When reheating, add a little water and simmer until quite dry and oily once more.)

5 Trim the hard ribbed edge from the banana leaf and discard any yellowed parts. Cut the leaf into 8 pieces, the first 4 about 14cm (6in) wide and the remaining 4 about 20cm (8in) wide. Wipe clean both sides of the cut pieces. Place each of the smaller pieces on top of a larger one, shiny sides facing outwards.

6 Along half of each of the inner banana leaves, smear a little cracked coconut cream, then sprinkle on a few basil leaves. Spread on a layer of the coconut mixture before repeating alternate layers of small amounts of Thai basil, kaffir lime leaves and fresh, uncracked coconut cream. Place the fish on top, then repeat the layering but in reverse.

7 Fold the inner banana leaf over to cover the filling, then wrap the outer banana leaf around this parcel quite tightly. Secure with wooden cocktail sticks, at least 3 per parcel.

8 Barbecue or grill the parcels, turning occasionally, for up to 30 minutes, depending on the degree of heat. The outer leaves should char; the inner leaves are used for serving.

HOR MOK HOI SHENN STEAMED SCALLOP CURRY

Mussels, clams, prawns and almost any fish, either saltwater or fresh, are happy alternatives to the scallops in this curry. Traditionally, the coconut cream is stirred in gradually, in one direction, to ensure that the cream does not separate during the cooking. I am not sure whether it is important to stir in one direction, but the cream should be added slowly. It is also imperative to have the cream at room temperature. If it is too cold it will not bind with the fish. It must be coconut cream, too – if the thinner milk is used it will introduce too much water and the mixture will be bound to separate and appear curdled. Some versions of this curry omit the fish purée and instead base it on a combination of fresh coconut cream, curry paste and eggs. This makes a rich but very loose custard that requires gentle steaming. Once the mixture is made, it is normally steamed in a container fashioned from banana leaves. Sometimes a green coconut is used as the container. I've used scallop shells here. Serve with rice, as part of a meal.

serves 4

rich, salty and slightly hot

50g (1³⁄₄oz) filleted white fish, such as turbot or sea bass

120ml (4fl oz) coconut cream (p241), cool but not too cold

1¹⁄₂–3 tbsp fish sauce

pinch of white sugar (optional)

1 small egg

5 kaffir lime leaves, very finely shredded

4 medium to large scallops, without the coral, each cut into 3 slices

4 scallop shells, boiled in heavily salted water for several minutes to clean

handful of Thai basil leaves

1 'bai yor' leaf, very finely shredded (optional)

a few pieces of red chilli julienne

a few coriander leaves

Red curry paste

6-8 dried red chillies, soaked and chopped

pinch of salt

2¹⁄₂ tbsp chopped garlic

4 tbsp chopped red shallots

4 tbsp chopped lemongrass

1 rounded tbsp chopped galangal

1 tsp chopped kaffir lime zest

1 tsp chopped coriander root

2 tsp Thai shrimp paste

good pinch of freshly ground white peppercorns

Thickened coconut cream

good pinch of rice flour

5 tbsp coconut cream (p241)

pinch of salt (optional)

1 First make the curry paste (p242).

2 Purée the fish in a blender, then pass through a sieve. Combine 4 tbsp of the curry paste with the fish purée. Work in the coconut cream, adding it gradually while stirring gently – and in the same direction – to ensure that the cream is thoroughly incorporated. Season the 'mousse' with fish sauce and sugar. Finish with the egg. The mixture should have a rather sticky texture and silken sheen, and taste salty and slightly hot. Stir in most of the shredded kaffir lime leaves (reserve some for garnish) and the scallops.

3 Generously line the prepared scallop shells with the Thai basil and then the optional *bai yor*. Spoon in the scallop curry mixture. Steam in a Chinese steamer over a gentle heat for about 15 minutes. When the 'mousse' is slightly firm, it is cooked. Be careful not to overcook or it will split.

4 Meanwhile, make the thickened coconut cream. Mix the rice flour with 1 tbsp of the coconut cream to make a slurry. Bring the remainder of the coconut cream up to the boil, then stir in the rice flour mixture to thicken. Season with salt, if liked. Pass the thickened cream through a fine sieve to remove any lumps, if necessary.

5 Spoon the thickened coconut cream over the curry and garnish with the reserved kaffir lime leaves, the red chilli and coriander leaves.

GENG GWIO WARN YORD MAPRAO GREEN CURRY OF HEART OF COCONUT

Green curries lend themselves to many variations. Given the Thai manner of eating, they usually include a meat, bird or fish. But there is a strong tradition of vegetarianism in this Buddhist country and at some time all Thais refrain from meat, whether it be to commemorate a solemn occasion, or more regularly, say, once a week or throughout a whole month. Heart of coconut is an ideal vegetable for a curry. Its toothsome crunch offers a wonderful textural contrast. However, this is not a common vegetable to be found, so baby corn, Asian aubergines of any type or even pumpkin can make a happy alternative. Make sure that the curry itself includes plenty of Thai basil to round out the flavours and at the end of cooking has a little coconut oil dappling its surface.

serves 4

thin, hot and salty

5 tbsp cracked coconut cream (p241)

150g (5^1/$_2$oz) elegantly cut heart of coconut

4–5 baby corn, each cut in half lengthways

2^1/$_2$ tbsp fish sauce, or to taste

500ml (16fl oz) coconut milk (p241)

a few picked pea aubergines (optional)

3 kaffir lime leaves, torn

3 young green chillies, deseeded and thinly sliced at an elegant angle

handful of Thai basil leaves

Green curry paste

1 heaped tbsp bird's eye chillies

1 long green chilli, deseeded

pinch of salt

1 rounded tbsp chopped galangal

2^1/$_2$ tbsp chopped lemongrass

1 tsp chopped kaffir lime zest

1 tsp chopped coriander root

1 tsp chopped red turmeric

2^1/$_2$ tbsp chopped red shallots

2 tbsp chopped garlic

1 tsp yellow beans

good pinch of finely ground white peppercorns

1 First make the curry paste (p242).

2 Heat the cracked coconut cream, add 4 tbsp of the curry paste and fry over a high heat for 5 minutes, stirring regularly. During this time, add the heart of coconut and the corn. Fry until the paste looks scrambled and smells cooked, then season with fish sauce.

3 Moisten with the coconut milk. Bring to the boil and add the remaining ingredients. Check the seasoning and adjust if necessary, then serve.

GENG GWIO WARN GUNG GREEN CURRY OF PRAWNS WITH AUBERGINES AND BASIL

This is quite a thin curry, commonly served with spiced salted beef. Kaffir lime leaves, fresh long chillies and Thai basil are essential garnishes, to give the dish its characteristic savour. Various aubergines are common but not always used. Sometimes breadfruit, corn or heart of coconut are included. Tradition dictates that the prawns be added to the frying curry paste, but I feel that this can lead to such quick-cooking items being overcooked, as they then continue simmering after the coconut milk is added. I think it is better – and safer – to add the prawns once the curry is made, when adding the vegetables. Almost any meat or fish can be used in place of the prawns; if more resilient, the meat or fish can be fried with the paste.

serves 4

thin, salty and hot

5 tbsp cracked coconut cream (p241)

2¹/₂ tbsp Kreaung Geng Geng Gwio Warn (p242)

1¹/₂–3 tbsp fish sauce, to taste

250ml (9fl oz) coconut milk (p241) and/or chicken or prawn stock

3 apple aubergines, stalk removed and each cut into sixths (if cut in advance, keep in salted water to prevent discoloration)

100g (3¹/₂oz) picked pea aubergines

8–12 good quality large, raw prawns, cleaned and deveined

3–4 kaffir lime leaves, torn

3 young green chillies, deseeded and thinly sliced at an elegant angle

handful of Thai basil leaves

1 rounded tbsp shredded wild ginger

1 Heat the cracked coconut cream, add the *kreaung* (curry paste) and fry over a high heat for about 5 minutes, stirring regularly, until fragrant. Make sure the paste is quite oily.

2 Season with fish sauce, then moisten with the coconut milk or stock, or a mixture of the two. Bring to the boil, then add the apple and pea aubergines. Simmer for a few minutes to cook before adding the prawns. Continue to simmer until they too are cooked.

3 Finish with the remaining ingredients, then allow to rest for a minute or so before serving. The curry should have a dappling of separated coconut cream floating on top.

GENG GARI FAK TONG AROMATIC CURRY OF PUMPKIN

The curry paste recipe here is from a very old cookbook written by Thanpuying Pliang Pasonagorn, a noble cook from the late 19th century. The light and delicate spicing makes it perfect for a vegetarian curry. While pumpkin is a good standard, almost any root vegetable, such as potatoes (sweet or regular), mooli or taro, are good alternatives. Serve with the cucumber relish on the opposite page. This cuts through the coconut cream to reveal the various spices, and so the aromatic curry is immeasurably improved.

serves 4

salty and aromatic

1 litre (1³/₄ pints) coconut milk (p241)

pinch of salt

200g (7oz) peeled pumpkin flesh, cut into bite-size chunks

120ml (4fl oz) cracked coconut cream (p241)

1 rounded tbsp palm sugar

4 tbsp light soy sauce

4 red shallots, sliced and deep-fried (p239)

Ajad Dtaeng Gwa (p276), to serve

Aromatic curry paste

4–5 dried long red chillies, deseeded, soaked and chopped

large pinch of salt

2¹/₂ tbsp chopped lemongrass

1 rounded tbsp chopped galangal

1 rounded tbsp chopped red turmeric

2 tsp chopped coriander root

4 tbsp chopped red shallots

4 tbsp chopped garlic

2¹/₂ tbsp roasted, ground and sieved Thai coriander seeds (p354)

1 rounded tbsp ground white pepper

1 First make the curry paste (p242).

2 Put the coconut milk in a medium-sized saucepan, add the salt and bring to the boil. (I like to mix in a little water, which helps to prevent the coconut milk from splitting as the pumpkin cooks.) Add the prepared pumpkin and simmer gently over a moderate heat for about 10 minutes or until tender. Drain, reserving the cooking liquid, and set aside.

3 Heat the cracked coconut cream in a small pan, add 4 tbsp of the curry paste and fry over a moderate heat for about 5 minutes or until it is quite fragrant. Stir regularly to prevent the paste from scorching. Season with the palm sugar and soy sauce.

4 Moisten with 250ml (9fl oz) of the pumpkin stock, then add the pumpkin and reheat if necessary. Check the seasoning and adjust accordingly. Serve sprinkled with the deep-fried shallots and accompany with the cucumber relish.

AJAD DTAENG GWA CUCUMBER RELiSH

This subtle pickle is a popular accompaniment to many dishes as its sweet and sour taste counterbalances any richness and oiliness that is so often a part of a Thai meal.

serves 4

5 tbsp white vinegar

1 rounded tbsp white sugar

1-2 coriander roots

1 small head pickled garlic and 1 tbsp or so of its liquid (optional)

pinch of salt

$\frac{1}{2}$ small cucumber, quartered lengthways and sliced across

1 red shallot, finely sliced

1 rounded tbsp julienned fresh root ginger

a few thin rounds of small, long red chilli

pinch of coriander leaves

1 Combine the vinegar, sugar, $6\frac{1}{2}$ tbsp water, the coriander root, pickled garlic and its liquid, and salt in a small saucepan and bring to the boil. Remove from the heat when the sugar dissolves. Cool, then strain. The liquid should taste sour, sweet and a little salty, but not be too concentrated.

2 Mix together the remaining ingredients in the serving bowl and pour over the vinegar mixture.

< Pickling cucumbers
This cucumber variety can also be used to prepare the above relish. As the name suggests, these are perfect for pickling as they retain their fresh and crunchy texture.

GENG GARI GAI AROMATIC CURRY OF CHICKEN AND POTATOES

This gentle curry of Muslim origin is one of the most popular in the Thai repertoire, and its agreeable spiciness makes it a favourite with Westerners too. The distinguishing characteristic that defines a *gari* curry is the use of spices. Very often it is a ground spice mix purchased from the market or medicine shops but this old recipe is more specific. Beef or chicken are normally used, with a starchy root vegetable. *Gari* curries are always served with a cucumber relish.

serves 4

rich, salty and a little spicy

2 chicken legs, about 500g (1lb 2oz) in total

750ml (1¼ pints) coconut milk (p241)

pinch of salt

3–4 waxy potatoes, peeled and quartered

120ml (4fl oz) cracked coconut cream (p241)

1 rounded tbsp palm sugar

2½ tbsp fish sauce, or to taste

4cm (1½in) piece cassia, roasted

pinch of ground white pepper

pinch of chilli powder

1 generous tbsp coconut cream (p241)

4 red shallots, sliced and deep fried (p239)

Ajad Dtaeng Gwa (see opposite), to serve

Aromatic curry paste

3–4 dried red chillies, deseeded, soaked and chopped

pinch of salt

2½ tbsp chopped grilled red shallots

2½ tbsp chopped grilled garlic

1 rounded tbsp chopped galangal

2 tbsp chopped lemongrass

1 tsp chopped coriander root

1 tsp chopped red turmeric

seeds from 3–4 roasted Thai cardamom pods

pinch of white peppercorns, roasted

½ tsp coriander seeds, roasted

½ tsp cumin seeds, roasted

good pinch of fennel seeds, roasted

4–5 cloves, roasted

2 blades mace, roasted

1 First make the curry paste (p242).

2 Segment the chicken legs into thighs and drumsticks or cut into thirds. Trim off excess fat. Heat the coconut milk with the salt. Add the chicken and poach for about 30 minutes or until cooked.

3 Rinse the potatoes in cold running water for a few minutes to remove any excess starch, then cook in boiling salted water, or some of the chicken poaching stock, until cooked but still firm. Drain.

4 Meanwhile, heat the cracked coconut cream, add 5 tbsp of the curry paste and fry for at least 5 minutes or until fragrant with the spices. Season with the palm sugar and fish sauce. Moisten with the chicken poaching liquid, adding it ladle by ladle, until a medium-thick curry is achieved. Add the chicken and potatoes. Finish with the roasted cassia, ideally still smoking.

5 Check the seasoning: often a pinch each of white pepper and chilli powder will improve the taste. Spoon over the coconut cream, sprinkle with the deep-fried shallots and serve, with the relish.

GENG HANG LAE MUU CHIANG MAI PORK CURRY

There are many variations of this northern curry, which comes originally from Myanmar. Some versions are quite salty with little spice and no sugar. However, this curry, from Chiang Mai, is rich and spicy and sweetened by the pickled garlic and its syrup. Although chicken or beef could be used, pork is the most common meat. Most traditional recipes use both a fatty and a lean cut of pork.

serves 4

salty, aromatic and fatty

200g (7oz) boned pork belly

200g (7oz) pork ribs

4 tbsp vegetable oil

16 or so red shallots, peeled

250g (9oz) fresh root ginger, coarsely shredded

190g (scant 7oz) pickled garlic, peeled and heads cut in half

250ml (9fl oz) pickled garlic syrup

75g (2½oz) roasted peanuts (optional)

1½–3 tbsp palm sugar, to taste

5 tbsp fish sauce

5 tbsp tamarind water (p355)

stock or water

Chiang mai curry paste

10 dried long red chillies, deseeded, soaked and chopped

large pinch of salt

1 rounded tbsp chopped galangal

8 tbsp chopped lemongrass

2½ tbsp chopped fresh root ginger

1 rounded tbsp chopped red turmeric

10½ tbsp chopped red shallots

8 tbsp chopped garlic

1 rounded tbsp coriander seeds, roasted

2 tsp cumin seeds, roasted

3 star anise, roasted

2cm (¾in) piece cassia bark, roasted

4 cloves, roasted

seeds from 4 roasted Thai cardamom pods (optional)

1 First make the curry paste (p242).

2 Cut the pork belly and ribs into 2cm (¾in) cubes. I like to blanch the pork before cooking it in the curry paste: cover the meat with cold water and bring to the boil, then drain and rinse. This gives the curry a lighter, less porky taste.

3 Heat the oil in a large, deep-sided frying pan. Add 120ml (4fl oz) of the curry paste and fry until fragrant. Add the pork and simmer for several minutes, stirring regularly to prevent burning.

4 Add the whole shallots, ginger, pickled garlic, garlic syrup and peanuts (if using). Season the curry with palm sugar, fish sauce and tamarind water. Cover with stock or water and bring to the boil, then reduce the heat and simmer for 1 hour or until the pork is tender.

5 The finished curry will be quite oily. That is how it is meant to be. Check seasoning: it should be just a little sweet and sour, and perfumed with ginger and the spices.

GENG MUSSAMAN MUSLIM-STYLE CURRY OF DUCK WITH POTATOES AND ONIONS

This a rich and generously flavoured curry. It is most often made with beef or chicken, but I find duck is an appropriate and delicious variation. As with most Muslim curries, the pieces of meat are considerably larger than in curries of Buddhist origin. The duck, potatoes and onion are deep fried to enrich the curry as well as to prevent them from breaking up during the braising. I like to marinate the meat briefly in a little soy sauce, which gives the duck an inviting mahogany colour. The curry is cooked in a large amount of cracked coconut cream – its oiliness helps to make the complex spicing more unified and mellow – and is finished with fruit juice, normally Asian citron, but you can use puréed and sieved fresh pineapple.

serves 4

salty and aromatic

2 large duck legs or 3–4 duck breasts, about 300g (10oz) in total

4 tsp dark soy sauce

4 potatoes, peeled and cut into elegant pieces

vegetable oil for deep frying

8 small pickling onions or red shallots, peeled

4 tbsp peanuts

500ml (16fl oz) coconut milk (p241)

good pinch of salt

1 piece cassia, 2 x 3cm (³/₄ x 1¹/₄in), roasted

5 or so cardamom pods, roasted

4 Thai cardamom leaves, roasted

500ml (16fl oz) cracked coconut cream (p241)

250–325g (9–11oz) palm sugar, to taste

250ml (9fl oz) tamarind water (p355)

120ml (4fl oz) fish sauce, or to taste

250ml (9fl oz) Asian citron or pineapple juice

Mussaman curry paste

8–12 dried red chillies

5 tbsp coriander seeds

2¹/₂ tbsp cumin seeds

1 rounded tbsp cardamom pods

5 or so cloves

2 pieces cassia

2 star anise

150g (5¹/₂oz) unpeeled shallots

160g (5³/₄oz) unpeeled garlic cloves

60g (2oz) chopped lemongrass

5 tbsp chopped galangal

salt

1 First make the curry paste. Roast the chillies and all the spices, individually, in a wok. Remove the seeds from the cardamom pods, then grind with the other spices. Sieve. Combine all the remaining ingredients and roast them in the wok, with a little water to prevent them from scorching, until brown and fragrant. Allow to cool slightly, then peel the shallots and garlic. Grind the browned fresh aromatics in a pestle and mortar to make a purée, then work in the ground spices.

2 Trim the duck legs of excess fat and skin. Segment the legs. If using breasts, cut them into cubes. Briefly marinate the duck in the soy sauce.

3 Rinse the potatoes in cold running water to remove excess starch. Drain well and dry. Heat vegetable oil in a large wok, then deep fry the potatoes until they are golden. Remove and drain. Deep fry the onions; drain. Then deep fry the duck until it too is golden. Remove and drain. Finally, deep fry the peanuts; drain. Set all of the deep-fried items aside.

4 Season the coconut milk with the salt and bring to the boil in a saucepan. Add the duck, the cassia, cardamom pods and leaves, and deep-fried peanuts. (There should be enough coconut milk to cover the duck.) Simmer until the duck is almost cooked: 10 minutes for breast, 30 minutes for leg. Add the deep-fried potatoes and then, a few minutes later, add the onions. Simmer until everything is just cooked.

5 Meanwhile, in a medium pot, heat the cracked coconut cream and add 500ml (16fl oz) of the curry paste. Reduce the heat and simmer for no less than 10 minutes, stirring regularly to prevent the paste from catching. Be careful, as it may splutter as it fries and it is damned hot. Cook until it is redolent of the spices. If the paste is not oily enough, moisten with some of the fat skimmed off the duck poaching liquid. When the paste is oily, hot and sizzling, season it with palm sugar. Continue to simmer as the sugar dissolves and begins to deepen the colour of the curry.

6 Add the tamarind water and continue to cook, then add the fish sauce. Carefully add the coconut poaching liquid from the duck, followed by the spices, then the potatoes, onions and duck. Simmer for several more minutes, then stir in the juice. Check the seasoning; the curry should be spicy, oily and quite thick. Put to the side for several minutes to allow the flavours to ripen, then serve.

MAINLAND SE ASIA

Cambodia, Laos and Vietnam have had the fortune – good and bad – to be a cultural and military crossroads for centuries. Armies and artisans, conquerors and cooks have traversed the area, making its history one of empire, artistic accomplishment and extraordinary cuisines. Curiously, perhaps, while China's very significant influence in the area can be linked to military dominance, the equally significant Indian influences were never military. The South Asians, it seems, came, traded and cooked, but never fought.Curry is rooted in the spicy cooked-down foods that date back to ancient times, and were recorded in Sumerian and Mesopotamian texts. Scholars generally agree that the word curry has its roots in the Tamil word *kari*, this referring to spices, sauces and stews. 'Curry' itself seems to be an English corruptive form of the Tamil word, first appearing in European references in the late 16th and early 17th centuries.

Curries do not have to be hot, and the spicy mixtures that underlie them can be powders or pastes, or a combination of the two. The powders you buy in shops are primarily turmeric, cumin, coriander and pepper. In general Asian, South Asian and Southeast Asian use, however, the palette is considerably broader, and may include chillies, mustard seed, cinnamon, and black and white peppers for hot notes; cloves, anise, fennel, nutmeg and mace for sweetish notes; and fenugreek, bay leaves, poppy seeds and allspice for expansive flavour notes. In Cambodia, Laos and Vietnam, lemongrass, coriander root and galangal may also appear – these lending uniquely Southeast Asian flavours to the dishes.

The spectrum of flavours and ingredients beyond the spicy basics is tremendous, ranging from pungent vegetables and fresh fish, to richly flavoured fowl, and white and – less often – red meats. What distinguishes Cambodian, Laotian and Vietnamese curries, however, is their relative lightness in comparison to their Indian cousins. They are also unique in other ways. For example, they can be custards, as in the Cambodian steamed curried snails (p298); they can be noodle soups, as in the Laotian Kao Soi (p310); and they can be stir-fries, skipping any rich coconut sauce altogether.

Unlike the rice-based meals of the rest of Asia, curries in this region often employ starches other than rice as the main staple. Baguette, for example, is a crisp, baked bread derived from the familiar French variety, a remnant of the French colonial era here. It is widely enjoyed with curry, and used to soak and scoop up rich sauces. Significantly, the Southeast Asian baguette has been regionalized: half the length and perhaps a bit fuller than its French cousin, it is made with a combination of white wheat and rice flours, rendering a lighter-textured loaf.

Side dishes play an important role in Cambodian, Laotian and Vietnamese curry-based meals. Lightly stir-fried leafy greens balance the unguent curry stews, providing contrasting colours and textures while broadening the range of vitamins and minerals in the meal. Pickled vegetables, too, play an important role. Lightly brined and mildly spiced, they help with the digestion of rich foods. Their crunchiness introduces variety of texture to the braised and tender morsels of curried meals and their intense colours brighten the table, contrasting with the often earthy hues of the main dishes.

As refrigeration is close to non-existent in broad areas of Cambodia, Laos and Vietnam, fresh ingredients are essential, so going to market several times a day is normal and expected. Asian households often have food sitting on a table at room temperature throughout the day, stored in shade, covered with insect netting, and available for snacking. The food is unlikely to be kept for the next day.

Indian and other South Asian meals often employ milk-based cheeses, yogurt and yogurt drinks such as *lassi* to mediate the heat of their spicier curries. Such milk-based products are relatively rare in Cambodia, Laos and Vietnam, so cooks here often use fatty coconut milks and creams in their main curry dishes to the same effect.

In summary, the delightfully surprising thing about Southeast Asian curries is their diversity, their broad range of influence and their significant degree of sophisticated cooking. Regional variations can be subtle, as in the variations found in Vietnam, or so different as to be separate categories of cooking, as in the nature of Laotian versus Cambodian dishes. Not just spicy – as might be assumed – and always interesting, these recipes cover dishes exploring the spectrum from mild to very hot, from simple to complex, and from bitter to sweet.

Corinne Trang

Making a savoury base >
Stir-fry curry paste with palm sugar and minced pork until golden.

THE TASTE OF MAINLAND SE ASIA

1. dried large red chillies
2. red Thai chillies
3. palm sugar
4. Vietnamese coriander
5. dill
6. coriander leaves and stalks
7. coriander root
8. pea aubergines
9. annatto seeds
10. tamarind pulp
11. shrimp paste
12. *prahoc*
13. peanuts
14. cumin seeds
15. coriander seeds
16. green cardamom pods
17. star anise
18. fresh root ginger
19. galangal
20. turmeric root
21. kaffir lime leaves
22. kaffir lime
23. wild ginger
24. lemongrass
25. Thai basil leaves

THE RAW MATERIALS

With the ever-increasing interest in cooking, the popularity of the Internet and on-line shopping, and the expansion of available ingredients in local shops, foods that at one time were thought of as 'exotic' are becoming more familiar. Where once only soy sauce was available, now you can find fish sauce, tamarind pulp and fresh lemongrass, for example. The Western palate has also developed, and fusion dishes show up in restaurants everywhere. Southeast Asian flavours are a large part of this trend. These are the key flavouring ingredients that will enable you to create Cambodian, Laotian and Vietnamese curries at home.

Palm sugar

FISH SAUCE

An indispensable seasoning in Southeast Asian cooking, fish sauce (*nuoc mam*) is made from a specific type of anchovy. Once salted, the fish are layered in wooden barrels and then left to ferment for 3 months. The juices are extracted and poured back into large barrels or earthenware jars and fermented for another 12 months or longer. The first extraction is the most prized, because it is 100 per cent pure fish sauce – this is generally used as a last-minute seasoning at table. Second and third grade fish sauces are made using the same fish, with salt water added to further ferment them. These lesser grade fish sauces, which are also delicious, are primarily used in cooking or for making dipping sauces.

VIETNAMESE CORIANDER

Also called Vietnamese mint and *rau ram* in Vietnam, this herb has narrow, pointy, dark bluish-green leaves and a strong floral aroma. There is no substitute, but you can use fresh coriander for a very different yet still Asian flavour.

DILL

Also known as Laotian coriander, dill is widely used in Laotian and Vietnamese cooking, and is especially enjoyed with seafood dishes. Believed to soothe the stomach, tender dill fronds are generally added fresh and in small quantities to cooked dishes. This pungent herb has an aroma reminiscent of sweet grass.

PALM SUGAR

This is produced from the boiled sap of the coconut palm. It is also called coconut sugar.

GALANGAL

Also called galingale, this rhizome (underground root-like stem) is used in herbal and spice pastes. Its flavour

Fresh dill >

is unique: less spicy than ginger, to which it is related, yet citrussy. Galangal is pale yellow throughout, including its translucent skin, although when young it has a pinkish hue. There is no substitute for it. Fresh or frozen galangal is best – dried slices and ground galangal are less pungent.

ANNATTO SEEDS

These tiny, rust-red, triangular seeds are used for colouring food, as well as to dye fabrics. Annatto seeds are available whole or ground or as an extract.

CHiLLiES

Asia first gained knowledge of chillies after the 15th-century voyages of Christopher Columbus – Spain introduced chilli-hot foods to South Asia, and from there the influence spread across greater Asia. Several kinds of chillies are used in this region's curries, and they range in heat from mildly hot and sweet large red chillies, similar to the New Mexico chilli, to Thai chillies and the tiny, thin bird's eye or bird chillies, both of which are extremely hot. Dried large red chillies are an important part of the Cambodian spice paste called Kroeung (p295).

PEANUTS

Unsalted roasted peanuts are widely used in Asian cooking, lending a crunchy texture and earthy, nutty note, as well as a thickening quality.

SHRiMP PASTE

Pungent, dark, greyish-purple shrimp paste is strong and salty in flavour.

< Star anise

Cambodian shrimp paste, which is only produced in the Cambodian coastal region of Kampot, is the preferred seasoning for making curries in this region, but it is not widely available elsewhere. However, excellent versions are produced in Malaysia, Indonesia and Thailand, and make perfectly acceptable substitutes. Before storing shrimp paste in the refrigerator it should be wrapped well in several layers of cling film so that its pungent aroma is not transferred to other foods in the fridge.

CARDAMOM

Also known as the 'grain of paradise', this spice is used in its whole form (green pods), or the tiny, sticky black seeds are taken out of the pods and ground to a powder. Cardamom has a unique pungent aroma and slightly bitter yet sweet, warm flavour.

COCONUT

Coconut milk, cream and oil are major ingredients in curries of this region, lending naturally sweet and rich flavours to tame spicy ingredients, especially chillies. You can make your own coconut milk and cream (p241).

PRAHOC

This unique, chunky fish paste is the backbone of Cambodian cooking; similar versions are used in Laotian food as well. It is the strongest of all the fermented fish-based products of Southeast Asia. *Prahoc* is made from gouramy, grey featherback or mud fish fillets, which are soft and easily flaked, and is light to medium grey in colour, from the fish's skin pigment. The preferred version is made using boneless fish fillets, with or without rice as a fermenting agent. This is labelled 'Siem Reap Style'.

Peanuts

STAR ANiSE

Shaped like a star (hence its name), this spice has a strong liquorice flavour that is warm and sweet. It is widely used in Southast Asian cooking.

KAFFiR LiME

Kaffir limes have little juice, and instead are prized for their zest (the green part of the peel) and leaves. The zest is widely used in Southeast Asian curry pastes for its bitter, citrus and floral notes. There is no real substitute, but for a different, yet still citrussy, flavour you can use regular lime zest. Fragrant kaffir lime leaves have strong lime and floral notes. They are best if fresh, although frozen leaves are also good. If slicing or chopping, remove the woody central rib first.

CORiANDER LEAVES

Widely used fresh all over Asia, coriander leaves have a floral and somewhat citrussy aroma that perfectly complements Asian foods, including spicy curries.

CORiANDER ROOT

The root of the coriander plant, rather than the green stalks and leaves, is used in curry pastes, in part because it is white – it keeps a yellow or red curry paste from turning green, for example. The root can be stored, in cold water to cover, for up to 1 week in the refrigerator; the water should be changed daily.

CORiANDER SEEDS

Available whole or ground, coriander seeds are round or oval, about the size of rice grains, with longitudinal ridges. Coriander has been widely used as a spice for thousands of years.

THAi BASiL

Dark green with purplish stalks and flowerbuds, Thai basil has a pungent liquorice-like flavour. Added fresh to soups or stir-fries, it gives a sweet note. Italian basil is not a good substitute.

CUMiN SEED

This strongly flavoured spice is one of the most important ingredients in most Asian curry powders and other spice mixes. Roast cumin seeds in a dry pan before grinding to a fine powder.

TURMERiC

Also known as curcuma (from its botanical name), turmeric is a rhizome with brown skin and bright orange flesh. When fresh it has a subtle earthy, spicy flavour. Turmeric is most widely available in dried ground form and it is this that is used as a colourant, giving curries their distinctive yellowish-orange hue.

WiLD GiNGER

Variously known as Chinese keys, fingerroot and lesser galangal in English, and *krachai* in Southeast Asia, this rhizome looks like a knob with long slender fingers or tentacles. It is widely used in herbal and spice pastes and to flavour soups and stews. Similar in flavour to galangal, it is available fresh, frozen, in brine or as dried powder, though the latter tends to be flavourless.

PORK

Relatively inexpensive in Asia, pork is occasionally used to enhance and deepen the flavour of vegetarian and seafood dishes.

PEA AUBERGiNE

Only a bit larger than green peas, pea aubergines grow in clusters like grapes. They are slightly bitter in flavour, and tender yet still firm when cooked. Pea aubergines are best used fresh – the longer they are kept, the more bitter they will become. Although most often associated with Thai food, they are used in cooking throughout maritime and mainland Southeast Asia.

TAMARiND

Tamarind is used to 'sour' foods, or make them tangy. The whole fruit, which resembles a large, brittle, brown bean pod, contains a pasty pulp, fibres and seeds. Solid blocks of tamarind pulp, with fibres and seeds, are most commonly available, and for use the pulp is soaked to yield tamarind water (p355), in the proportion of 4 tbsp of pulp and 250ml (9fl oz) lukewarm water. While the tamarind tree is native to eastern Africa, it is now widely grown in many other parts of the world, including Asia.

LEMONGRASS

Much used in Southeast Asian cooking, lemongrass is a tall, clumping grass, yellow to light green in colour. Before use, remove the tough, outer layers, starting from the hard root end. About 20cm (8in) of the tender inner stalk can be used. When making a spice or herbal paste, lemongrass should go into the mortar first, as it takes great effort to break down the fibres.

PREPARING DRIED CHILLIES

In general, large smooth chillies are much less hot than small wrinkly chillies. Both are used dried and fresh. When dried, chillies are normally rehydrated before adding to a recipe. They may be deseeded too, to make them less hot. When preparing chillies, you may want to wear plastic or rubber gloves, as there is an alkaloid in chillies, called capsaicin, that can irritate your skin. After preparing chillies, thoroughly wash your hands with soapy water.

1 Put the chillies in a bowl of lukewarm water and place a small plate on top to keep them submerged. Leave to soak until soft and fully rehydrated (this can take as long as 15–30 minutes, depending on the size of the chillies).

2 Drain the chillies and pat dry with kitchen paper. Tear the chillies open and remove the stalks, veins and seeds. (It is the seeds and veins in a chilli that contain the heat.)

3 Chop the chillies, then grind in a mortar for a curry paste or use according to the recipe instructions.

Ground roasted chillies
Roast dried chillies (mildly hot red chillies or very hot bird's eye or bird chillies) in a wok or pan over a moderate heat, stirring regularly to prevent scorching, until they change colour and smell toasted. Allow to cool, then grind to a coarse or fine powder in a pestle and mortar, a clean coffee grinder or a spice mill. The powder will keep well in an airtight container in a dark, cool place for up to 1 year.

KROEUNG CAMBODIAN HERBAL PASTE

This is an all-purpose Cambodian herbal paste. Similar in many ways to Indian and, especially, Thai curry pastes, it belies the idea that Cambodia does not have curry pastes, or curries in general for that matter. *Kroeungs* come in several versions that include yellow (using additional turmeric), green (using green lemongrass leaves) and red (using red chillies), just like Thai curry pastes. It is essentially (or arguably) the foundation to many Cambodian hybrid curries, and contains seven main ingredients: lemongrass, galangal, wild ginger (*krachai*), garlic, shallot, kaffir lime zest and turmeric. Other more complex *kroeungs* may also include kaffir lime leaves, coriander root and chillies. For a basic curry base, stir-fry the paste with 1 tbsp Indian curry powder and 1 tbsp or more shrimp paste, until it becomes two shades darker. Add thick coconut milk and/or stock and proceed as you would with other types of curries, adding meat, poultry or seafood, and vegetables.

1 stalk lemongrass, outer leaves removed then chopped

30g (1oz) galangal, chopped

30g (1oz) wild ginger

2 large garlic cloves, crushed

1 large shallot, chopped

grated zest of 1 kaffir lime

4 kaffir lime leaves (optional)

3 tbsp finely chopped coriander root (optional)

30g (1oz) turmeric root, chopped, or ½ tsp ground turmeric

Other ingredients

2 lemongrass leaves (if making a green *kroeung*), chopped

extra 15g (½oz) turmeric root or ¼ tsp ground turmeric (if making a yellow *kroeung*)

2–4 dried large red chillies (if making a red *kroeung*), soaked until soft, deseeded and chopped

1 Traditionally this paste is made using a mortar and pestle, pounding the most fibrous ingredients first as they will need more pulverizing than anything that is tender. However, it is easier, and quicker, to use a mini food processor or blender: blend the ingredients, adding water (1 tbsp at a time and as is necessary) to ease the process. The amount of water, if needed, all depends on how naturally juicy the ingredients are.

2 The paste is always best freshly made, but can be kept in an airtight container in the refrigerator for 2–3 days.

CARI K'HOM CAMBODIAN RED CURRY PASTE

This red-coloured curry paste is a variation on the basic *kroeung* (p295), and closer to the Indian (rather than the Thai) roots of much Cambodian cooking. In general, Cambodian curry pastes are lightly spiced, using mild to moderately hot chillies. Note that unlike a *kroeung*, this curry paste also includes dried spices similar to those used in Indian cooking.

2 tbsp coconut oil

2 dried large red chillies, soaked, deseeded and coarsely chopped, or 1 tbsp mild or hot paprika

7.5cm (3in) cinnamon stick, broken into pieces

1 tsp grated nutmeg

2 star anise

5 cardamom pods

1/2 stalk lemongrass, outer leaves removed then sliced

2 kaffir lime leaves

2 tbsp coarsely chopped coriander root

4 large garlic cloves, coarsely chopped

2 medium shallots, coarsely chopped

7.5cm (3in) piece galangal, chopped

1 tbsp shrimp paste

1/2 tsp ground turmeric

1 Heat the oil in a frying pan over a moderate heat. Stir-fry the chillies, cinnamon, nutmeg, star anise, cardamoms, lemongrass, kaffir lime leaves, coriander root, garlic, shallots and galangal for about 5 minutes or until fragrant and lightly toasted.

2 Transfer the ingredients to a blender. Add the shrimp paste and turmeric and blend until smooth, adding water (1 tbsp at a time and as is necessary) to ease the process. The paste can be kept in an airtight container in the refrigerator for up to 3 days.

< Grated nutmeg
Widely used in Asian cuisines, grated nutmeg adds a warm aroma and a woody flavour to curries.

PRAHOC KROEUNG K'TIH CURRIED FERMENTED FISH AND PORK DIP

Seasoned with the fermented fish paste called *prahoc*, this is an example of the unique flavour combinations Cambodian cuisine has to offer. Serve the dip with plain rice and with crunchy raw vegetables, such as green beans, cabbage, cucumber or aubergine, and fruit in season.

serves 4

rich, mildly sweet and spicy

2 tbsp *prahoc*

4 tbsp coconut oil

225g (8oz) coarsely minced pork

4–5 tbsp red *Kroeung* (p295)

4 tbsp palm sugar or granulated sugar

250–350ml (9–12fl oz) thick coconut milk (p241)

125ml (4fl oz) tamarind water (p355)

4–6 kaffir lime leaves, bruised

100–150g ($3^1/_2$–$5^1/_2$oz) pea aubergines

salt

1 Crush the *prahoc* with 5 tbsp hot water in a bowl, then leave to soak for 10 minutes. Pass through a sieve set over a bowl, pressing the *prahoc* solids against the sieve. Discard any remaining solids and reserve the extract.

2 Heat the coconut oil in a saucepan over moderately high heat and stir-fry the pork, breaking it up, for about 5 minutes or until lightly golden. Stir in the *kroeung* and sugar and cook for 1 minute or until fragrant. Add the coconut milk, tamarind water, *prahoc* extract and kaffir lime leaves and bring to the boil. Reduce the heat to moderately low, add the pea aubergines and season to taste with salt. Cook for a further 5 minutes.

3 Remove the kaffir lime leaves and transfer to a serving bowl. Serve at room temperature.

Pea aubergines >
Always add pea aubergines at the end of the cooking (as in the above recipe) to retain their crunchy texture.

AMOK CHOUK STEAMED SNAILS IN CURRY CUSTARD

Amok is a curried coconut custard that is generally steamed in a small container hand-formed from a section of banana leaf. A speciality of Malaysia, hybrid versions appear in both Thai and Cambodian cooking. While freshwater fish such as catfish is used in many *amok* recipes, this delicious and dramatic version uses snails, and the snails and custard are cooked in the shells. Serve this as an appetizer or light lunch or as part of a dinner with vegetables and rice on the side. Be sure to buy canned Burgundian snails, which are usually sold in a packet with clean shells. The exact snail-to-custard ratio will depend on the relative size of the snail and shell; the custard should not overflow the shell.

serves 4

aromatic, mildly sweet and spicy

4–5 tbsp red Kroeung (p295)

500ml (16fl oz) thick coconut milk (p241)

1 tbsp shrimp paste

1 tbsp fish sauce

2 tsp palm sugar or granulated sugar (optional)

1 large egg, beaten

grated zest of ½ kaffir lime

salt

1 stalk lemongrass, leaves separated and cut into 24 pieces, each 10cm (4in) long

24–36 snail shells, well cleaned

24–36 cooked Burgundian snails (about 2 cans), rinsed and drained

6 kaffir lime leaves, very finely julienned

4 red Thai chillies, deseeded and very thinly sliced into rounds

1 In a mixing bowl, stir and mash together the *kroeung*, half of the coconut milk, the shrimp paste, fish sauce and sugar to a smooth consistency. Add the remaining coconut milk, the egg and kaffir lime zest and mix well. Season with salt, if necessary.

2 Fold a piece of lemongrass leaf and set it inside a snail shell so both ends of the leaf stick out. Half fill the shell with the coconut mixture. Place a snail in the centre and fill with more coconut mixture. Set the snail, open end up, on a bamboo steaming rack. Repeat with the remaining lemongrass pieces, shells, coconut mixture and snails. As you fill the steaming rack, the snails will butt up against each other and find enough support to stand. (If using a 6 or 12-portion stainless steel or ceramic snail plate, simply set the snails directly on the plate, and the plate on the bamboo steaming rack.)

3 Half fill a wok with water and set the covered bamboo steamer on top (the base of the steamer should not touch the water). Bring to the boil over a high heat, then reduce to moderately low and steam the snails for about 15 minutes or until the custard is set but still moist.

4 Serve the snails hot, garnished with the kaffir lime leaves and chillies. To eat, simply pull out the lemongrass strands, dislodging the snail in the process.

KARI TREY CATFISH CURRY WITH RICE NOODLES

In Cambodia, fish accounts for 70 per cent or more of the protein in the daily diet, and catfish, caught in the Tonle Sap (Great Lake) near Siem Reap and the Mekong River, has long been one of the most widely eaten fish. White fleshed and mild in flavour, it absorbs all the spices and herbs a curry sauce has to offer. In this recipe tender catfish morsels complement crunchy bamboo and water spinach. Thin, delicate rice noodles make a perfect canvas on which the exotic flavours and contrasting textures meet. If using fresh, round rice noodles (spaghetti shaped) dip them in boiling water for a few seconds to heat them. If using dried rice sticks (linguine shaped), rehydrate them in water until pliable, then cook in boiling water for 1–2 minutes.

serves 4

sweet, savoury and mild to spicy

3 tbsp coconut oil

4–5 tbsp yellow Kroeung (p295)

1 tbsp shrimp paste

1¹/₂ tbsp palm sugar

175g (6oz) coarsely minced pork (optional)

1 litre (1³/₄ pints) thick coconut milk (p241)

900g (2lb) catfish fillets, cut into 5cm (2in) pieces

1 stalk lemongrass, outer leaves discarded then sliced

6 kaffir lime leaves, bruised

1 large bamboo shoot, parboiled and thinly sliced lengthways

1 bunch of water spinach, halved crossways

fish sauce to taste

450g (1lb) fresh thin, round rice noodles or rice sticks, cooked (see above)

red Thai chillies, deseeded and thinly sliced into rounds

1 Heat the coconut oil in a pot over a moderately high heat and stir-fry the kroeung and shrimp paste, breaking up the paste with the back of a spoon, for about 2 minutes or until just golden and fragrant. Add the palm sugar and pork and stir-fry, breaking up the pork fully, for about 5 minutes or until cooked and lightly golden.

2 Reduce the heat to moderately low. Add the coconut milk, catfish, lemongrass and kaffir lime leaves. Cook for 5 minutes. Add the bamboo shoots and water spinach, cover and cook for a further 5 minutes. Adjust the seasoning with fish sauce.

3 Place a serving of rice noodles on each of 4 plates. Ladle the fish curry into 4 bowls. Serve with the chillies on the side. To eat, simply grab some noodles with chopsticks and dip them in the coconut curry, adding chillies to taste.

SARAMAN CARDAMOM AND GINGER BEEF CURRY WITH PEANUTS

Full of meat such as beef or duck and rich by Asian standards, Saraman is often served in restaurants or prepared for special occasions, when it is eaten in modest quantities. A classic Cambodian-style braised curry, it has dominant cardamom and ginger flavours, and the addition of peanuts helps to thicken the stew to a *crème anglaise* consistency. Serve over rice or with baguette (p322) for soaking up the 'gravy', with pickled vegetables (p315) and stir-fried leafy greens as side dishes.

serves 4

rich, creamy, nutty and mild to spicy

85g (3oz) fresh root ginger, finely grated

675g (1½lb) boneless beef shin steak or thin flank, cut into 4cm (1½in) cubes

2 tbsp coconut oil

2 dried large red chillies, soaked, deseeded and torn in half

1 tsp coarsely chopped galangal

4 large garlic cloves, crushed

1 large shallot, coarsely chopped

1 stalk lemongrass, outer leaves discarded then sliced

7.5cm (3in) cinnamon stick

2 star anise

7 green cardamom pods

1 tsp grated nutmeg

½ tsp ground mace

1½ tbsp finely chopped coriander root

¼ tsp ground turmeric

3 tbsp vegetable oil

1 tbsp shrimp paste

1 litre (1¾ pints) thick coconut milk (p241)

4 tbsp palm sugar or granulated sugar

4 tbsp tamarind water (p355)

2 tbsp fish sauce

75g (2½oz) unsalted roasted peanut halves

salt

2–4 red Thai chillies, deseeded and thinly sliced (optional)

1 Squeeze the grated ginger in your hand to extract the juice into a bowl. Discard the dry fibres. Add the beef to the bowl and toss to coat with the ginger juice, then leave to marinate for 30 minutes.

2 Meanwhile, heat the coconut oil in a saucepan over a moderate heat and stir-fry the chillies, galangal, garlic, shallot and lemongrass until fragrant. Add the cinnamon, star anise, cardamoms, nutmeg and mace and stir-fry for 5–7 minutes or until fragrant and lightly toasted. Transfer the ingredients to a blender. Add the coriander root and turmeric and blend until smooth, adding water (1 tbsp at a time as is necessary) to ease the process. Set this curry paste aside.

3 Heat the vegetable oil in a large pot over a moderately high heat and stir-fry the shrimp paste, breaking it up with the back of a spoon, for 15–30 seconds or until a shade darker. Add half of the coconut milk and the curry paste. Stir well. Add the beef. Cook for 20 minutes, stirring occasionally.

4 Reduce the heat to low and add the remaining coconut milk, the sugar, tamarind water, fish sauce and peanuts. Season with salt, if necessary. Simmer, covered, for 1½–2 hours or until the meat is fork tender, adding more coconut milk if the stew thickens too much. Serve garnished with chillies.

KARI MOUAN CHICKEN CURRY WITH YOUNG JACKFRUIT

This Cambodian chicken curry is a sensual delight. Jackfruit, which is widely grown and eaten throughout Southeast Asia, is sweet with floral notes when ripe. The unripened fruit, although not as complex in flavour, is used much in the same way a vegetable would be in savoury dishes. In this curry, crunchy young jackfruit morsels complement the tender chicken, giving the dish a wonderful range of textures. If you cannot find fresh jackfruit, brined jackfruit in cans or jars, sometimes labelled 'young green jackfruit', makes a good substitute. Be sure to soak and rinse the brined jackfruit in several changes of water before use. Serve Kari Mouan with rice or baguette (p322) and stir-fried leafy greens.

serves 4

light and aromatic

1 chicken, about 1.1kg (2½lb)

3 tbsp coconut oil

4–5 tbsp red Kroeung (p295)

1 tbsp shrimp paste

1 tbsp Vietnamese Cari (p314) or store-bought Indian curry powder

1½ tbsp palm sugar

1 litre (1¾ pints) thick coconut milk (p241)

1 stalk lemongrass, outer leaves discarded then sliced

6 kaffir lime leaves, bruised

225–350g (8–12oz) young jackfruit chunks

fish sauce to taste

1 Remove the legs from the chicken and split them at the joint into thighs and drumsticks. Remove the wings and discard the tips. Split the chicken in half down the breastbone. Cut out the back and discard or reserve for making stock. Cut each breast crossways into 2 equal pieces. You should have 10 pieces in total.

2 Heat the oil in a large pot over a moderately high heat. Add the chicken pieces, skin side down, and brown for about 10 minutes, turning to colour all sides. Remove the chicken from the pot.

3 Add the *kroeung* and shrimp paste and stir-fry, breaking up the paste with the back of a spoon, for about 2 minutes or until just golden and fragrant. Add the curry powder and palm sugar and stir for a further minute or until fragrant.

4 Reduce the heat to moderately low. Return the chicken to the pot and add the coconut milk, lemongrass and kaffir limes leaves. Cover and cook for 20 minutes. Add the jackfruit, adjust seasoning with fish sauce and cook for a further 10 minutes. Serve hot.

< Young jackfruit chunks
Known for its meat-like flavour, young jackfruit gives a rich, thick texture to gravies.

KORE LAOTIAN ALL-PURPOSE CURRY PASTE

Laotian curries are hybrids, taking their herbal base from Thai curries and their flavourful dry spice notes from Indian curries in making a basic paste. Accordingly, the fresh ingredients lemongrass, galangal, ginger, kaffir lime zest, shallots, garlic, chillies and coriander root, and the dry spices cumin, turmeric and coriander seed make up the foundation of any good Laotian curry. Sometimes a Laotian curry paste will include a small amount of Indian curry powder to deepen and broaden the dry spice flavour.

1½ tsp cumin seeds

1 tbsp coriander seeds

1 stalk lemongrass, outer
   leaves discarded
   then chopped

30g (1oz) galangal, chopped

grated zest of 1 kaffir lime

3 large garlic cloves, crushed

1 large shallot, chopped

3 tbsp finely chopped coriander root

30g (1oz) turmeric root, chopped, or
   ½ tsp ground turmeric

30g (1oz) fresh root ginger, chopped,
   or ½ tsp ground ginger

4 or more green or red Thai
   chillies, deseeded

2 tsp shrimp paste

1 tbsp Indian curry powder (optional)

1 Heat a dry frying pan over a moderate heat and roast the cumin and coriander seeds for about 2 minutes or until fragrant.

2 Put the lemongrass, galangal, kaffir lime zest, garlic, shallot, coriander root, turmeric, ginger, chillies and roasted cumin and coriander seeds in a blender. Blend the ingredients to a smooth consistency, adding water (1 tbsp at a time and as is necessary) to ease the process. Add the shrimp paste and curry powder, if using, and blend well.

3 The paste can be kept in an airtight container in the refrigerator for up to 3 days.

Turmeric root >
Along with adding colour,
turmeric root gives an
earthy aroma to curries.

KORE POU GALI STIR-FRIED YELLOW CURRIED CRABS

This seafood curry is a stir-fry rather than the more usual stewed dish. The fierce cooking heat elevates the aromas of the herbs and spices, caramelizing their natural sugars and intensifying the overall flavour of the dish. Kore Pou Gali is prepared using small, rice paddy-raised freshwater crabs, but any small crabs will do as long as they are halved or quartered to allow the curry flavours to mingle with the natural juices of the crabmeat. The dish is a perfect appetizer or light lunch served with steamed sticky rice and pickled vegetables (p315). As with many Laotian foods, this can be served at room temperature and eaten with the hands. Some Lao cooks make this curried crab using only Indian curry powder; others use a fresh curry paste such as the one called for here; and still others combine the two. These approaches betray the cultural underpinnings of Laotian food. Equally delicious stir-fries can be made using cut-up lobster, clams or mussels.

serves 4

light and spicy-hot

4 tbsp vegetable oil

5 tbsp Laotian Kore (p305) or store-bought Thai curry paste

1 tsp Indian curry powder (optional)

8 small crabs, about 225g (8oz) each, halved or quartered

2 spring onions, thinly sliced diagonally

1 Heat the oil in a wok over a high heat and stir-fry the curry paste for about 5 minutes or until golden and fragrant. Add the curry powder, if using, and stir-fry to blend well.

2 Reduce the heat to moderate and add the pieces of crab, tossing them to coat each piece with the curry paste. Cover the wok and cook for 5 minutes. Toss the crabs again and cook, covered, for a further 5 minutes.

3 Transfer the crabs to a serving platter and garnish with the spring onions.

GANG KEO GOUNG GREEN PRAWN CURRY WITH FRESH DILL

Fresh dill, sometimes referred to as Laotian coriander, is widely used in Laos for fish or other seafood dishes. Never used dried or cooked, the dill fronds are added at the last minute as a garnish. Here they enliven a green prawn curry, also helping to mellow the sometimes intense flavour of kaffir limes leaves. Eat this curry at room temperature with steamed sticky rice on the side: with your fingers, pinch and shape a small amount of rice into a ball and dip into the curry, eating prawn along with dill in the same bite.

serves 4

lemony and sweet

3 tbsp vegetable oil

5 tbsp Laotian Kore (p305) or store-bought Thai curry paste

1 tbsp shrimp paste

1 tbsp palm sugar or granulated sugar

500ml (16fl oz) thick coconut milk (p241)

500ml (16fl oz) chicken or vegetable stock

4–6 kaffir lime leaves, bruised

fish sauce to taste

2 large waxy potatoes, peeled and cut into 2.5cm (1in) pieces

675g (1½lb) raw tiger prawns, peeled and deveined

1 bunch of dill

1 Heat the oil in a pot over a moderately high heat and stir-fry the curry paste for about 2 minutes or until just golden and fragrant. Add the shrimp paste (breaking it up) and palm sugar, and stir-fry for 1 minute or until fragrant. Reduce the heat and add the coconut milk, stock, kaffir lime leaves and fish sauce to taste. Add the potatoes, cover the pot and cook for 20 minutes.

2 Add the prawns and stir well, then cover again and cook for about 5 minutes or until they turn pink. Serve hot, garnished with dill fronds.

KAO SOI NOODLES WITH PORK IN RED CURRY BROTH

This curry noodle soup is a speciality of the Laotian northern region of Luang Namtha and is similar to a dish of the same name from northern Thailand. It is widely believed, however, that Kao Soi originated in Myanmar. This version combines coconut milk with a light pork stock, creating a delicious, subtle broth. The steaming liquid is poured over raw vegetables, and it is completed with tender rice noodles and bits of sweet pork. If preparing the dish with Laotian Kore, omit the optional Indian curry powder in that recipe, as it is added here.

serves 4

spicy, rich and aromatic

450g (1lb) boned pork shoulder

60g (2oz) fresh root ginger

6 spring onions, 4 of them crushed and 2 thinly sliced diagonally

2 tbsp fish sauce, or to taste

2 tbsp vegetable oil

5 tbsp Laotian Kore (p305) or store-bought Thai red curry paste

1 tbsp Indian curry powder

1 tsp shrimp paste

1 tbsp palm sugar

225g (8oz) coarsely minced pork

1 litre (1¾ pints) thick coconut milk (p241)

8 kaffir lime leaves, bruised

450g (1lb) fresh, thin, round rice noodles, or 225g (8oz) dried rice sticks, soaked in water until pliable

150–175g (5–6oz) Chinese leaf, cut into 3mm (1/8in) julienne

1 bunch of watercress, large stalks discarded

100g (3½oz) beansprouts

25g (scant 1oz) mint leaves, torn

25g (scant 1oz) coriander leaves, torn

1 lime, quartered

1 Bring 1.5 litres (2¾ pints) water to the boil and add the pork shoulder, ginger, crushed spring onions and 2 tbsp fish sauce. Reduce the heat and simmer, partly covered, for about 1½ hours or until the liquid has reduced by half. Transfer the pork to a cutting board to cool, then slice thinly and cover with cling film. Set the broth aside.

2 In another pot, heat the oil over a moderately high heat and stir-fry the curry paste for 2 minutes or until just golden and fragrant. Add the curry powder, shrimp paste (breaking it up) and palm sugar, and stir-fy for about 1 minute or until fragrant. Add the minced pork and cook, stirring to break it up, for about 7 minutes or until just golden. Reduce the heat and add the coconut milk, pork broth and kaffir lime leaves. Adjust seasoning with fish sauce. Cover and simmer for 30 minutes.

3 Bring a pot of water to the boil. If the fresh rice noodles are cold, heat in the boiling water for 5 seconds; if they are at room temperature, skip this step. If using rehydrated rice sticks, cook them for 3 minutes. Drain.

4 Divide the noodles among 4 large Asian-style soup bowls and top with Chinese leaf, watercress, beansprouts and sliced pork shoulder. Bring the spicy coconut broth to the boil, then ladle into the bowls. Garnish with mint and coriander, squeeze a lime wedge over each serving and serve hot.

KANG SOH BAMBOO SHOOT SALAD

This bamboo shoot salad is believed to have originated in the mountains of northern Laos, which are known for their particularly delicious wild bamboo shoots. While any bamboo shoot can be the basis for a tangy and savoury salad, slender, young winter shoots are prized for their tenderness – shoots cultivated past the winter season, eg in spring or summer, tend to be more fibrous and less juicy. Always use a good quality fish sauce that is golden amber in colour to ensure a fresh and clean flavour (black indicates excessive ageing). If using fresh bamboo shoots, peel and parboil for 15 minutes to get rid of any natural toxins, then drain. If using canned bamboo shoots, be sure to select whole shoots; drain and parboil them for 2 minutes to remove any canned flavour.

serves 4

refreshing, crunchy and mild

1 small shallot, halved

1 large garlic clove, crushed

2 tbsp fish sauce

2 tbsp lime juice

1 red Thai chilli, deseeded and thinly sliced

450g (1lb) bamboo shoots, halved and thinly sliced lengthways

1 spring onion, thinly sliced diagonally

1/2 bunch of coriander, stalks discarded

toasted sesame seeds

1 Heat a dry frying pan and char the shallot and garlic over a moderate heat for about 2 minutes, turning to colour all sides. Allow to cool, then finely chop the shallot and garlic.

2 Mix together the fish sauce, lime juice, shallot, garlic and chilli in a large bowl. Cover and set aside for 20 minutes.

3 Add the bamboo shoots, spring onion and most of the coriander leaves to the bowl and toss to coat with the dressing. Transfer the salad to a serving platter and garnish with the remaining coriander leaves and toasted sesame seeds.

CARI ViETNAMESE ALL-PURPOSE CURRY POWDER

In contrast to other Southeast Asian cuisines, Vietnamese curries employ powders rather than pastes. This powder is based on traditional Indian curry powder, which can be used as a substitute if necessary. Freshly ground spices make for deep flavours and rich aromas. If you enjoy authentic flavours, making your own curry powder from scratch will be something you want to try. Freshly made versions differ from place to place and cook to cook, of course. This one includes star anise, a spice not generally included in Indian curry powders but enjoyed in Vietnam.

8 curry leaves

2 star anise

1-2 dried red chillies, deseeded (optional)

4 tbsp coriander seeds

2 tsp cumin seeds

1/2 tsp mustard seeds

1 tsp fenugreek seeds

1/2 tsp whole cloves

1 tsp black peppercorns

1 tbsp ground turmeric

1 tsp ground ginger

1 tsp grated nutmeg

1/2 tsp ground cinnamon

1 Heat a dry frying pan over a moderate heat. Add the curry leaves, star anise, red chillies (if using), coriander, cumin, mustard and fenugreek seeds, cloves and peppercorns and roast, constantly shaking the pan to prevent the ingredients from burning, for about 1 minute or until a shade darker. Remove from the heat and leave to cool.

2 Transfer the spices to a spice mill or clean coffee grinder and process to a fine powder. Put into a jar and add the turmeric, ginger, nutmeg and cinnamon. Close the jar and shake to blend. Store the curry powder in a dark, cool place, where it will keep for 3-6 months.

< Star anise pods
This spice is not only used to infuse a liquorice flavour in dishes, but also to beautify them.

RAU CHAY CHUA PICKLED VEGETABLES

Pickled vegetables are an integral part of the Southeast Asian diet, considered essential accompaniments to meals. Believed to aid digestion of rich, fatty or oil-based dishes, pickled vegetables are appropriately served with curries, 'cutting' the fat while 'lifting' and cleansing the palate to allow a deeper enjoyment of the food.

serves 4–8

crunchy, sweet and sour

450g (1lb) ridge cucumbers, peeled (optional) and deseeded

450g (1lb) mooli, peeled

450g (1lb) carrots, peeled

3 tbsp sea salt

100g (3½oz) caster sugar

350ml (12fl oz) white rice vinegar

1 Cut the cucumbers and mooli into sticks 5mm (¼in) thick and 4cm (1½in) long. Cut the carrots into sticks of the same length but 3mm (⅛in) thick.

2 Put the vegetables in 3 separate colanders set over mixing bowls. Sprinkle each vegetable with 1 tbsp salt and toss, then leave to drain for 1 hour.

3 Gently squeeze any remaining juice out of the vegetables, then transfer them to a large re-sealable plastic bag.

4 In a bowl, whisk together the sugar and rice vinegar until the sugar is completely dissolved. Add this pickling liquid to the vegetables. Close the bag, squeezing out any air. Leave to marinate for 3 hours before serving. You can keep the pickles in the refrigerator for a week or two; the longer they are kept the softer they will be and the more pronounced the pickle flavour.

Salted lemonade Believed to aid digestion, this unsweetened lemonade (called *da chanh muoi*) made with salt-preserved lemons (sometimes limes) is enjoyed at the end of a meal, either served at room temperature or chilled with ice cubes. It is also drunk during the day as a thirst quencher and restorative, particularly in warm weather. The ratio of lemon to water given here can be adjusted to taste. For 1 serving, rinse ⅓ preserved salt-brined lemon and put in a bowl. Crush the lemon with a fork. Place 1–1½ tbsp of the crushed lemon in a large glass. Add ice cubes to taste, if using, and top up with 250ml (9fl oz) still or sparkling mineral water. Stir a few times, then drink. While best made fresh, large quantities (full pitchers) can be prepared a few hours ahead of time and kept in a cool place or chilled.

Ridge cucumbers >

The mild, juicy flavour and the crispy texture of these cucumbers make them perfect for an assorted vegetable pickle.

CARI GA CHICKEN CURRY WITH SWEET POTATOES AND CARROTS

Vietnamese curries are a speciality of the south of the country, where the Indian culinary influences are pronounced. While herbal pastes are generally employed in Cambodian or Laotian curies, they are absent from Vietnamese versions, and fresh herbs such as lemongrass and kaffir lime leaves are used whole as flavour enhancements. Another difference is that for a chicken curry such as this one, the Vietnamese cook will marinate the chicken in a sweetened curry powder before cooking. Potatoes are an integral part of Vietnamese curries, with the preferred type being sweet white yam. Serve this with rice or baguette (p322).

serves 4

rich, slightly spicy and fragrant

1 chicken, about 1.1kg (2½lb)

2 tbsp Vietnamese Cari (p314) or store-bought Indian curry powder

1 tsp caster sugar

1 tsp salt

4 tbsp vegetable oil

2-3 white yams or sweet potato, peeled and cut into 2.5cm (1in) cubes

3 large garlic cloves, crushed

2 shallots, cut into wedges

1 litre (1¾ pints) thick coconut milk (p241)

2 tsp annatto seed extract (optional)

2 stalks lemongrass, outer leaves removed then bruised

2 kaffir lime leaves

2 tbsp fish sauce

3 large carrots, peeled and cut into 4-5cm (1½-2in) long pieces

salt

1 Remove the legs from the chicken and split them at the joint into thighs and drumsticks. Remove the wings and discard the tips. Split the chicken in half down the breastbone. Cut out the back and discard or reserve for making stock. Cut each breast crossways into 2 equal pieces. You should have 10 pieces in total.

2 Mix together 1 tbsp of the curry powder, the sugar and salt in a large bowl. Add the chicken and toss well to coat. Marinate for 1 hour.

3 Heat the oil in a large pot over a moderately high heat and brown the yams all over for about 5 minutes. (The yams should be browned only, not cooked through.) With a slotted spoon, transfer the yams to kitchen paper to drain.

4 Add the chicken, skin side down, to the pot and cook for about 10 minutes, turning to brown all sides. With a slotted spoon, transfer the chicken to kitchen paper to drain.

5 Add the garlic and shallots to the pot and stir-fry for about 5 minutes or until lightly golden. Add the remaining curry powder, the coconut milk, annatto seed extract, lemongrass, kaffir lime leaves, fish sauce and carrots, then return the chicken and yams to the pot. Bring to the boil. Reduce the heat to a gentle boil, cover and cook for 20 minutes or until the chicken and yams are tender.

CARI CHAY VEGETABLE AND TOFU CURRY

Tofu, which originated in China millennia ago, came into Vietnamese cuisine during China's thousand-year rule of Vietnam, from 100BCE to 1000CE approximately. Today, with the high cost of meat (usually reserved for special occasions and holidays) and the religious preferences of vegetarian Buddhism, tofu still plays an important role in the country's cooking. Cari Chay combines tofu, bamboo and Asian aubergine in a relatively light dish suitable for any season. It is subtle with a light coconut milk broth spiced with curry powder. The last-minute addition of Vietnamese coriander lends a floral finish. Serve with rice or baguette (p322).

serves 4

light, sweet
and lemony

3 tbsp vegetable oil

2 large garlic cloves, crushed

1 large shallot, thinly sliced

1–1½ tbsp Vietnamese Cari (p314) or store-bought Indian curry powder

1 tbsp palm sugar

1 litre (1¾ pints) thick coconut milk (p241)

juice of 1 lime

2 tbsp fish sauce (optional)

2 tsp annatto seed extract (optional)

2 stalks lemongrass, outer leaves discarded then bruised

2 kaffir lime leaves, bruised

salt

900g (2lb) firm tofu, cut into 2.5cm (1in) cubes

1 large boiled bamboo shoot, thinly sliced

2 Asian aubergines, halved lengthways and cut into 2.5cm (1in) pieces

24 Vietnamese coriander leaves or Thai basil leaves

1 Heat the oil in a pot over a high heat and stir-fry the garlic and shallot for about 5 minutes or until they are golden. Add the curry powder and palm sugar and continue to stir-fry for 1 minute or until fragrant. Add the coconut milk, lime juice, fish sauce, annatto seed extract, lemongrass and kaffir limes leaves. Bring to the boil, then reduce the heat to low. Adjust the seasoning with salt and add the tofu, bamboo shoot and Asian aubergines. Simmer, covered, for 10–15 minutes or until the aubergines are tender.

2 Serve garnished with Vietnamese coriander or Thai basil.

RAU MUONG XAO STiR-FRiED WATER SPiNACH

Also known as water convolvulus, swamp cabbage or swamp morning glory in English, and *rau muong* (Vietnamese), *bongz* (Laotian) and *trakuon* (Cambodian), this leafy green vegetable is abundant in Southeast Asia. Prized for being versatile, flavourful, nutritious and well textured, it has tender, narrow and pointy leaves with crunchy hollow stalks. Water spinach can be added whole to soups or to stir-fries such as this one, where it is seasoned with fish sauce, garlic and a pinch of sugar. Thought of as a wonderful embodiment of the ancient Chinese philosophy of yin-yang, or balanced opposites, it combines tender and crunchy textures in each bite.

serves 4

savoury, crunchy and tender

2 tbsp vegetable oil

2 large garlic cloves, chopped

450g (1lb) water spinach

1 tbsp fish sauce, or 1 tbsp (1–2 cubes) fermented bean curd

pinch of sugar

pepper to taste

1 Heat the oil in a frying pan or wok over a high heat and stir-fry the garlic for about 2 minutes or until fragrant and lightly golden. Add the water spinach, fish sauce, sugar and pepper and cover the pan. Cook for 5 minutes.

2 Remove the lid, toss a few more times and serve hot.

BANH MI SAIGON BAGUETTE

Originating from the French colonial era of the mid-1800s to mid-1900s, Banh Mi is made from a mixture of rice and wheat flours. Shorter (about half the length) and lighter than their French cousins, and sometimes almond shaped rather than long and slender, these breads have become an integral part of the everyday Vietnamese and Cambodian diet. In lieu of the more traditional rice or noodles, baguette is often eaten with coconut curries, where it is used as a scoop. Smeared with butter, it is also enjoyed for breakfast; when sliced lengthways and filled with pork, vegetables and chilli paste it is a popular lunchtime sandwich.

makes 4

15g (½oz) fresh yeast
350ml (12fl oz) lukewarm water
140g (5oz) rice flour
350g (12oz) white bread flour, plus extra for kneading
2 tsp salt

1 Put the yeast in a small bowl and add the lukewarm water. Stir until dissolved.

2 Sift the flours and salt into a large mixing bowl. Make a well in the centre and add the yeast liquid. With a wooden spoon incorporate the wet and dry ingredients until fully combined. The dough should be soft, not wet, and definitely not stiff.

3 Turn the soft dough on to a floured work surface and knead for about 5 minutes or until smooth and elastic. Shape into a ball. Grease a large mixing bowl and place the dough ball in it. Cover with cling film and leave to rise at warm room temperature for 3 hours or until doubled in size.

4 Knock back the dough, bringing the sides towards the centre. Turn out the dough on to a floured work surface and knead for 2 minutes, then shape into a ball once again. Divide the dough into 4 equal pieces. Make sure they are separated by 5cm (2in) or so, then cover them with cling film and leave to rise at warm room temperature for 2 hours or until doubled in size.

5 Knock back each piece of dough, rolling and pulling it (against the work surface) back into a ball. Stretch each ball roughly into a 1cm (½in) thick rectangle, then roll into a slender, almond-shaped loaf with tapered ends. Cover the cling film and leave to rise at warm room temperature for 1 hour or until almost doubled in size.

6 Remove all but one rack from your oven. Place the rack at the bottom and set a pizza stone on it. Preheat the oven to 230°C (450°F/Gas 8).

7 Sprinkle a peel or baking sheet with flour and place 1 or 2 shaped breads on it. Score each bread 3 times on the diagonal using a clean razor blade or sharp knife. Slide the breads on to the hot stone and bake for 20–25 minutes or until golden. Transfer the loaves to a wire rack and leave to cool for 1–2 hours before eating.

OUTPOSTS

Comforting, celebratory and diverse, South Asian cooking styles have travelled well across thousands of miles, amassing worldwide acclaim from curry aficionados and connoisseurs alike. There are few classic cuisines that have evolved and been embraced by host countries in the same way as Indian food. Encapsulated in the blending of favourite spices is a cosmopolitan appreciation of global cooking styles. From South African *masalas*, Caribbean stews, colonial British curries and Japanese-inspired spice formulas, the variety and versatility of curry in all its guises have impressive credentials.

Over centuries, the sustained and successive movement of slaves, followed by indentured labour, economic emigrés and businessmen, laid the foundation for the changing flavours of displaced Indian kitchens. Familiar food and preparations – the aroma of toasted cumin seeds, the rhythmic pounding of *masalas* and a pot of bubbling rice on the fire – were the only culinary handles to a country left far behind. Adept home cooks soon learnt to adapt meals to suit the produce of their newly adopted country. And in doing so, they won over the local populace and enriched national cuisines. Even in Japan, where Indian-style dishes arrived via the tenuous route of the Western palate, curries are malleable enough to be included on restaurant menus and for quick, accessible home cooking.

One of the tenets of Asian hospitality is sharing home-cooked food with family and friends, making sure that there's enough to go around. Even in homes with meagre resources there's usually an extra portion prepared 'for the pot' or as a token offering to the gods. For unexpected guests, a handful of chopped vegetables added to chicken curry, or a fistful of peas tossed into rice as it simmers, is a life-saver. Whether in Durban, Glasgow or Trinidad, cooks will all give a nod to their cultural heritage in the same way. Recipes are accommodating and rarely regimented – making an Indian curry is pretty much a laid-back affair so nobody holds back from putting in their own add-ons.

At the same time, top chefs have fashioned a new approach, elevating curries to fine dining status, and these interpretations are an acknowledgement of the curry's versatility. Local produce – Jamaican chillies, Japanese noodles or succulent Scottish salmon – are as likely to be found on modern menus as are the traditional stalwarts such as fresh coriander, green chillies and *garam masala*. The global reach of Indian cooking and the curry has long since crossed national boundaries, and is a tribute to, and an endorsement of, entrepreneurial flair, acculturation and experimentation.

Frying spices >
Toast curry leaves, cinnamon and mustard seeds in hot oil

From hearty African staples to Cape Malay curries, fiery Indian *masalas* and European mainstays, modern South African kitchens are a melting pot of world cuisines. Despite apartheid and its attempts at racial segregation, for centuries culinary curiosity for other cooking styles has tempted tastebuds into trying new and adventurous dishes. Indian and Cape Malay dishes have stood the test of time, seasoning South Africa's meals with sweetly spiced offerings, succulent kebabs and an array of pickles and *sambals*.

To appreciate South Africa's richly diverse food history, it's worth tracing the journey of immigrants, settlers and slaves who made the arduous journey across the seas hundreds of years ago. Their arrival transformed the culinary scene, as they brought with them an appreciation for kitchen specialities traced to what is now Indonesia and India. Cape Malays, the descendants of the original slave population, are skilful cooks, and evoke a love of flavoursome Southeast Asian cooking, often combining sweet fruity flavours with tart-tasting tamarind and aromatic spices. Their culinary heritage is celebrated in the kitchen with exotic sun-kissed produce, including lemon leaves, fennel seeds, cinnamon and cardamoms.

In the 19th century, Indian labourers were brought to Natal to work in the sugar-cane fields. Because time for cooking was limited, curries were adapted to suit the needs of the day, with many dishes taking on a fiery stew-like character that included an assortment of pulses, beans and herbs. Spotting a new market, Indian entrepreneurs, particularly from the Gujarati community, established trade links, plying spices, foodstuffs and textiles. Many settled in eastern and southern Africa, adapting their curries to take in local ingredients, such as cornmeal and African pulses. In Kenya, this acculturation process went even further, with Indian 'curries' adopting Swahili titles for local consumption. In South Africa, decades of a shared immigrant experience and a common identity forged around surviving apartheid have tended to ease traditional caste differences and regional and linguistic variance. In the main, culinary and cultural diversity has been swapped for an all-embracing approach to pan-Indian cooking, notable for its distinctive South African character.

From Bobotie, Cape Malay's tasty take on shepherds' pie, to Bunny Chow, a seriously spicy, curry-filled bread loaf, it is family food cooked for everyday meals that really showcases the best flavours. Indian-inspired South African cooking can never be fussy or fanciful. The crackle of curry leaves, the nutty aroma of popped mustard seeds, and the sweet whiff of toasted fennel seeds is always within sniffing distance. Indian cooking, in all its guises, is as steeped in South African culinary culture as biltong, *boerewors* (farmers' sausages) and the ultimate in barbecues, the *braai*.

Roopa Gulati

AFRICA

BUTTER BEAN CURRY

Durban ground spice *masalas* are sold by weight from market stalls, and there's a different spice blend for almost every style of curry. One favourite is 'mother-in-law's tongue' *masala* – and what a lashing of chillies it unleashes. In this recipe, which is also called sugar bean curry, I've recreated my own mother-in-law's special spice blend. It's milder than many *masalas* and has an almost nutty character, spiked with the bite of refreshingly sharp chillies. The creamy blandness of butter beans works especially well with the pungency of Indian spices.

serves 4

warmly spiced and aromatic

3 tbsp vegetable oil

1 tsp mustard seeds

2 sprigs of curry leaves (about 2 tbsp leaves)

3–4 fenugreek seeds

2 onions, diced

3cm (1¼in) piece fresh root ginger, finely chopped

3 garlic cloves, finely chopped

2 green chillies, deseeded and chopped

4 plum tomatoes, skinned and chopped

1 carrot, peeled and cut into 3cm (1¼in) chunks

¾ tsp ground coriander

¼ tsp ground turmeric

½ tsp red chilli powder

¾ tsp ground cumin

½ tsp ground *garam masala*

1 red pepper, deseeded and cut into 3cm (1¼in) chunks

75g (2½oz) green beans, cut into 3cm (1¼in) lengths

400g canned butter beans, drained

2 tbsp chopped coriander leaves

1 Heat the vegetable oil in a *karahi* or wok. When hot, toss in the mustard seeds, followed by the curry leaves and fenugreek seeds. After about 30 seconds, the spices will give off a nutty aroma.

2 Add the onions and soften over a low heat for about 10 minutes. Stir in the ginger, garlic and green chillies and continue frying until the onions are flecked golden.

3 Turn the heat up slightly, add the chopped tomatoes to the pan and cook until thickened and darkened in colour. Tip in the carrot and sprinkle over the ground coriander, turmeric, chilli powder, cumin and *garam masala*. Fry briskly for 1 minute before pouring over 150ml (5fl oz) hot water. Cover the pan and simmer for 10–15 minutes or until the carrots are just tender.

4 Stir in the red pepper and green beans and continue cooking, uncovered, for 10 minutes or until the vegetables are softened.

5 Add the butter beans and pour in another 150ml (5fl oz) hot water. Half cover the pan and simmer for a further 10 minutes. You might need to add more water as the beans cook.

6 Garnish with chopped coriander and serve with boiled rice.

Butter beans >
These starchy, buttery beans add volume and richness to the curries they are used in.

CRAB AND MANGO CURRY

Brimming with sunshine ingredients, this delectable curry from the Maldives marries tropical fruit with sizzling spices and fresh seafood. As with many Asian-inspired dishes, once you get a feel for the ingredients, feel free to experiment – try adding a few cloves, green chillies or white peppercorns, for example. Other fruits that work well with seafood curries include star fruit, papaya and pineapple.

serves 4

tangy and slightly sweet

juice of 1 lime

$^1/_4$ tsp ground turmeric

$^3/_4$ tsp cracked black peppercorns

8 uncooked crab claws

1 firm, slightly under-ripe mango, cut into 2cm ($^3/_4$in) cubes

1 tbsp palm sugar or muscovado sugar

Masala

4 tbsp vegetable oil

$^3/_4$ tsp mustard seeds

2 sprigs of curry leaves (about 2 tbsp leaves)

4cm (1$^5/_8$in) cinnamon stick

1 large onion, sliced

2 red chillies, deseeded and chopped

3 garlic cloves, finely chopped

2cm ($^3/_4$in) piece fresh root ginger, finely chopped

$^1/_2$ tsp ground cumin

$^1/_2$ tsp chilli powder

1 tsp fennel seeds, roasted and ground (p354)

4 large plum tomatoes, skinned and finely chopped

1 Combine the lime juice with the turmeric and cracked peppercorns. Coat the crab claws in the spiced juice and leave on one side.

2 Heat the oil in a *karahi* or wok and add the mustard seeds – they should start popping almost straight away. Toss in the curry leaves and cinnamon stick. After about 30 seconds, once all the spluttering has settled down, add the sliced onion. Turn down the heat, cover the pan and soften the onions for about 5 minutes.

3 Stir in the chillies, garlic and ginger and cook for a further minute before adding the ground cumin, chilli powder and ground fennel. Stir to mix everything together, then tip in the tomatoes. Fry this *masala* until the tomatoes have cooked down and most of the liquid has evaporated.

4 Add the crab claws to the pan along with any spiced lime juice from the bowl. After a few seconds, add the mango cubes and sprinkle over the sugar. Turn the heat up high and continue frying for about 10 minutes or until the crab claws turn colour and the meat is tender. If the *masala* looks like it is catching on the bottom of the pan, add a dash of water now and again.

5 You'll need a small hammer or a pair of crackers to break open the crab shells for eating – it's quite a messy affair, but great fun. Serve with flatbreads or rice.

MTUZI WA SAMAKI KENYAN FISH CURRY

Fiery, broth-like curries, sharpened with tamarind and enriched with coconut milk, are typical of the Gujarati-inspired dishes from East Africa. Most Gujaratis are vegetarian, and although this curry is made with fish, the recipe also works well with vegetables – green beans, baby aubergines and chunks of carrot make a tasty combination. The best accompaniment to this dish would be generous helpings of rice, enough to soak up the delectably soupy *masala*.

serves 4

soup-like and tangy

juice of 1 lime

1 tsp cracked black peppercorns

600g (1lb 5oz) haddock fillet, skinned and cut into 5cm (2in) pieces

6 tbsp vegetable oil

Spice mixture

2 dried red chillies

3/4 tsp coriander seeds

3/4 tsp cumin seeds

1 tsp mustard seeds

1/4 tsp ground turmeric

Masala

1 red onion, finely chopped

1 red pepper, deseeded and shredded

1 red chilli, finely shredded

4 garlic cloves, finely chopped

250g (9oz) plum tomatoes, skinned and finely chopped

200ml (7fl oz) thick coconut milk (p241)

125ml (4fl oz) tamarind water (p355), or to taste

1 To make the spice mixture, roast the chillies and seeds, then grind to a powder (p354). Combine with the turmeric. Leave on one side.

2 Combine the lime juice with the cracked peppercorns and pour over the fish. Heat the oil in a deep-sided frying pan. Pat the fish dry with kitchen paper, then fry for about 1 minute on each side until lightly coloured but not quite cooked through. Using a slotted spoon, transfer the fish to a plate, cover with foil and leave on one side while you make the masala.

3 Add the red onion to the pan you used for frying the fish. Cover and cook for about 5 minutes or until softened. If the onion looks like it is catching on the bottom of the pan, add a dash of water. Tip in the red pepper, chilli and garlic, and continue frying, uncovered, for 10 minutes or until the onions are on the verge of turning colour. Stir in the spice mixture and fry briskly for 1 minute.

4 Stir in the chopped tomatoes and bring to the boil, then pour in 200ml (7fl oz) water. Simmer the curry for about 15 minutes or until thickened.

5 Pour in the coconut milk and add enough tamarind water to lend a pleasant tang. The curry shouldn't be too thick – aim for something almost broth-like in consistency.

6 Return the fish to the pan and simmer for 5–10 minutes or until cooked through. Serve hot.

PLANTAIN CURRY

Kwazulu Natal has a large Indian population and as a result there are plenty of South Indian-inspired dishes to season its diverse cooking styles. Affordable and plentiful, plantains are a staple food for many locals, and make a versatile curry that can be served as a side dish or snack. This recipe, inspired by my mother-in-law, Ambi Pillay, is lighter than most, because she steams the plantains before frying them with peppery curry leaves and popped mustard seeds. Deliciously tart, it's particularly good served with spiced and pickled chillies and relishes.

serves 4

mildly spiced and light

4 plantains

3 tbsp vegetable oil

³/₄ tsp mustard seeds

¹/₂ tsp cumin seeds

1 sprig of curry leaves
(about 1 tbsp leaves)

1 onion, finely chopped

3cm (1¹/₄in) piece fresh root
ginger, finely chopped

2 green chillies, deseeded
and chopped

pinch of ground turmeric

2 tbsp chopped coriander leaves

lemon juice, to sharpen

1 Put the unpeeled plantains in a steamer basket set over a pan of simmering water. Steam for about 10 minutes – they should still be quite firm to the touch.

2 While the plantains are cooking, make the *masala*. Heat the oil in a *karahi* or wok and toss in the mustard seeds followed by the cumin seeds and curry leaves. As soon as the seeds pop and sizzle, tip in the onion, ginger and green chillies. Turn the heat down low, cover the pan and cook for about 10 minutes or until the onion is softened.

3 When the plantains are cool enough to handle, strip off the peel with a sharp knife and grate along their length so you have long coarse shreds. It's best to do this just before you add them to the onion mixture because they discolour really quickly.

4 Add the turmeric to the *masala* while still on the heat and stir well to combine. Tip in the grated plantains and fry for a further 5–7 minutes, keeping an eye on them – you want them to keep some texture and bite. If it looks like it is sticking, add a dash of water.

5 Sprinkle with the chopped coriander, sharpen with a squeeze of lemon and serve with boiled rice.

BUNNY CHOW CURRIED BEANS IN A LOAF

The final word in South African street food, Bunny Chow began life as an affordable and filling meal for workers in the city. No one is quite sure when it originated, but most people believe it's named after a *baniya*, an Indian term for a trader, who coined the idea of filling bean curry into a hollowed-out bread loaf. The word *baniya* has been shortened to 'bunny', and 'chow' translates to mean food. Besides beans, there's a choice of vegetable, chicken and lamb Bunny Chows – they're all incredibly spicy and best enjoyed late at night with plenty of cold beer.

serves 4

full-flavoured and fiery

1 large white sandwich loaf, unsliced

4–6 tbsp vegetable oil

3 sprigs of curry leaves (about 3 tbsp leaves)

2 onions, diced

5cm (2in) piece fresh root ginger, shredded

2 tsp crushed dried chillies

1 potato, about 150g (5½oz), peeled and diced

400g canned chopped tomatoes

1 tsp ground *garam masala*

150g (5½oz) green beans, roughly chopped

2 cans (400g each) kidney beans

juice of 1 small lemon

large handful of coriander leaves, chopped

1 Lay the loaf flat and slice a 3cm (1¼in) layer horizontally off the top. Reserve the top. Pull out most of the crumb from the loaf, leaving 1cm (½in) thick sides on the bread case. Set aside.

2 Heat the oil in a large saucepan and toss in the curry leaves. After about 10 seconds, turn the heat down low and stir in the onions, ginger and chillies. Cover the pan and cook for 10–15 minutes or until the onions are really soft. Uncover and continue frying the onions until they are tinged golden.

3 Add the diced potato, cover the pan again and cook for about 10 minutes or until they're almost tender. Lift the lid every few minutes and give the potatoes a good stir to prevent them from sticking to the bottom of the pan.

4 Tip in the tomatoes and *garam masala* and fry briskly until the tomatoes darken in colour and the *masala* thickens. Stir in the green beans and cook for 1 minute. Add the kidney beans along with the liquid from the cans. Stir well, then bring to the boil and simmer for about 10 minutes or until the curry thickens.

5 Preheat the oven to 180°C (350°F/Gas 4).

6 Sharpen the curried beans with the lemon juice and stir in the chopped coriander. Ladle the hot curry into the hollowed-out loaf, taking care to stop short of filling it right to the top. Replace the lid, pushing down well, so that the bread has a chance to soak in the *masala*. Wrap the loaf in foil and bake for 15 minutes.

7 Bring the filled loaf, still wrapped in foil, to the table. Place on a big board and unwrap. Break open the four corners and tuck in – no cutlery needed!

BOBOTIE SPiCED MiNCE BAKED WiTH SAVOURY CUSTARD

Brought to South Africa by Southeast Asian slaves in the 17th century, Bobotie is a tribute to Cape Malay cooking styles and Islamic culinary influences. Boer settlers used to bake their interpretation of Bobotie inside a hollowed-out pumpkin. Today, it's usually baked in a round pot, with most cooks adding their own special twist – perhaps a handful of raisins or dried apricots, or more chillies for added strength.

serves 4

mild and slightly sweet

2 slices white bread, crusts removed
125ml (4fl oz) milk
2 tbsp vegetable oil
50g (1^3/$_4$ oz) butter
2 onions, roughly chopped
2 red chillies, deseeded and chopped
4 large garlic cloves, finely chopped
600g (1lb 5oz) minced lamb
2^1/$_2$ tsp mild curry powder
^{3}/$_4$ tsp ground cinnamon
^{3}/$_4$ tsp cracked black peppercorns
grated zest and juice of 1 lemon
1 tbsp Mrs Ball's Extra Hot Chutney, or other hot mango chutney, chopped
1 tsp demerara sugar
1 tbsp blanched almonds, halved
6 lemon leaves or fresh bay leaves

Savoury topping
2 large eggs
100ml (3^1/$_2$fl oz) single cream
100ml (3^1/$_2$fl oz) milk
^{1}/$_4$ tsp crushed black peppercorns
pinch of grated nutmeg

1 Tear the bread into rough pieces, place in a small bowl and pour over the milk. Leave on one side for about 10 minutes.

2 Meanwhile, heat the oil in a flameproof casserole and, when hot, add the butter. Tip in the onions and chillies and cook until golden. Add the garlic and minced lamb and continue frying, stirring frequently, until the meat browns. Sprinkle over the curry powder, ground cinnamon, peppercorns and lemon zest. Stir and fry over a moderate heat for a further 5 minutes to cook the spices.

3 Squeeze excess milk from the soaked bread, then add the bread to the mince. Stir well to break up any lumps. Add the lemon juice, chutney, sugar and almonds. Remove from the heat and leave to cool before turning the meat mixture into a 1 litre (2 pint) pie dish. Roll the lemon or bay leaves into cigar shapes and stand them upright in the spiced meat. They should peep through the lamb.

4 Preheat the oven to 180°C (350°F/Gas 4).

5 Whisk together the eggs, cream and milk and stir in the peppercorns. Pour this savoury custard over the mince and sprinkle with grated nutmeg. Set the pie dish in a roasting tin half filled with hot water. Bake for about 25 minutes or until the topping is golden and set.

6 Serve with boiled rice or baked sweet potatoes. Bobotie also works well with a crisp salad and some tangy chutney.

The labourers of the 1800s who were shipped over from the Indian subcontinent and China to work the plantations of the Caribbean left their mark in the best possible place – the bellies of the Caribbean people. From Arrival Day in 1845 to the present, the colours, flavours and textures of Indian cooking pervade meals from breakfast through dinner and are enjoyed on holidays and high-days as well as at the many Indian festivals and religious days celebrated throughout the islands. Just as those of African and Indian descent have mixed and married and blurred their ethnic descent, so the foods of these countries have jumped into the cooking pot and mixed themselves together to produce a vibrant cuisine.

Indian immigration to Trinidad spanned the period 1845–1917, and during this time over 140,000 Indians were transported to Trinidad and Tobago alone. These indentured labourers arrived to replace the black African workers who had been released from slavery in 1833. The Indians were a displaced population over 12,000 miles from home; the continuation of their culinary traditions offered comfort as they adapted to their new country. Today, Indo-Caribbeans form a large part of the population in Guyana, Surinam, and Trinidad and Tobago. Smaller groups live elsewhere in the Caribbean, especially in Barbados, Jamaica, Grenada, Martinique and Guadeloupe.

In Trinidad and Tobago 42 per cent of the population is of Indian descent, and it is here that you find the largest variety of Indo-Caribbean dishes in the islands. The vast majority of street food is Indian-based: a typical early morning scene in Port of Spain, Trinidad, sees labourers and lawyers in the same queue waiting for their day to start with a delicious snack called 'doubles' (p349), which is generally eaten by the roadside, accompanied by ice-cold coconut water drunk from the cracked-open nut.

One of the most popular Indo-Caribbean street snacks is the *roti*. In India this is the name for a flatbread, but in the islands a *roti* is the bread with its curried filling. The bread by itself is called a *roti* 'flap' or 'skin', and it can be filled with just about any curry: goat, prawns, chicken, beef or chickpeas and vegetables. Bread is the most popular partner for curry in the Caribbean, although it is also served with rice. In fact, it was the Indian and Chinese labourers who introduced rice to the area.

The influence of curry even permeates the music of the region. 'Chutney' is not only a condiment to accompany curry but is also the name given to the Indian version of soca and soul. Drawing inspiration from the rhythms of pan and rap as well as Indian folk and Bollywood film music, chutney songs have become immensely popular.

Judy Bastyra

CARIBBEAN

THE RAW MATERIALS

SPRING ONIONS

Known as scallions or 'cives' in the islands, these are an integral part of any fresh seasoning mix. Combined with celery, chives, parsley, *chandon beni* and garlic, they make 'green seasoning', which is used in Trinidad to season meat, poultry and fish.

CHILLIES

It is hot chillies (or hot peppers, as they are called) that give Caribbean cooking its distinctive flavour. There are many varieties used, including Scotch bonnets, tiny bird or bird's eye chillies and 'seasoning peppers', but it is the Scotch bonnet that is the most popular. It is extremely hot, with a distinctive aroma and fruity flavour. It is so-named because it resembles a little bonnet. Seasoning peppers also have a strong flavour, but they don't have the heat of the other chillies. If you are unable to find hot Caribbean chillies, a Caribbean hot pepper sauce will give a more authentic flavour than using other fresh chillies.

CHANDON BENI

Also called culantro (*Eryngium foetidum*), the leaves of this pungent wild herb are used as a flavouring in Trinidad and Tobago as well as on many of the Spanish islands. It is known by many other names: shadow bennie, shado beni, shadon bene and chandon beni, among them. All seem to be descended from a French vernacular name, *chandon beni*, meaning 'blessed thistle', because the plant has thistle-like leaves. In Jamaica it is known as 'fit weed', because it is thought to cure fits. Fresh coriander leaves are a good substitute.

CURRY POWDER

Unlike most other countries where curry is cooked, in the Caribbean curries are seasoned with locally manufactured curry powders. Each mix is a little bit different, with the spices and the proportions used varying according to local tastes. None of the curry powders is very hot. 'Colombo' is a special mixture of Indian spices used in Guadeloupe when making a curry.

THYME

This aromatic herb is used throughout the Caribbean, but especially in Trinidad and Tobago as an integral part of the 'seasoning mix'.

Chandon beniAlso called culantro (Eryngium foetidum), the leaves of this pungent wild herb are used as a flavouring in Trinidad and Tobago as well as on many of the Spanish islands. It is known by many other names: shadow bennie, shado beni, shadon bene and chandon beni, among them. All seem to be descended from a French vernacular name, chardon beni, meaning 'blessed thistle', because the plant has thistle-like leaves. In Jamaica it is known as 'fit weed', because it is thought to cure fits. Fresh coriander leaves are a good substitute.

ALLSPICE

Allspice is the dried berry of a tropical tree that is cultivated in Jamaica. The flavour is like a mixture of cloves, black pepper, cinnamon and nutmeg, which is why it is called allspice. Its other names are pimento and Jamaica pepper. It is one of the core ingredients in many Jamaican dishes, such as jerk, as well as curries. Allspice is used much in the same way as cloves, either whole or ground to a powder.

< **Allspice berries**

'RIVER LIME' CURRIED DUCK

As you drive through the countryside in Trinidad you will often see groups of Indo-Caribbean people gathered on a river bank, relaxing, enjoying each other's company, drinking icy-cold Carib beer and generally having a good time. This is what is known as a 'river lime', and curried duck is one of the dishes often cooked in a 'dutchie' over an open fire by the river. Dutchie is a local term for a 'Dutch pot', which arrived in the Caribbean islands in the mid 1600s from the Netherlands, brought by the early explorers who used these cooking vessels on their expeditions into the interior. Made from aluminium scraps and river sand, the dutchie (also called a 'coal pot') is still used all over the Caribbean.

serves 4–6

strong and full-flavoured

1 duck, about 2.25kg (5lb), skinned, trimmed of excess fat and cut into serving pieces

1 bunch of thyme, stalks removed

1 tbsp finely chopped fresh root ginger

2 garlic cloves, pounded to a paste

1 red onion, cut into small dice

5 'seasoning peppers', finely chopped, or 1 Scotch bonnet chilli, deseeded and finely chopped

1 bunch of *chandon beni* or coriander leaves, chopped

5 tbsp Trinidadian curry powder

1 tbsp ground turmeric

1 tbsp roasted cumin seeds

4 tbsp vegetable oil

900ml–1.2 litres (1½–2 pints) coconut milk (p241)

1 Scotch bonnet chilli

salt and pepper

1 Season the duck with the thyme leaves, ginger, garlic, onion, seasoning peppers, *chandon beni* and 1 tbsp curry powder. Allow to marinate overnight, if possible.

2 Mix the remaining curry powder, the turmeric and cumin with 4 tbsp water. Heat the oil in a heavy frying pan, add the spice mixture and fry for 12 minutes or until browned. Add the duck and stir well to coat with the spices. Cook for 15 minutes to brown the duck on all sides.

3 Add the coconut milk and bring to the boil. Lower the heat to a simmer and add the whole Scotch bonnet chilli. Cover and cook for about 1¼ hours or until the duck is tender.

4 Remove the lid and simmer for a further 10 minutes or until the liquid has reduced a little. Season with salt and pepper. Serve immediately, garnished with a few extra chopped chandon beni or coriander leaves. Serve with rice.

Thyme >
The earthy and peppery thyme, can withstand long, slow cooking, imparting a spicy, understated flavour.

TRINIDADIAN ROTI CURRIED PRAWNS IN SPLIT PEA FLATBREAD

One of the most popular street foods in Trinidad is roti, which can best be described as curry parcels – flatbreads wrapped around various curries and then eaten like a hot sandwich. *Roti* vendors are found throughout Trinidad and Tobago, but one of the best places is in St James, down Port of Spain. On Friday nights the place is buzzing. The bars are full and people spill out on to the street. The action continues into the early hours, with fresh *rotis* being made throughout the night. The secret to this simple prawn filling is the 'green seasoning' (p342).

serves 6

warmly spiced

900g (2lb) raw medium-sized prawns, peeled

1 tsp finely chopped garlic

1 large onion, finely chopped

3 tbsp curry powder, preferably Trinidadian

2 tbsp vegetable oil

2 medium potatoes, about 225g (8oz) in total, cut into cubes, boiled for 5 minutes and drained

1 tsp salt

1 Scotch bonnet chilli, deseeded and finely sliced

1 tbsp finely chopped *chandon beni*, or 2 tbsp finely chopped coriander leaves

6 Dhalpurie Roti (p348)

Green seasoning

1 bunch of spring onions, coarsely chopped

2 tbsp coarsely chopped chives

2 tbsp coarsely chopped parsley

3 tbsp chopped *chandon beni* or coriander leaves

4 garlic cloves, peeled

1 First, make the green seasoning. Put all the ingredients in a food processor or blender with 4 tbsp water and process until very finely chopped, almost puréed. (This makes more seasoning than is needed for the recipe, but the remainder can be kept in the fridge for up to 1 week. For keeping longer, substitute 1 tbsp cane or white vinegar for all the water.)

2 Season the prawns with the garlic, half the onion and 4 tbsp of the green seasoning, tossing well. Set aside for 30 minutes.

3 Mix the curry powder with 4 tbsp of water to make a paste. Heat the oil in a frying pan, add the remaining onion and cook for 6 minutes to soften. Add the curry paste and cook for 1 minute. Stir in the potatoes and cook over a low heat for 5 minutes.

4 Add the prawns with the salt and chilli and stir for 1-2 minutes to coat the prawns with the curry mixture. Pour in 125ml (4fl oz) water and cook on a high heat for 3-5 minutes or until the prawns have turned pink and are cooked through. Do not overcook, or the prawns will become tough. Stir in the *chandon beni* or coriander and serve hot, wrapped in the *roti*.

JAMAICAN GOAT CURRY

No Jamaican party would be complete without a pot of goat curry. Goat is a very popular meat throughout the Caribbean, but it is a real Jamaican speciality – another Jamaican dish called 'Mannish Water', which is a soupy stew made from all parts of the goat, is meant to have aphrodisiac properties. You can use either the leg or the rib cut of the goat. Traditionally it is cooked on the bone, which the butcher cuts for you into manageable pieces, and sucking the bones is part of the enjoyment (Jamaicans believe that the meat is always sweeter next to the bone). This recipe uses boned leg of goat, but with the bone cut up and added to the pot during cooking, to give extra body to the sauce. If you are unable to find goat, lamb tastes just as good. In Jamaica this is served with rice and peas, and fried plantain.

Serves 4-6

mild, creamy and meaty

2kg (4½lb) leg of goat, boned (bones reserved), washed, dried and cut into 2.5cm (1in) cubes

2 tbsp finely chopped chives

2 Scotch bonnet chillies, 1 deseeded and chopped, the other left whole

4 garlic cloves, finely chopped

1 tsp ground allspice

1 small bunch of thyme, leaves chopped

4 tbsp Caribbean curry powder

2 tbsp vegetable oil

2 onions, finely chopped

1 tbsp grated fresh root ginger

1 tsp salt

400ml (14fl oz) coconut milk (p241)

1 Ask the butcher to cut up the bones for you. Season the cubes of meat with the chives, chopped chilli, half the garlic, the allspice, half the thyme and 2 tbsp of the curry powder. Cover and marinate for at least 4 hours, preferably overnight.

2 Heat the oil in a large flameproof casserole, or 'dutchie' (p343), and add the remaining garlic and thyme, the onions and ginger. Cook for about 5 minutes or until the onions start to turn golden.

3 Mix the remaining curry powder with 4 tbsp of water. Add to the pot and cook, stirring, until all the liquid has evaporated. Add the cubes of goat meat and cook over a low heat for 5 minutes or until the meat is seared all over, stirring constantly to prevent it from sticking to the pot.

4 Add the bones, salt and whole chilli, then pour over the coconut milk and 250ml (9fl oz) water. Bring up to the boil. Reduce the heat to low, cover and simmer for 2 hours.

5 Remove the lid and continue cooking for about 30 minutes or until the meat is soft and tender and the sauce is thick and glossy. Serve hot.

DHALPURIE ROTI GROUND SPLIT PEA FLATBREAD

There are two types of *roti* 'skins' or 'flaps' in Trinidad. One is plain and the other is stuffed with split peas. The latter is known as Dhalpurie Roti, or just Dhalpurie. *Roti* may be folded around a curry and eaten with the hands like a sandwich, or served to accompany a curry, with the torn pieces of *roti* being used as a utensil to scoop up the curry. Once made, *roti* can be frozen, then reheated in the microwave.

makes 12

mild and filling

2 heaped tbsp caster sugar

2 eggs

400ml (14fl oz) full-fat milk

750g (1lb 10oz) plain flour

1 tbsp salt

¹/₂ tsp baking powder

4 tbsp vegetable oil

4 tbsp vegetable oil or melted margarine, or a mixture, for cooking

Split pea filling

225g (8oz) split peas

¹/₂ tsp ground turmeric

2 tsp salt

3 garlic cloves, chopped

1 tbsp vegetable oil

1 tbsp ground cumin

1 To make the filling, put the split peas into a pan with the turmeric, half the salt and the garlic. Cover with water, bring to the boil and boil for 15–20 minutes or until cooked but still firm. Drain well and allow to cool.

2 Grind the split peas to a powdery paste in a food processor or coffee grinder. Heat the oil in a frying pan and fry the split pea paste over a moderate heat for 1 minute, stirring constantly to prevent it from sticking to the pan or burning. Add the cumin and remaining salt to taste. Set aside while you make the dough.

3 Mix the sugar and eggs with the milk in a large jug, stirring until the sugar has dissolved. Sift the flour into a large mixing bowl and stir in the salt and baking powder. Gradually add the egg and milk mixture and knead lightly to make a soft dough. Take care not to work the dough too much or it will become stretchy. Cover with a damp cloth and leave to rest for 15 minutes.

4 Add the oil and mix lightly. Divide the dough into 12 pieces and shape each into a ball. Open each one and place 2–3 tbsp of the split pea mixture inside. Pull the sides over to enclose the filling and re-form into balls. Dredge lightly with flour, then carefully roll out the filled balls very thinly, using enough flour on the work surface to prevent sticking.

5 Heat an oiled griddle or *tawa* and place a rolled-out *roti* on top. Cook for 1 minute, then turn over and brush with oil or melted margarine. Cook for ¹/₂ minute, then turn over again and brush with oil or margarine. Remove and set aside while you cook the remaining roti in this way. Serve hot.

DOUBLES BARA AND CURRIED CHICKPEAS

Doubles consists of two delicate pancake-type breads called *bara* filled with lightly curried chickpeas (*channa*), served with hot pepper sauce and mango chutney. My favourite Doubles vendor is George, who is located just outside the Brooklyn Bar in Port of Spain. Confusingly, just a few yards away there's another vendor selling Doubles, with a huge sign saying 'George X'. This is George's ex-wife.

serves 8-12

mild and appetizing

250g (9oz) dried chickpeas, soaked overnight

2 tbsp vegetable oil

1 large onion, finely chopped

4 garlic cloves, finely chopped

2 tbsp mild curry powder

1 tsp ground cumin

1 tsp salt

1/4 tsp chopped Scotch bonnet chilli or hot pepper sauce (optional)

chopped *chandon beni* or coriander leaves

Bara

350g (12oz) plain flour

1 1/2 tsp instant yeast

1/2 tsp caster sugar

1/2 tsp salt

1 tsp ground turmeric

1/2 tsp ground cumin

2 tablespoons melted margarine

250ml (9fl oz) vegetable oil for deep-frying

1 Drain the chickpeas, then put them in a pan of fresh salted water. Bring to the boil and boil for 15-20 minutes or until hey are tender. Drain well.

2 Heat the oil in a large frying pan, add the onion and garlic and cook for a few minutes until golden. Stir in the curry powder and pour in 4 tbsp water. Cook for another few minutes. Stir in the chickpeas and cook for a further 5 minutes. Pour in 250ml (8floz) of water and season with the cumin, salt and chilli. Bring to the boil, then reduce the heat to low, cover and cook for 15 minutes or until the chickpeas are soft and juicy, adding more water if necessary. Keep warm while you make the bara (or reheat for serving).

3 Mix the flour, yeast, sugar, salt, turmeric, cumin and margarine together in a bowl. Add about 250ml (9fl oz) warm water to make a soft dough. Knead for a few minutes, then return to the bowl. Cover and set aside for 15 minutes.

4 Form the dough into 24 balls. On an oiled work surface, using your fingertips, pat each ball flat into a thin pancake about 8cm (3 1/4in) in diameter.

5 Heat the oil for deep-frying in a deep-sided frying pan. When the oil is hot, fry the *bara* one at a time: add to the oil and fry for just 5-7 seconds or until the dough starts to bubble, then turn over and fry for another 5-7 seconds. Remove with a slotted spoon and drain on kitchen paper. Keep warm in a low oven while you fry the remaining *bara*.

6 Serve by making a sandwich: place 2 tbsp of curried chickpeas between a pair of *bara*, adding some *chandon beni* plus hot pepper sauce and/or mango chutney to taste.

< Scotch bonnet chillies
These colourful chillies are very hot and have a deep, smoky flavour. They are mostly used in Caribbean cuisine.

LEILA'S GUYANESE CHICKEN CURRY

A Guyanese friend of mine gave me this delicious recipe, which I have used time and time again. What makes it slightly different to other Caribbean curry recipes is that you make your own spice mix and then combine it with some ready-made curry paste. The spice powder can be kept in an airtight container for several weeks. Although the recipe is for chicken, both lamb and beef would taste equally delicious. I have skinned the chicken, making the dish less fatty. Also, without the skin, the spices can seep further into the chicken meat.

serves 4–6

warmly spiced and aromatic

1 tsp ground turmeric

1 tbsp Madras curry paste

2 tbsp vegetable oil

1 large onion, finely chopped

5 garlic cloves, finely chopped

1 tsp grated fresh root ginger

2 red chillies, chopped

1 chicken, about 1.6kg (3¹/₄lb), skinned and cut into 8–10 pieces

4 medium tomatoes, skinned and chopped

6 curry leaves

2 medium potatoes, peeled and quartered

Curry powder

2 tbsp coriander seeds

1 tbsp cumin seeds

1 tbsp cardamom pods

1 tsp black peppercorns

1 tsp cloves

1 cinnamon stick

2 tsp black mustard seeds

1 To make the curry powder, roast and grind all the spices (p354). Mix 2 tbsp of the curry powder with the turmeric and curry paste. Add 2 tbsp water and mix well.

2 Heat the oil in a large heavy-based saucepan and fry the chopped onion, garlic, ginger and chillies until golden brown. Add the curry mixture and fry for 3–5 minutes, stirring constantly to ensure that the mixture does not burn. Add the chicken pieces to the saucepan and turn them so that they are thoroughly coated with the spice mixture.

3 Add the tomatoes and curry leaves and cook for 1 minute, then add the potatoes and 125ml (4fl oz) water. Cover the saucepan and simmer for 20 minutes or until the chicken is cooked. Stir the curry occasionally during the cooking, to make sure that it does not stick to the pan. Serve immediately with rice or *roti*.

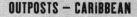

Indian cuisine is omnipresent in Britain – so much so that Chicken Tikka Masala has been voted Britain's favourite national dish. Two centuries of colonial presence in the Indian subcontinent fostered a much-flaunted love affair with the Indian kitchen, and Britain, reinventing a centuries-old culinary heritage, has made 'going out for a curry' and 'having a take-away' celebrated symbols of multiculturalism.

The British *memsahib* adapted Indian *masalas* to suit Western palates, and in so doing 'authenticity' went out of the window. Colonial-style curries were made up of meat, fried with a curry paste before being stewed in water. Anglicized curries, made popular by returning expatriates, were often embellished with chopped bananas, shredded coconut and raisins, a style of cooking virtually unknown in South Asia.

South Asian immigrants arrived in Britain's big cities from India, Bangladesh, Pakistan, Sri Lanka and East Africa during the sixties and seventies, and many entered the restaurant and catering industry. Adept at adapting menus to suit local tastes and expectations, the South Asian restaurant sector has been the success story of the second half of the last century.

Most Indians prefer lamb or chicken curry made with meat cooked on the bone, the advantage being that while the meat simmers, it makes its own flavoursome sauce. In Britain, however, meat cooked this way can be tricky to negotiate on the plate, especially with cutlery, which might explain why boneless meat is preferred.

While menus at many high street curry houses have remained largely unchanged over the past two decades, the emergence of newer styles of cooking at fine restaurants has elevated modern Indian cooking to a privileged position. More recently, supermarkets have developed new product ranges championing regional gems, including Keralan fish curry and *biryani* from Hyderabad.

But it's the tried-and-tested stalwarts of Indo-British cooking that continue to hold their own, such as Madras Curry (p363), creamy *kormas* and Chicken Tikka Masala (p365). The difference today is that there's a culinary curiosity to lift the lid off the Indian spice box and cook authentic recipes at home.

Roopa Gulati

BRITAIN

ROASTING AND GRINDING SPICES

Dry-roasting whole spices makes them more aromatic and brings out their flavour. It also dries them and makes them easier to grind to a powder.

1 Heat a small, heavy-bottomed frying pan or griddle over a moderate heat. Add the whole spices and roast for about 1 minute, stirring constantly or shaking the pan to prevent the spices from scorching.

2 As soon as they start to darken and you catch the lovely spicy aroma, remove from the heat and tip the spices on to a plate. Cool.

3 Transfer the spices to a mortar and grind to a fine powder using the pestle. Alternatively, use a spice mill or clean electric coffee grinder.

4 For a very fine result, pass the powder through a sieve to remove any remaining bits of husks and seed.

TAMARIND WATER

As a general guide, use a walnut-sized piece or about 30g (1oz) of pulp and 125ml (4fl oz) water. To make thick tamarind water, use twice as much pulp.

1 Break a piece of tamarind pulp from the block, put it in a bowl and cover with hot water.

2 Leave to soak for 10–15 minutes or until the pulp has softened, then squeeze and mash the pulp with your fingers to loosen and separate the fibres and seeds.

3 Strain the thick brown water through a sieve into a bowl; discard the solids. Tamarind water can be stored in the fridge for 2 weeks.

MADRAS FIERY CURRY PASTE

This paste can be used in various chicken and vegetable curries. Curry leaves mixed with dried chillies and other spices give it a hot, lemony flavour. Mix a small quantity of the paste in a curry for a sharp, but palatable taste.

makes 400g (14oz)

150ml (5fl oz) vegetable oil

1 tsp mustard seeds

5 sprigs of curry leaves

2 tsp sugar

1 tsp salt

Spice paste

6 garlic pods, peeled

20g (³/₄oz) ginger

10 dried red chillies

1 tbsp cumin seeds

1 tbsp coriander seeds

250ml (9fl oz) wine or malt vinegar

Dry mix

1 tsp *garam masala* powder

1 tbsp paprika

½ tsp ground turmeric

1 Put all the ingredients for the spice paste in a blender and grind to make a paste. Mix together the ingredients for the dry mix, add it to the spice paste and blend into the paste.

2 Heat the oil in a frying pan. Add the mustard seeds and cook over a moderate heat until they crackle.

3 Add the curry leaves and sauté for 5 seconds or until the leaves begin to release their aroma.

4 Add the spice paste and cook for 10 minutes over a moderate heat.

5 Reduce the heat and simmer for 5 minutes or until the *masala* settles to the base.

6 Add sugar and salt and check the seasoning. Set aside to cool, then transfer the paste to an airtight container and store for up to 1 month.

ROGAN JOSH LAMB CURRY WITH AROMATIC SPICES

More upmarket than earthy *baltis* (p181), Rogan Josh evolved from Kashmiri roots and was one of the earliest curries to achieve mainstream popularity on British high streets. It isn't a chilli-laden curry, but it does have an appealingly intense flavour. Kashmiri chillies, noted for their mildness and bright colour, are traditional but not that easy to get hold of; paprika makes a super substitute. If you can, make this curry a day ahead, to give the *masala* a chance to mature and mellow.

serves 4

mild and fragrant

1 large onion, roughly chopped

4–5 garlic cloves, roughly chopped

4 tbsp vegetable oil

1 brown cardamom pod, split (optional)

8 green cardamom pods, split

2 cinnamon sticks, 3cm (1¼in) each

1 dried bay leaf

5 cloves

¾ tsp black peppercorns

1 blade mace

600g (1lb 5oz) boned shoulder or leg of lamb, cut into 3cm (1¼in) cubes

125g (4½oz) plain yogurt

Spice mix

2 tsp fennel seeds, roasted and ground (p354)

¾ tsp ground coriander

¾ tsp ground cumin

2 tsp mild paprika

½ tsp chilli powder

½ tsp ground ginger

¼ tsp ground turmeric

1 To make the spice mix, combine all the ingredients. Leave on one side.

2 Put the onion in a food processor, add a dash of water and blend to a smooth paste. Tip the onion paste into a small bowl. Alternatively, you can grate the onion. Blend the garlic in the food processor with 1 tbsp water, then transfer to another bowl.

3 Heat the oil in a wok or *karahi* over a moderate heat and add the brown and green cardamoms, cinnamon sticks, bay leaf, cloves, peppercorns and mace. Swirl everything around in the hot oil for about 30 seconds or so, until the spices give off a nutty whiff. Add the onion paste to the pan, turn down the heat and fry until golden. Stir in the garlic paste and continue cooking for 1 minute.

4 Tip the lamb into the pan, turn the heat up and fry for about 10 minutes or until browned. If it looks like it is catching on the bottom of the pan, add a couple of tablespoons of water. Stir in the spice mixture. Gradually add the yogurt to the pan, stirring well between each addition. Pour in enough hot water to barely cover the lamb, then cover the pan and simmer, stirring occasionally, for about 40 minutes or until the lamb is tender and the sauce thickened.

5 If, at the end of cooking, the *masala* is a little thin, take the lamb out of the pan and boil the liquid until thickened. Return the meat to the curry and serve piping hot.

DHANSAK LAMB WITH LENTILS AND TAMARIND

In its purest form, Dhansak is a labour of love to prepare and far removed from often formulaic British interpretations. This lamb curry, with its blend of spiced lentil and vegetable purée with refreshingly tart tamarind, marries modern cooking styles with the rich culinary heritage of the Parsees. In India, Dhansak is always made with lamb, but variations with chicken are just as popular in Britain.

serves 4

sweet and tart

6 garlic cloves, roughly chopped

3cm (1¹/₄in) piece fresh root ginger, roughly chopped

4 tbsp vegetable oil

1 star anise

2 onions, very finely chopped

600g (1lb 5oz) boned shoulder or leg of lamb, cut into 3cm (1¹/₄in) cubes

³/₄ tsp ground coriander

¹/₂ tsp each cracked black peppercorns, ground cinnamon, crushed cardamom seeds, chilli powder and ground cumin

Lentils

25g (scant 1oz) split *gram* lentils (*chana dal*)

25g (scant 1oz) split red lentils (*masoor dal*)

1 small aubergine, diced

handful of fresh fenugreek leaves or mustard greens

75g (2¹/₂oz) pumpkin flesh, diced

To finish

125ml (4fl oz) tamarind water (p355), or to taste

1 rounded tsp palm sugar

2 tbsp shredded mint leaves

1 Wash the *gram* lentils and pour over enough water to cover. Bring to the boil and simmer for about 15 minutes or until half cooked. Add the red lentils, diced aubergine, fenugreek leaves and pumpkin. Simmer until the lentils and vegetables are very soft. Remove the pan from the heat and leave the lentil mixture to cool slightly before blending to a smooth purée. Transfer it to a bowl and leave on one side.

2 Put the garlic and ginger in the rinsed-out blender and pour over 100ml (3¹/₂fl oz) water. Process to make a thin paste, then transfer to a small bowl.

3 Preheat the oven to 170°C (325°F/Gas 3).

4 Heat the oil in a flameproof casserole over a moderate heat. Add the star anise and leave to sizzle for a couple of seconds, then stir in the onions and fry until just beginning to turn golden.

5 Add the meat to the pan and cook, stirring frequently, until browned. Gradually stir in the garlic and ginger paste. Sprinkle over all the spices and fry for 1 minute, stirring all the time. Pour over enough hot water to reach three-quarters of the way up the meat. Bring the curry to boiling point, then cover the pan and transfer to the oven. Cook for about 40 minutes or until the meat is tender.

6 Stir the puréed lentil mixture into the curry and continue cooking for 10 minutes. To finish, add enough tamarind water to sharpen the flavour, and stir in sugar to sweeten. You should aim for a sweet-sour taste. Serve garnished with the mint and accompanied by rice.

CHICKEN KORMA CREAMY CHICKEN CURRY WITH NUTS

Served at Indian banquets and high street curry houses all over Britain, *kormas* come in many guises. The mild creamy sauce is best suited to timid palates, so *korma* is often suggested as a first taster of Indian cooking. South Asian *kormas* are steeped in regal tradition, and even today remain the ultimate party dish. What makes the evolution of British-style *kormas* so intriguing is that they're a global celebration of curry rather than being solely derived from a single regional cuisine. You could use lamb instead of chicken. Just remember to give it a longer cooking time, adding more water as it simmers.

serves 4

mild and aromatic

1/4 tsp saffron threads

3 tbsp vegetable oil

1 tbsp *ghee* or clarified butter

1 blade mace

5 cloves

6 cardamom pods, split

4cm (1⅝in) cinnamon stick

1 onion, very finely chopped

3cm (1¼in) piece fresh root ginger, roughly chopped

6 garlic cloves, roughly chopped

4 boned chicken thighs, about 600g (1lb 5oz) in total

1/2 tsp mild chilli powder or paprika

1 tsp ground coriander

1/2 tsp ground *garam masala*

Browned onion paste

1 onion, thinly sliced

salt

vegetable oil for deep-frying

Nut paste

1 tbsp cashew nuts

1 tbsp almonds, blanched

To finish

75ml (2½fl oz) thick coconut milk (p241)

75ml (2½fl oz) single cream

1 tbsp chopped coriander leaves

1 For the browned onion paste, sprinkle the sliced onion with salt and set aside for 20 minutes. Pat the onion dry with kitchen paper. Heat vegetable oil in a deep-fryer or wok and fry the onion slices until golden. Drain on kitchen paper. Transfer the warm fried onion to a food processor. Add 2 tbsp hot water and process until smooth. Leave on one side.

2 For the nut paste, soak the cashew nuts and almonds in boiling water, covered, for 30 minutes. Drain the nuts, reserving 2–3 tbsp of the liquid. Grind the nuts to a paste in a food processor, helping them along their way with a dash of the soaking liquid.

3 Put the saffron threads in a small bowl and cover with 2 tbsp hot water. Leave to soak for at least 10 minutes. Meanwhile, heat the oil in a *karahi* or wok and add the *ghee*. Once melted, stir in the mace, cloves, cardamom pods and cinnamon stick. Swirl the spices around for about 30 seconds. When you catch a warm nutty aroma, add the chopped onion. Turn the heat down low and cook for about 5 minutes or until the onion is soft but not coloured.

4 While the onion is cooking, put the ginger and garlic in a food processor and add 2 tbsp water. Blend to a smooth paste. Add this paste to the onions and fry, stirring well, for a further 1 minute. Stir in the nut paste and continue cooking, stirring all the time, for 2–3 minutes or until most of the liquid has evaporated.

5 Add the chicken pieces to the pan along with the chilli powder, ground coriander and *garam masala*. Combine everything and fry for 5 minutes to cook the spices. Pour over about 125ml (4fl oz) water and turn the heat down low. Cover the pan and simmer for 10 minutes or until the chicken is cooked, stirring occasionally. If the curry looks like it is catching on the bottom of the pan, add a dash more water.

6 Add the browned onion paste and stir to combine. Pour the coconut milk and cream over the curry. Bring to a simmer, then add the saffron and its soaking liquid. Scatter over the chopped coriander and serve piping hot with *naans*.

MADRAS CURRY FIERY LAMB CURRY

You're likely to draw a blank if you go to Chennai and ask for a Madras Curry – it's almost as British as Lancashire Hot Pot. Take a culinary journey around numerous curry houses, and you'll find as wide a variety of Madras curries as there are number of restaurants. What they do all have in common is fiery chilli heat. Simple to make at home, Madras Curry tastes far better than take-away meals, and you remain in charge of how many chillies go into the pot.

serves 4

chilli-hot and robust

3 tbsp vegetable oil

2 onions, very finely chopped

250g (9oz) plum tomatoes, skinned and finely chopped

2 tsp tomato purée

600g (1lb 5oz) boned shoulder or leg of lamb, cut into 3cm (1¼in) chunks

150ml (5fl oz) thick coconut milk (p241)

Dry spice blend

1 tsp coriander seeds

1 tsp cumin seeds

½ tsp mustard seeds

3-4 dried red chillies

½ tsp black peppercorns

Coconut paste

¼ tsp ground turmeric

½ tsp ground cinnamon

4 garlic cloves, roughly chopped

2cm (¾in) piece fresh root ginger, roughly chopped

3 tbsp freshly grated coconut

3 tbsp white wine vinegar

1 To make the spice blend, roast and grind the spices (p354). Leave on one side.

2 For the coconut paste, combine all the ingredients in a food processor and process until smooth. You might need to add a dash of water to help it along its way.

3 Heat the oil in a large flameproof casserole and fry the onions until golden. Stir in the tomatoes, tomato purée and dry spice mixture. Cook briskly, stirring frequently, for about 10 minutes or until the sauce has thickened.

4 Add the meat to the pan and fry over a high heat until it starts to colour. While the meat is cooking, gradually add the spiced coconut paste. Turn the heat down low and pour over enough hot water to reach three-quarters of the way up the meat. Cover the pan and simmer for about 30 minutes or until the lamb is tender.

5 Just before serving, add the coconut milk and gently reheat the curry, stirring frequently. Serve with rice or Indian breads.

Coriander seeds >
These seeds impart a warm, floral fragrance to *masala* mixes.

CHICKEN TIKKA MASALA

The popularity of Chicken Tikka Masala is testament to Britain's centuries-old love affair with Indian food. Don't be shy with the garlic and ginger – this dish is big on bold flavours. Simple to make, this curry also embraces other ingredients. For a vegetarian version, cut a block of *paneer* or tofu into large cubes and add the pieces, without marinating, to the tomato sauce at the end of cooking.

serves 4

rich and full-flavoured

6 boned chicken thighs, about 675g (1½lb) in total, skinned

juice of 2 limes

1 tsp paprika

1½ tsp cumin seeds

½ tsp coriander seeds

2 shallots, roughly chopped

4 large garlic cloves, roughly chopped

4cm (1⅝in) piece fresh root ginger, roughly chopped

2 green chillies, deseeded and roughly chopped

125g (4½oz) plain Greek-style yogurt

½ tsp ground *garam masala*

1 tbsp vegetable oil

Sauce

400g canned chopped tomatoes

1 rounded tsp tomato purée

handful of coriander leaves, roughly chopped

3cm (1¼in) piece fresh root ginger, grated

1 tsp lime juice

½ tsp caster sugar

50g (1¾oz) unsalted butter

125ml (4fl oz) single cream

1 Cut the chicken thighs into 3cm (1¼in) chunks. Combine the lime juice and paprika and mix with the chicken. Leave on one side while you roast and grind the cumin and coriander seeds (p354).

2 Put the shallots, garlic, ginger and chillies into a food processor. Drain the lime juice and paprika mixture from the chicken and add to the onion mixture. Process until smooth. Tip into a mixing bowl and stir in the yogurt, *garam masala* and add half the coriander and cumin powder.

3 Pour the spiced yogurt mixture over the chicken, turning every piece so that it's evenly coated. Cover with cling film and marinate overnight in the fridge. If you can, flip the chicken over once or twice while it's marinating.

4 Preheat the grill, with the grill pan in place, to its hottest setting.

5 Take the chicken out of the yogurt marinade and arrange on the hot grill pan. Drizzle with the oil and grill for about 5 minutes on each side or until beginning to char around the edges. Pour any cooking juices into a bowl and skim off any fat. Keep the chicken warm while you make the sauce.

6 Combine the tomatoes, tomato purée, coriander leaves, ginger, lime juice, sugar and remaining cumin and coriander powder in a blender or food processor and process until smooth. Heat the butter in a saucepan and, when melted, add the spiced tomato mixture and cream. Bring to simmering point, then strain in the reserved cooking juices and add the cooked chicken pieces. Reheat and serve piping hot, with Indian breads.

PRAWN BALTI

Having more in common with Birmingham than Pakistan, *baltis* are a star attraction for curry aficionados. Putting together a *balti* is a theatrical affair, best appreciated when ingredients are showered into a cavernous *karahi* and flash-fried over a fierce heat. Expect robust garlicky notes, plenty of onions and a sprinkling of tingling chillies – perfect for mopping up with an obliging *naan*. No one's really sure how they came into being - *balti* means 'bucket' in Punjabi – hardly a prosaic description. However, chances are that *batti*, which means food, could well have been the inspiration behind naming Birmingham's most-loved curry.

serves 4

warmly spiced

500g (1lb 2oz) raw king prawns, peeled but last tail section left on

juice of 1 lime

1¹⁄₂ tsp paprika

Masala

3 tbsp vegetable oil

1 red onion, diced

4cm (1⁵⁄₈in) piece fresh root ginger, finely shredded

2 garlic cloves, finely chopped

2 green chillies, shredded

1 red pepper, deseeded and shredded

400g canned chopped tomatoes

¹⁄₄ tsp ground turmeric

¹⁄₄–¹⁄₂ tsp red chilli powder

¹⁄₄ tsp ground cinnamon

¹⁄₂ tsp ground *garam masala*

¹⁄₂ tsp ground coriander

¹⁄₂ tsp caster sugar

2 tbsp coarsely chopped coriander leaves, to garnish

1 Put the prawns in a bowl, squeeze over the lime juice and stir in the paprika. Stir well, then leave on one side while you make the *masala*.

2 Heat the oil in a *karahi* or wok set over a moderate heat and fry the onion for about 5 minutes or until softened and just beginning to turn golden. Add three-quarters of the ginger, followed by the garlic, chillies and shredded red pepper. Continue frying for 1 minute.

3 Turn the heat up and add the tomatoes, turmeric, chilli powder, cinnamon, *garam masala*, ground coriander and sugar. Cook briskly until the tomatoes have thickened and darkened in appearance. Pour in about 150ml (5fl oz) hot water, stir well and turn the heat down low.

4 Add the prawns, along with any lime juice from the bowl, and simmer for 3–4 minutes or until they turn pink and are tender.

5 Garnish with chopped coriander and the remaining shredded ginger before serving.

Curry was first introduced to Japan around the middle of the 19th century, by chefs who came with the British traders. The first published Japanese curry recipe in 1872 was 'Curried veal or fowl served with white rice'. In fact, it was not an authentic Indian curry but a curried meat stew, which Westerners adapted from the original. Having travelled to the West, curry was brought back to the East, but this time bypassing India and starting a new life.

This was when Japan, a closed country for the preceding 200 years, opened up its borders to the outside world and also stopped being a vegetarian nation. Many people found eating meat quite intriguing but very challenging. Curry helped to overcome this by disguising the smell of meat with spices and a thick sauce. Also, stewed meat was more tender and easier to chew than grilled.

Over time, 'Curry Rice', or, as it is sometimes called, 'Rice Curry', successfully settled into the Japanese diet. Other meat dishes, such as beef steak, pork cutlet and hashed beef, were introduced at around the same time. They are still called *Yo-Shoku*, which means 'Western food'. Eating these exotic foods was seen to be a sophisticated thing to do by open-minded Japanese people. Today, numerous 'curry houses' can be found all over Japan, and curry is the most popular dish made at home. Ever since the introduction of ready-to-use curry roux (p370) in shops and supermarkets in the sixties, Curry Rice has been a regular dish in the repertoire of Japanese home cooks. Seasonal vegetables can be added to the standard combination of potato, carrot and onion, and seafood such as prawns, clams, squid or canned tuna can be used instead of meat.

In Japan there are those who like Japanese and European curries, those who prefer Indian curries and those who want to eat other Asian curry varieties. One thing all have in common is that they eat them with sticky, white, short-grain Japanese rice, not Basmati rice. This preference is a good example of the 'Japan-ization' of foreign food. Another example is the way curry is combined with traditional Japanese dishes, such as curry and noodles or curry pancake.

At home, curry is eaten with just a spoon. However, at a restaurant the same curry may be served with a European table setting. The Japanese pickles that accompany the curry are presented in a special silver dish and the waiter bows to you politely before pouring curry sauce from a silver saucepot on to your plate of rice. As with so many other aspects of Japanese life, the serving of curry can be quite a formal affair.

Yasuko Fukuoka

JAPAN

THE RAW MATERIALS

Seven vegetable pickles (right) and Pickled Japanese shallots

CURRY ROUX MIX

Solid blocks of 'curry roux mix', which look like bars of chocolate, are sold in shops and supermarkets in Japan alongside other special flavourings such as 'fond de veau' or 'bouquet garni extract' – as if curry roux were also part of French cuisine. Using instant curry roux cuts the preparation time enormously. Consequently, not many Japanese venture to make their own roux at home anymore.

SEVEN VEGETABLE PICKLES

Often coloured a bright red, these sweet pickles (which are called *fuku-jin-duke* in Japanese) were devised to be served with Japanese curry dishes as a substitute for Indian chutney. They contain mooli, shiso perilla leaves, white sesame seeds, small aubergines, sword bean pods, cucumber and lotus root, all of which are finely shredded and pickled in a shoyu-based liquid.

The Japanese never make these pickles at home as the ingredients are not widely available, even in Japan, and the pickling method has remained a closely guarded secret since it was first created by a small specialist shop about 150 years ago. Fuku-jin-duke can easily be found in Japanese or Chinese food shops.

PICKLED JAPANESE SHALLOTS

The Japanese shallot is smaller and sweeter than the European type, and the pickling liquid used to make *rakkyo* is sweeter than a Western pickle. You can make a nice substitute by mixing 1 tsp honey into a cup of pickled pearl onions along with their pickling liquid and leaving overnight.

KARASHI-DUKE RADISHES PICKLED WITH MUSTARD

This is easy to make, and gives you an idea of the kinds of pickles served with a curry in Japan. It goes well with the recipes on the following pages.

Makes 1kg (2¼ lb)

1kg (2¼lb) red radishes, trimmed

1 garlic clove, crushed

45g (1½oz) fine sea salt

100g (3½oz) caster sugar

1 tbsp Japanese or English mustard powder

2 x 5cm (¾ x 2in) strip *dashi-konbu* (optional)

1 Put the radishes, garlic and salt in a large re-sealable plastic bag. Close and seal the bag, then 'massage' the bag with your hands for 2–3 minutes, to rub the salt into the radishes and garlic. Some radishes will be cracked or broken up.

2 Add the sugar, mustard powder and *konbu*. Shake the bag to mix all the ingredients together well. Leave overnight in the refrigerator. The pickles will be ready to eat the following day, and will keep for a week in the fridge.

DASHI SOUP STOCK

Below is the traditional method for preparing Dashi, using seaweed and dried bonito flakes. For instant stock, simply dissolve a 5g sachet (about 1 heaped tsp) *dashi-no-moto* granules in 1.4 litres (2½ pints) warm water.

Makes 1.4 litres (2½ pints)

10 x 5cm (4 x 2in) piece of *dashi-konbu*

35g (1¼oz) *katsuo-bushi* or *kezuri-bushi*

1 Put the *konbu* in a large pan and pour in 1.4 litres (2½ pints) water. Bring to the boil. When the water boils, reduce the heat and remove and discard the *konbu*.

2 Add the *katsuo-bushi* and boil over a low heat for 2 minutes. Strain the stock through a sieve into a bowl. Discard the contents of the sieve.

CURRY NANBAN SOBA CURRY NOODLE WiTH CHiCKEN

A relatively recent innovation, Curry Noodle is a fusion of two favourite dishes that the Japanese love with a passion: noodles in hot soup and a light curry sauce. Three types of noodle can be used: *soba* (buckwheat noodles), *udon* (thick white wheat noodles) or *ramen* (Chinese-style yellow wheat noodles). *Soba* are used here. If the curry roux and soup are all made at home from scratch, it is a quite laborious dish to cook. However, to save time, Japanese cooks often make the stock with *dashi-no-moto* granules, available from Japanese food shops, and curry roux mix (p370). Then you only need to cook the chicken and noodles.

serves 4

savoury and warming

1.4 litres (2½ pints) Dashi (p371)

250g (9oz) chicken thighs, skinned and cut into bite-sized pieces

1 onion, cut into 8 segments lengthways

150ml (5fl oz) *shoyu*

150ml (5fl oz) *mirin*

400g (14oz) dried *soba*

1 spring onion, cut into thin rings

8 mange tout, blanched for 1 minute, then cut diagonally into thin slivers

Curry roux

3 tbsp vegetable oil

1 onion, thinly sliced lengthways

2 garlic cloves, finely chopped

2cm (¾in) piece fresh root ginger, finely chopped or grated with a Japanese grater

3 tbsp plain flour

2½ tbsp mild Japanese or Indian curry powder

1 tbsp tomato ketchup

1 tbsp mango chutney

1 First make the curry roux. Heat the oil in a saucepan and fry the onion, garlic and ginger over a low heat for 20–30 minutes or until golden. Add the flour and curry powder and stir until the oil in the pan has been absorbed. Add the ketchup and chutney, mixing thoroughly. Remove from the heat and set aside.

2 To make the soup, pour the *dashi* stock into a large pan and bring to the boil. Add the chicken and onion and simmer for 5 minutes, skimming off any scum from the surface. Reduce the heat to low.

3 Scoop out about 500ml (16fl oz) of stock and mix little by little into the curry roux to make a smooth, thick paste. Pour the roux mixture into the rest of the stock in the large pan, then add the *shoyu* and *mirin*. Mix thoroughly. Bring to the boil, then reduce the heat and leave to simmer gently while you cook the *soba*.

4 Bring a large pan of water to the boil. Add the *soba* and cook for about 5 minutes or as instructed on the package. As with Italian pasta, *soba* should be cooked al dente and eaten as swiftly as possible. Drain the *soba*, then pop it into the soup. Mix well.

5 Ladle the soup into 4 deep soup bowls. Sprinkle with the spring onion and garnish with the mange tout. Serve immediately.

Spring onions >
A common garnish in Asian cuisines, spring onions add colour, freshness and a mild onion flavour to dishes.

CURRY RICE

This dish is popular with Japanese of all ages. If using a shop-bought curry roux mix (p370), break the roux bar into chunks and add them to the pan after the potato and carrot and bringing the stock to the boil.

serves 4

thick and slightly sweet

450g (1lb) Japanese rice

2 tbsp vegetable oil

50g (1³/₄oz) butter

250g (9oz) stewing beef, cubed

1 onion, cut into 8 chunks lengthways

2 potatoes, peeled and each cut into 4–6 pieces

1 carrot, peeled and cut into 2cm (³/₄in) pieces

1 bay leaf

700ml (24fl oz) beef or vegetable stock

Curry roux

1 onion, thinly sliced lengthways

2 garlic cloves, finely chopped

2cm (³/₄in) piece fresh root ginger, finely chopped or grated with a Japanese grater

2 tbsp mild Japanese or Indian curry powder

4 tbsp plain flour

1 tbsp mango chutney

2 tbsp tomato ketchup

2 tsp *shoyu*

salt and white pepper

1 Put the rice in a bowl and wash under cold running water for 2 minutes. Drain in a sieve. Pour 550ml (18fl oz) water into a large pan with a tight-fitting lid, add the rice and set aside to soak.

2 Heat the oil and half of the butter in a frying pan until the butter melts, then fry the beef over a moderately high heat until browned all over. Remove with a slotted spoon and place on a plate.

3 To make the curry roux, add the sliced onion to the frying pan and reduce the heat to low. Fry for 30–40 minutes or until the onion is soft and well browned. Stir in the garlic, ginger and curry powder and fry for 2 minutes. Add the flour and stir to absorb the oil. Add the chutney, ketchup and *shoyu* and mix well. The roux should look like a thick brown paste. Remove from the heat.

4 Now start cooking the rice. Place the lid tightly on the pan and bring to the boil. As soon as you hear a bubbling noise, turn the heat down to low and simmer for 10 minutes or until the bubbling noise disappears and a faint crackling noise starts. Remove the pan from the heat, without lifting the lid, and leave aside for at least 10 minutes before checking the rice.

5 While the rice is cooking, melt the remaining butter in another deep pan and add the onion chunks and then the browned beef. Fry for 3 minutes. Add the potatoes, carrot and bay leaf and pour in the stock. Bring to the boil. Reduce the heat and simmer for 20 minutes or until the potatoes and carrot are tender. Skim off any scum from the surface.

6 Scoop out about 500ml (16fl oz) of the hot stock and add to the curry roux in the frying pan. Mix well into a smooth and runny mixture. Add this to the rest of the stock in the deep pan and stir in thoroughly. Add salt and pepper to taste. Bring back to the boil and cook for a further 2 minutes.

7 Serve the curry on a bed of warm rice, with some pickles if you like (pp370–371).

KATSU CURRY CURRY RiCE WiTH PORK STEAKS

The word *katsu* is derived from 'cutlet' and generally means a piece of deep-fried boneless meat. Pork is widely used for this dish, although chicken breast is also popular. The pork rests on a bed of rice and the curry sauce is spooned over. Serve with Japanese *ton-katsu* sauce or Worcestershire sauce and pickles (pp370–371).

serves 4

mild, rich and meaty

4 pork loin steaks, about 150g (5½oz) each

2 tbsp plain flour

1 egg, beaten

25g (scant 1oz) fine, dry white breadcrumbs

vegetable oil for deep-frying

450g (1lb) Japanese rice, freshly cooked (see Curry Rice, p373)

Curry roux

2 tbsp vegetable oil

25g (scant 1oz) butter

1 onion, thinly sliced lengthways

2 garlic cloves, finely chopped

2cm (¾in) piece fresh root ginger, finely chopped or grated with a Japanese grater

2 tbsp mild Japanese or Indian curry powder

4 tbsp plain flour

1 tbsp mango chutney

2 tbsp tomato ketchup

2 tsp *shoyu*

Curry sauce

1 tbsp vegetable oil

1 onion, thinly sliced lengthways

400g (14oz) button mushrooms, halved or quartered if large

½ cooking apple, grated with skin

1 small carrot, peeled and grated

1 stick celery, finely chopped

600ml (1 pint) vegetable stock

salt and ground white pepper

1 To make the curry roux, heat the oil and butter in a frying pan, add the onion and reduce the heat to low. Fry for 30–40 minutes or until the onion is soft and brown. Stir in the garlic, ginger and curry powder and fry for 2 minutes. Add the flour and stir to absorb the oil. Add the chutney, ketchup and *shoyu* and mix well. Remove from the heat and set aside.

2 Next make the curry sauce. Heat the oil in another frying pan and fry the onion for 3 minutes. Add the mushrooms and fry until soft. Add the apple, carrot and celery and fry for 5 minutes over a moderately low heat. Pour in the stock and bring to the boil. Stir in the curry roux little by little and add salt and pepper to taste. Cover and leave to simmer gently, stirring occasionally.

3 With a sharp knife, make shallow cuts around the edge of the pork steaks to prevent them from curling up when fried. Season the steaks. Dust lightly with flour, then dip in beaten egg and coat with breadcrumbs, patting them on well.

4 Heat oil for deep-frying to 160°C (325°F). Fry the pork steaks for about 3 minutes per side or until the breadcrumbs are golden brown and the meat is thoroughly cooked. Drain on kitchen paper, then cut the meat into strips about 2cm (¾in) wide. Make a bed of rice on each plate and arrange the pork on top. Spoon over the hot curry sauce and serve immediately.

GLOSSARY

Asian celery
Also known as wild celery, this has a very strong, bitter flavour. Similar in appearance to flat-leaf parsley, it is often used as a flavouring in stir-fries and soups.

Bai yor leaf
Otherwise known as Indian mulberry leaf, this is a tobacco-like plant with a bitter, earthy flavour. In Thailand and the Philippines, young *bai yor* leaves may be shredded and added to curries. It is not readily available in the West.

Balti
Made of heavy cast iron, this cooking vessel is similar to a wok with handles on both sides. It is used to prepare traditional Pakistani dishes and stir-fried dishes.

Betel leaf
These are used in Thailand, mostly as an edible wrapping for certain hors d'oeuvres. They can be replaced with spinach leaves.

Biryani
The original Persian spelling is *biriani*, meaning 'fried', and refers to a spicy dish of meat and basmati rice flavoured with saffron. The Moghul version was often elaborately garnished with gold leaf.

Cha-om
Not widely available in the West, this green herb is in fact the leaves of the Thai Acacia tree. It has a bitter, nutty flavour and is commonly used in Laos and Thailand in soups, curries, omelettes and stir-fries.

Choy sum or Choi sum
Also known as Chinese flowering cabbage, this is a very popular vegetable in Cantonese cuisine, as well as being widely used throughout Asia and the West. It is sold as bunches of leaves, and can be used raw in salads or lightly boiled or steamed to add to meat dishes.

Dal
This can refer to either split lentils (or other pulses) as an ingredient, or, more generically, to a dish containing beans, peas or lentils.

Dalcha
Mostly cooked by South Indian Muslims as an accompaniment to *biryani*, it is a combination of lentils cooked together with meat or vegetables.

Dum cooking
This is a century-old, traditional cooking method of the Indian Muslim community. In this method food is cooked in a thick, heavy-bottomed copper or brass vessel known as *handi*. The *handi* is sealed on the top by dough, to ensure that the food is cooked in its own juices.

Halwa or Halva
Derived from the Arabic word for sweet, *hulw*, in India *halwa* refers to a semolina and sugar-based confectionery. The ingredients and flavourings vary widely, with the simplest recipe involving semolina being fried in *ghee* with syrup and raisins. In Pakistan, meanwhile, *halva* can be similar in texture and appearance to Turkish delight.

Jackfruit
A large fruit native to Southern India, but grown all over India and Sri Lanka. When unripe, it is treated more as a vegetable and added to savoury dishes. As it ripens it becomes much sweeter, and is mainly used in desserts.

Kadhai or karahi
Kadhai, or *karahi*, refers to an Indian wok, and also the dish it produces, namely a stir-fry. This method of cooking is popular with youngsters and amateur chefs, who do not want to spend hours in the kitchen.

Kadhi
Prepared in almost all the states of India, this light yellow gravy is made with yogurt or buttermilk, hot spices, ground turmeric and thickened with chickpea flour. The yogurt or the buttermilk balances the heat of the spices used in the gravy. *Kadhi* is cooked with vegetables such as okra, fresh fenugreek leaves or chickpea dumplings.

Korma
A cooking term which, in India and Pakistan, originally referred to a slow-cooked dish with a sauce. Nuts, yogurt and butter are the ingredients most commonly used to enrich an Indian *korma*.

Masala or Massalla
Meaning 'spice mixture', *masala* can refer to any combination of spices, ground or whole, hot or mild, as a powder or paste. These mixes form the basis for most Indian dishes, and vary widely from region to region. *Garam masala* (p31) is the best-known example, though again the blend will differ according to regional preferences. In terms of preparations, powders are generally preferred in North India, while pastes are favoured in the south.

Mirin
Similar in appearance to rice wine, *mirin* is a liquid sweetener used in Japanese cuisine. It is only used in very small quantites, often in the place of sugar and soy sauce. It has

a low alcohol content, and in the 17th and 18th centuries was even drunk as an alternative to sake.

Pandanus leaf
An important ingredient throughout Southeast Asia, predominantly as a flavouring in Thai, Malaysian and Indonesian cooking. They are added directly to rice dishes and desserts, allowing their delicate fragrance to infuse the food. Use fresh leaves where possible.

Popadum or Papadum
These are thin, round wafers made from dough and fried in oil until crisp. Chickpea flour and lentil flour are both commonly used, and various spices may also be added. In North India they tend to be spicier, whereas in the south a milder recipe is preferred, to balance the hotter local cuisine.

Qualiya
One of the several gravies in Indian cuisine, the *qualiya* gravy is fine, velvety yellow with a touch of saffron and cream. The cream makes the gravy smoother in texture and is cooked with aromatic *garam masalas*.

Raita
This is a cooling, yogurt-based condiment, popular as an accompaniment to fiery curries. The yogurt is seasoned with herbs and spices, including mustard, cumin, mint and coriander. In addition, various chopped vegetables may be added; cucumber is popular in western versions, though aubergine, potato and spinach are just as popular in authentic Indian *raita*.

Rice vinegar
Most Asian vinegars are brewed from rice; they have a lower acid content than malt vinegars and are relatively mild. Japanese brown rice vinegar is the best quality but is not so easy to find.

Shoyu
An essential ingredient in Japanese cuisine, shoyu is a soy sauce which strongly differs in flavour from its Chinese counterpart. This is due to the presence of wheat, which gives the Japanese sauce a sweeter, more alcoholic taste.

Siamese watercress
More commonly known in the West as water spinach and in Thailand as *pak bung*, this leafy vegetable has excellent nutritional qualities. Full of protein and minerals, it is an inexpensive addition for curries and stir-fries.

Snake beans
Also known as yard-long beans, these are excellent eaten raw when very fresh and firm. They can be used as a garnish, or lightly cooked in stir-fries.

Sugar cane vinegar
Popular in the Philippines, this vinegar is mild in flavour, not dissimilar to rice vinegar. It is dark yellow or brown in colour, and, unusually, is not at all sweet.

Tandoor
Essential to the way of life in North India and Pakistan, the tandoor is a clay oven used to bake breads and other dishes. It is the focal point of many homes, and some villages may even have a communal tandoor where gossip is as important as cooking. The fires are fuelled by charcoal and are often kept lit all day.

Tawa or Tava
A flat, circular pan, often made from cast iron, used in Indian cooking to make *chapattis* and *parathas*.

Yakhni
This rich stock from Kashmir is also known as *shorba*. Yakhni is generally cooked with mutton or lamb in yogurt and saffron along with aromatic spices, such as aniseed, fennel, cinnamon sticks, cloves and cardamoms, which gives it a unique taste.

Popadum or Papadum

INDEX

Page numbers in *italic* refer
to illustrations

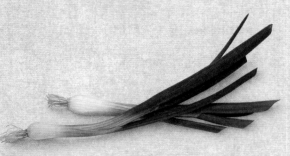

ACKNOWLEDGMENTS

DORLING KINDERSLEY WOULD LIKE TO THANK THE FOLLOWING:

Updated edition 2015
Tanvi Mishra for new photography; Deeba Rajpal for food and prop styling; Aditya Kapoor for his studio space; Nandita Talukder for her props; Roopam Baijal, Harnoor Channi-Tiwary and Madhumita Mitra for recipe testing; Gazal Bawa and Vikas Sachdeva for design assistance; Tarika and Anuja Naorem for editorial assistance; Sreshtha Bhattacharya, Pallavi Paul, Neha Samuel, Suparna Sengupta and Kriti Talwar for proofreading and Aparajita Barai and Namita for assistance.

First edition 2006
Editorial: All of the editorial contributors for being so efficient and accommodating throughout. Jeni Wright and Norma Macmillan for their tireless hard work and professionalism; Food stylists: Bridget Sargeson and Alice Hart; Prop stylist: Victoria Allen; Index: Hilary Bird; DTP: Adam Walker and Emma Hansen-Knarhoi; On behalf of David Thompson: Tanongsak Yordwai who prepared and styled David's food for photography.

Picture Credits
The publisher would like to thank the following for their kind permission to reproduce their photographs:

12–15 Susan Downing (Vivek Singh); **Manoj Siva** (Das Sreedharan); **Oliver Wright** (Mahmood Akbar); **Susan Downing** (Sri Owen); **Martin Brigdale** (David Thompson); **Christopher Hirsheimer** (Corinne Trang); **Sharron Gibson** (Roopa Gulati); **Mike Dennis** (Judy Bastyra); **Paul David Ellis** (Yasuko Fukuoka). **8–9 Dorling Kindersley: Rough Guides**. **121 Getty Images**: felipedupouy.com / Photodisc (br). **124 Getty Images**: felipedupouy.com / Photodisc (bl). **291 Dorling Kindersley: Rough Guides** (tr).

(Picture key: a-above; b-below/bottom; c-centre; f-far; l-left; r-right; t-top)

All other images © Dorling Kindersley. For further information see: **www.dkimages.com**